The
Age of
Giant
Corporations

The Age of Giant Corporations

A Microeconomic History of American Business, 1914-1984

A SECOND EDITION

Robert Sobel

Contributions in Economics and Economic History, Number 59

Greenwood Press
Westport, Connecticut • London, England

Library of Congress Cataloging in Publication Data

Sobel, Robert, 1913 Feb. 19-
    The age of giant corporations.

    (Contributions in economics and economic history,
ISSN 0084-9235   ; no. 59)
    Bibliography: p.
    Includes index.
    1. United States—Industries—History—20th century.
2. Industry and state—United States—History—20th
century. 3. Corporations—United States—History—
20th century. I. Title. II. Series.
HC106.S676   1984   338.7'4'0973   84-8955
ISBN 0-313-24582-7 (Lib. bdg.)
ISBN 0-313-24583-5 (pbk.)

An Updated Second Edition of *The Age of Giant Corporations:
A Microeconomic History of American Business, 1914-1970*, Contributions
in Economics and Economic History, Number 7

Library of Congress Catalog Card Number: 84-8955
ISBN: 0-313-24582-7 (lib. bdg.)
ISBN: 0-313-24583-5 (pbk.)
ISSN: 0084-9235
First published in 1984

Greenwood Press
A division of Congressional Information Service, Inc.
88 Post Road West
Westport, Connecticut 06881

Printed in the United States of America

10 9 8 7 6 5 4 3 2

For Ed Wheeler

Contents

Introduction

In 1913 the United States was a relatively isolated nation in the midst of a depression. For the most part, Americans lived in small towns or on farms and worked for themselves or for sole proprietorships or partnerships. Big business in the form of the trusts and holding companies was already a part of the national scene, and there were old giants in the fields of railroads, banks, and insurance, and newer ones in steel, meat packing, and petroleum, but these were islands in the industrial–commercial sea of small units. Despite antitrust laws and great debates over their use, the government's role in the economy was small. In 1913 President Woodrow Wilson still believed the tariff, not the Clayton Anti-Trust Act, to be the greatest force for industrial control. Like most Americans of his time, he seemed to harken back to Jeffersonian ideals more than anticipate the revolutionary industrial and political developments of the next half-century.

The world seemed simple and optimistic in 1913. When the Woolworth Building, stretching 793 feet into the air, was opened that year, it was hailed as a modern miracle. Grand Central Terminal, one of the most spacious buildings in the world, was also put into use in 1913, and it seemed the soul of strength, permanence, and power. The Panama Canal was completed in 1913, and the first Ford assembly line was put into operation. The Lincoln Highway Association, pledged to construction of a transcontinental motor route, held its first meeting that year. It was an age of Jules Verne and Tom

Swift, of industrial miracles that would change the face of the world. On the eve of World War I, H. G. Wells was able to write that man would soon be able to predict the future as easily as he then studied the past. "What will happen in centuries to come when men shall stand upon the Earth as on a footstool and laugh and reach out their hands amid the stars?" he asked. They would see progress, writ in large letters, was the answer Wells had to offer in 1913.

Seven years later Wells published his *Outline of History.* This work, written during the Great War, was to become the best-selling nonfiction book of the 1920s. In it the author admitted being a trifle too optimistic in 1913, but he averred that world government, peace, and universal religion were the destinies of mankind. As for business, he predicted that the world's "economic organization will be an exploitation of all natural wealth and every fresh possibility science reveals, by the agents and servants of the common government for the common good. Private enterprise will be the servant—a useful, valued, and well-rewarded servant—and no longer the robber master of the commonwealth."

The hero of Edward Bellamy's *Looking Backward, 2000–1887* fell asleep in 1887 to awaken in the year 2000. He found a land of plenty and peace, where private property for production had ceased to exist and all worked for the common good. Wells' vision of the future was similar in outline if not in detail. He too thought the future would see the development of a variety of democratic socialism and world government. But neither author told his readers how this would come about. And most significantly, *The Outline of History* contains references in its index to the Aar Valley, Bhurtpur, Hauran, and Sir William Harcourt, but none for John D. Rockefeller, the Rothschilds, Alfred Nobel, or J. P. Morgan. And in an index of almost fifty pages there is no reference to corporations. Today we are closer to the year 2000 than we are to 1920 or 1887, and it is already evident that Bellamy's and Well's predictions were far from the mark. While it is doubtless true that the past half-century has been marked by wars, insecurity, the destruction of values, and the rise of new political forces, in terms of power and influence it has been the age of the nation-state, and insofar as economic power is concerned, it has been the age of the corporation.

Whether due to accident, good fortune, native talents, or the mistakes of others, the United States was to become the dominant power in this age of the nation-state and the corporation. It would soon be realized that the one depended on the other. Without its great economic power, the nation would have been unable to survive, and this power has increasingly been concentrated in the hands of large corporations. This dominance dates back to World War I. In 1913, the United States was the world's leading debtor nation; four years later it was its greatest creditor. The gross national product, less than $40 billion in 1913, was double that figure before the end of the decade and, despite the interlude of depression in the 1930s, passed the trillion dollar mark in 1970. Today it stands at above $3.5 trillion. Indeed, the annual *increment* in GNP during most years of the 1960s was more than the *total* GNP in any year prior to World War I, and the increments in the 1980s exceeded the totals of the late 1940s, remarkable achievements even taking inflation into account.

The outlines for this tremendous growth were already present in 1917. In that year the five largest American industrial corporations in terms of revenues were U.S. Steel, Swift & Co., Armor & Co., Standard Oil of New Jersey, and American Smelting & Refining. Fifty years later Standard Oil was still one of the top five, American Smelting & Refining was a comparatively minor firm, and the other three were still giants but were overshadowed by new firms with greater growth. But all survived. Indeed, of the top twenty firms of 1917, only Midvale Steel & Ordnance and International Mercantile Marine had disappeared completely by 1984. There were, however, major changes in scale. The U.S. Steel of 1917 had $2.4 billion in assets and $1.3 billion in revenues, while the largest American corporation of 1983, Exxon, had assets of $62.3 billion, posted sales of $94.6 billion, and earnings of $5 billion. If placed side by side with the industrial corporations of today, the U.S. Steel of 1917 would rank below the top hundred in revenues.

The half-century before 1970 has been marked by the rise of new corporations in novel, previously unthought of fields, and the growth of companies that were comparatively small, young, and untested in industries that were just beginning to emerge in 1917. Ford had only $160 million in assets and $275 million in sales in 1917. It was the nation's largest automobile manufacturer, but it was still smaller than Singer Manufacturing and less than half the size of Bethlehem Steel. General Motors had $134 million in assets and was smaller than Chile Copper and Central Leather, both of which no longer exist. Texaco was not a major corporation in 1917; IBM was a small manufacturer of office supplies operating under a different name; Sears, Roebuck was the same size as the Koppers Company. Yet all were among the top ten industrial firms in 1970.

Information processing, which was not known in 1917, was a major industry in the mid-1980s, and most students of American business history expect it to be the largest before the end of the century. Coal mining, the nation's fourteenth largest industry in 1917, was a comparatively minor one in 1984, with most of the large concerns either out of business or engulfed by energy conglomerates. Railroads and producers of rail equipment bowed to the airlines and aerospace companies in terms of net worth and sales; the Pennsylvania and New York Central, premier American corporations in 1917, came together to form the Penn Central, which went bankrupt and is no longer involved with railroading. The aviation industry, virtually unknown in 1917, had undergone several major changes and by the 1980s was as interested in space exploration as in earthbound transportation.

This book, the first edition of which was issued in 1972, has been updated and now deals with the industries, corporations, and businessmen that have played major roles in the nation's economic growth during the seventy years since the outbreak of World War I.

The
Age of
Giant
Corporations

CHAPTER I

American Business During World War I

The world did not expect a major war in 1914. Since the last decade of the nineteenth century, there had scarcely been a year in which a major crisis did not threaten the peace, yet there had been no general war. The Western world had grown accustomed to tension and was certain that it could be ignored. In the spring of 1914, Kaiser Wilhelm II of Germany and Czar Nicholas II of Russia still sent genial letters to each other. Berlin and London continued secret discussions about financing the Baghdad railroad and had common interests in the Portuguese colonies. In January the Bank of England reduced its discount rate from 5 percent to 3 percent, and Berlin and New York quickly joined in the reduction. The easy availability of money testified to the fact that businessmen and bankers were equally convinced that the peace would be unbroken.

On June 28, Archduke Franz Ferdinand, nephew of Emperor Franz Joseph of Austria-Hungary and heir to the throne, was assassinated at Sarajevo. The world was stunned but expected that the matter would not get out of hand. On July 9, the London *Economist* reported that "the Norway visit of the Kaiser marks the beginning of the dead season in German politics." But the alliances fell into place during the next few weeks. On July 31, Germany sent ultimatums to France and Russia, the London Stock Exchange closed its doors for the first time in history, and all the other major exchanges, including the New York Stock Exchange, followed suit. On August 3,

3

Germany declared war on France. Within a matter of days, almost every major European power was involved in war, and the United States emerged as the world's leading neutral.

At the time, the United States was experiencing a mild depression. The per capita income of $335 in 1914 was some $19 less than it had been the year before. Business leaders were wealthier and more secure than they had been at the turn of the century, but they were wary of the reforming zeal of President Woodrow Wilson who, despite his sophistication and urbanity, was considered representative of agrarian elements in the Democratic party. Antitrust activities had increased during the first year of the Wilson administration, and the passage of the Clayton Anti-Trust Act and the low Underwood Tariff confirmed business anxieties regarding Wilson. Unwilling to take risks, and hesitant about mergers and expansion, business was at least partially responsible for the economic slowdown of 1914.

The business community—that is to say the nation's large businessmen—was disturbed but not overly concerned about the financial crisis accompanying the outbreak of war. To these men, the war could be a means by which they could overcome the antibusiness mentality in Washington and so enhance their industry positions and increase profits. Although the overwhelming majority of businessmen desired neutrality and many had important commercial connections with Germany, most hoped for an Allied victory from the first. After the war, Thomas Lamont of J. P. Morgan & Company told the Senate Special Committee to Investigate the Munitions Industry that "like most of our contemporaries and friends and neighbors, we wanted the Allies to win from the outset of the war." The younger Morgan was as direct. "Certainly we did the right thing [in granting large loans to the Allies]. We would do it again if we had to." Such men expected the United States to supply the Allies with war materials and thought to gain profits thereby; government interference was anticipated but could be overcome. Few thought the nation would have to enter the war as a belligerent.

The armed forces were as unprepared for war as the businessmen were unaware of the implications of economic involvement. In 1902, General William Crozier had spoken forcefully of the need for an expanded army, and intimated that the entire economy might have to be mobilized in case of a general war. Eight years later military and naval leaders suggested the establishment of a council of national defense, which would control the civilian economy as well as the military forces in a new war. Some businessmen joined in the call. Howard E. Coffin, a vice-president of Hudson Motor Company, was one of the first to speak of the need for general mobilization in time of war. "Twentieth century warfare demands that the blood of the soldier must be mingled with from three to five parts of the sweat of the man in the factories, mills, mines, and fields of the nation in arms." Coffin applauded the establishment of the Federal Trade Commission shortly after the war began, especially when its members indicated a desire to cooperate with businessmen rather than act as a brake on their actions. One member of the commission asked a business group to learn the value of teamwork, "by which is meant correlation of the efforts of the manufacturer, merchant, banker, and investor. . . . The creation of the Federal Trade Commission must prove to be a great benefit to our manufacturers and exporters."

Notwithstanding the views of men like Coffin and the conciliatory statements of the FTC, government preparations for hostilities or a state of emergency were almost nonexistent between 1914 and 1917. During this period, American businessmen and bankers acted to provide the Allies with needed aid. Private loans to the Allies were more than $1 billion in 1915 and 1916 and would surpass the $2.5 billion mark before the war ended. Most of this money, along with the bulk of Allied gold and dollar holdings, went to America to purchase war supplies.

In 1915 Allied agents placed heavy orders with most American firms willing and capable of filling requests for war materials. As a result, the economy boomed. In 1913 there was a danger that U.S. Steel would not be able to meet the interest on some of its bonds; by the end of 1915, the firm was operating at 90 percent of capacity, and its backlog of orders was double that of 1914. In 1915, the first full year of war, more than one-third of U.S. Steel's production went overseas. Pig iron output, 19 million tons in 1914, rose to 38 million tons the following year, and the price of Bessemer pig went from $14.70 a ton to $19.65. Iron and steel production rose from 41.4 million tons in 1914 to 75.3 million tons in 1917. Copper output rose from 1.2 million pounds to 1.8 million pounds in the same period. Sharply increased grain production, the result of American shipments to Europe, led to an upturn in orders for agricultural machinery.

This boom brought disadvantages as well as benefits however. Exports to Europe in American bottoms placed unprecedented strains on the shipping industry; Phelps Dodge was unable to accept new orders for copper wire in 1916; U.S. Steel's board of directors could not fulfill schedules for development of new facilities due to a lack of skilled manpower and the allocation of funds elsewhere. Bethelehem Steel found it necessary to discontinue production of steel rails, since most of that firm's capacity was needed for the shipbuilding and chemical industries. Railroads were forced to suspend expansion programs. The automobile industry searched for substitutes for steel and copper as the Allies bid up the price of these materials. During the neutrality period, tungsten went from $.75 a pound to $8.00 a pound and other raw materials rose as well. Inflation gripped the nation. Wages rose 28 percent in the neutrality period, but due to increases in the cost of living, real wages actually declined by 10 percent. Still, the unemployment of 1913 was replaced by widespread labor shortages in 1917. Much of this could be traced to the fact that

American exports rose from $2.3 billion in 1914 to $6.2 billion three years later.

The booming economy of 1914–1917, accompanied by shortages of strategic materials, led the government to act. A Naval Consulting Board which included businessmen, government officials, and scientists, was established to assist in the construction of shipyards. By 1915 the businessmen on the board, recognizing the need for similar committees with broader powers, formed the Industrial Preparedness Commission. Financed and manned entirely by businessmen, and with little government cooperation, the commission compiled a list of manufacturing establishments that could be adapted to war work in a national emergency. The businessmen chose Howard Coffin as their leader and by 1916 had, under his direction, established the possibility of converting some 20,000 plants to war work. The Chamber of Commerce, through its Committee on National Defense, cooperated with Coffin's group, and drew thousands of small businessmen into the drive.

Late in 1915 the federal government began to recognize the need for work such as that done by the Coffin Committee, and moved to give it semiofficial recognition. In 1916, Congress voted to establish the Council of National Defense, which consisted of cabinet officers and an advisory board of civilians, including Coffin, private speculator Bernard Baruch, Walter Gifford of American Telephone and Telegraph Company, and Julius Rosenwald of Sears-Roebuck Corporation. In announcing the formation of the council, President Wilson said:

> The Council of National Defense has been created because the Congress has realized that the country is best prepared for war when thoroughly prepared for peace. From an economical point of view there is now very little difference between the machinery required for commercial efficiency and that required for military purposes. In both cases the whole industrial mechanism must be organized in the most effective way. Upon this conception of the national welfare, the Council is organized in the words of the

act for "the creation of relations which will render possible in time of need the immediate concentration and utilization of the resources of the nation."

According to Wilson, the council's major tasks would be to assure satisfactory communication and transportation between various sectors of the economy and preparing plans for war mobilization.

One of the objects of the Council will be to inform American manufacturers as to the part they can play in national emergency. It is empowered to establish at once and maintain through subordinate bodies of specially qualified persons an auxiliary organization composed of men of the best creative and administrative capacity, capable of mobilizing to the utmost the resources of the country.[1]

The council established some 184,000 local groups which continued the job of compiling information begun by the Industrial Preparedness Commission. Perhaps more important than any actual work done, however, was the fact that it opened the way for greater government–business cooperation and marked the effective end of Wilson's campaign against big business. From December 7, 1916, when the council first met, to the conclusion of his administration, the President ordered no new antitrust prosecutions, and in some cases he suspended actions brought earlier.

Bernard Baruch was easily the most vigorous member of the council. In 1917 he suggested a detailed study of the metals industries be initiated so as to facilitate conversion to war production should it become necessary. The other members agreed, and the study was made; it became a model for future reports. Shortly thereafter Baruch was named chairman for

1. Grosvener Clark, *Industrial America in the World War* (New York, 1923), pp. 21–22.

raw materials, minerals, and metals. While in this post he was able to convince producers to hold down prices, especially in copper and certain chemicals.

On April 6, 1917, the President signed the American declaration of war, making the United States an associated power of the Allies. He knew that without a massive effort by industry the war could not be won. "Modern wars are not won by mere numbers," he said. "They are won by the scientific conduct of war, the scientific application of industrial forces." Still, there was little evidence that industrial preparations were accelerating in the summer of 1917.

Secretary of War Newton Baker was blamed for failing to organize the armies and their support elements. Senator George Chamberlain of Oregon, a Democrat and strong supporter of Wilson, conducted an investigation of war preparations in his capacity as chairman of the Senate Committee on Military Affairs. Chamberlain called many to testify, including Baker himself, who appeared for three days. On January 18, 1918, Chamberlain spoke of his findings before the National Security League, a private organization. "The military establishment of the United States has broken down," he claimed. "It has almost ceased functioning. I speak not as a Democrat but as an American." Theodore Roosevelt, who was in the audience, led the applause which followed. The former President had said several weeks before that, "To an infinitely greater degree than ever before, the outcome depends upon long preparation in advance, and upon the skillful and unified use of the nation's entire social and industrial no less than military power." Now he moved, through friends and political contacts, to push Wilson and Baker into action. Baker made several speeches in which he indicated his appreciation of the need for mobilization. "War is no longer Samson with his shield and spear and sword, and David with his sling," he told one conference. "It is the conflict of the smokestacks now, the combat of the driving wheel and the engine." When critics charged that his actions did not fit his words, Baker replied, "The situation is entirely satisfactory."

At first Wilson tried to defend Baker. Commenting on Chamberlain's speech, the President charged, "Senator Chamberlain's statement as to the present inaction and ineffectiveness of the Government is an astonishing and absolutely unjustifiable distortion of the truth." In private, however, he indicated that some action to speed up mobilization would have to be taken.

The War Industries Board, which was to have broad but undefined powers, was organized by the Counsel of National Defense in July 1917. Its chairman was Frank A. Scott of Warner-Swasey Co., and it included several prominent military and naval leaders, as well as many civilians who had previously served on the Council of National Defense. Baruch headed the raw materials section, and was granted more power when Scott was succeeded by Daniel Willard, president of the Baltimore & Ohio Railroad, who showed little skill at the job. The board faltered due to lack of definition and leadership, however, and Willard indicated a desire to be relieved. Secretary of the Treasury William McAdoo urged Wilson to name Baruch to the post of chairman. This was done on March 4, 1918, both as recognition of Baruch's skill and in the hope that the new chairman would be able to still the critics. With the appointment went increased powers, many of which were taken from the War Department. In effect, Baruch was to be given command of the mobilization effort.

As it developed, Baruch's job was to mold the entire economy into a smoothly running, integrated operation. At the time his task was compared with that of Henry Ford in automobiles, only Baruch had to deal with almost every conceivable problem, whereas Ford only had to worry about the backward and forward integration of a single industry. Clearly such a task would have been impossible to accomplish without an organizational program and delegation of responsibilities.

The WIB quickly undertook control of every aspect of the civilian economy and tried to direct it toward the war effort. Not even during World War II, and certainly not during the Civil War, did such wide-scale mobilization take place under a single agency. Unused to these controls, some businessmen balked. William Durant of General Motors and Henry Ford were uncooperative during the neutrality period, but changed their attitudes once war was declared. Despite Assistant Secretary of the Navy Franklin D. Roosevelt's remark that until Ford "saw a chance for publicity free of charge, he thought a submarine was something to eat," the motor genius did a remarkable job. By mid-1918 he was not only able to meet all Allied and American demands for tractors, but could fill civilian orders as well. Ford met the British requests for ambulances, and in 1917 tried to convert his Highland Park plant to the production of airplanes. Without knowing much about the machines, he proposed to construct 150,000 a year if the British could send him a German model of the best type, so that he could copy some of its features. Ford's interest in aircraft did not end with the armistice; in the 1930s he became a major airplane manufacturer.

In time Baruch came to be considered a wonder worker, and his reputation for efficiency and knowledge soared. Although his mandate was broad, he was never the "economic dictator" his opponents thought him to be, but he did go to great pains to create the illusion of vast powers and all-knowing agents. He knew that some businessmen and bureaucrats could be brought into line if they believed he was more influential with the President than was actually the case.

Some businessmen—especially the nation's "giants"—railed at what they considered Baruch's arbitrary actions. When the steel industry's leaders, headed by Elbert Gary of U.S. Steel, refused to go along with WIB directives as to the mobilization of the companies, Baruch called a meeting and presented the industrialists with an ultimatum: cooperate or have the government take over the plants. Whether Baruch could have obtained the President's support in this matter was questionable. In any case the matter was resolved without a final test of wills. Gary and his colleagues fell into line, although Baruch was warned, "They'll never forgive you as long as you live." For the duration of the war the steel industry operated under price agreements set down by the WIB. Baruch later claimed they were not unduly harmed.

> The steel industry accepted these new prices in good faith and they remained almost unchanged till the end of the war. It has been estimated that this regulation of steel prices saved the government more than a billion dollars. The steel industry also did a superb job of production; but there is no question that profits, especially of the great integrated companies, were still excessive.[2]

Frank W. Taussig, the noted economist who at the time was a member of the Price Fixing Committee of the WIB, put it this way:

> The prices fixed were in all cases reached by agreement with representatives of the several industries. In strictness, they were agreed prices rather than fixed prices. The agreements were usually reached in cordial cooperation with the producers concerned, and thus were in reality voluntary. There were cases, however, in which they were agreements only in name. The representatives of some industries, though they accepted them, did so virtually under duress. In these cases the Committee to all intents and purposes decreed prices and was enabled to impose them under the form of agreement, by a more or less veiled threat of commandeering and also by the certainty that public opinion would condemn those who failed to accede.[3]

In practice, this meant the individual corporation had the option of accepting contracts under the WIB price structure

---

2. Bernard Baruch, *Baruch: The Public Years* (New York, 1960), pp. 66–68.
3. Benedict Crowell and Robert F. Wilson, *How America Went to War: The Giant Hand* (New Haven, 1921), pp. 78–79.

or rejecting them. Thus, Bethlehem Steel refused to supply the government with steel rails at what the firm considered an unfair price. But Bethlehem was a leading ship builder prior to the war, and grew rapidly during the conflict, with all its major contracts under the WIB prices. In addition, the company became a major producer of gun carriages and a supplier of bombs under these arrangements. Jones & Laughlin Steel Company refused several contracts urged upon it by the WIB, but was the leading American producer of barbed wire and toluol, the latter a coal tar derivative made from the byproducts of iron manufacture.

Profits of leading corporations rose during the war, but not as much as Baruch indicated. The rise in earnings and gross income from 1913 to 1917 was sizable as America went from the bottom of a mild depression to a prosperity based on supplying the Allies. But when the nation entered the war, price controls, new taxes, and inflation ate up most of the extra profits. For example, U.S. Steel's gross receipts rose from $1.23 billion in 1916 to a peak of $1.74 billion in 1918, but the corporation's earnings fell almost 20 percent. On the other hand, charges to plant accounts rose sharply, as demands for new capacity increased. U.S. Steel's 1914 assets were $1.73 billion; by 1918 they had risen to $2.57 billion. In the same period, du Pont's assets rose from $78 million to over $300 million. Similar figures could be given for most leading producers of war supplies.

Although the WIB tried to hold the line on prices and make fair allocations of scarce commodities, its most difficult job was the conversion of the civilian economy to the products of war. The American economy had not undergone as drastic a conversion since the Civil War, when no overall plan existed and a good deal of misdirected effort was made. By 1917, however, the American businessman was more sophisticated and the government more accustomed to the exercise of power over the economy.

In November 1917, Chairman Willard of the WIB was asked

by Alexander Legge, then vice-president of International Harvester Corporation and soon to become Baruch's chief aide, to select someone to take charge of the conversion effort. Willard responded by naming to the post George N. Peek, vice-president of Deere and Company and an old friend of Legge's. Peek was charged with locating new facilities for government projects, advising industry of government needs, and studying "future war requirements and from time to time making such recommendations to the chairman as the exigencies of the situation require."

Eventually Peek gained great powers, and used them effectively to mobilize the copper and iron producers for the war effort. In addition, he formulated programs of regional development so as to ease transportation bottlenecks and produce war goods more quickly and cheaply. Together with C. A. Otis, former head of the Cleveland, Ohio, Chamber of Commerce, Peek placed a large volume of orders in the upper Ohio region, primarily because Otis was able to obtain the cooperation of manufacturers there, who took these factors into consideration when subcontracting or purchasing raw materials. Eventually Peek worked out a program based on twenty-one industrial regions, each with an advisor whose job it was to coordinate plans of war production. This regional decentralization not only made Barauch's job easier, but it also gave many businessmen a sense of being closer to the government and the mobilization projects, while at the same time having more autonomy than might have been the case if the directives came from Washington. The Resources and Conversion Section operated smoothly during the war, and the lessons learned from the experience were not lost on either government or business. The decentralized corporation of the next decade was often patterned after the WIB plans and operations, while many agencies of the New Deal during the thirties were fashioned after the World War I models.

The major problem in dealing with large firms was that of persuasion, but once the boards of directors were either talked or coerced into cooperation, they operated well and with few hitches. The problem then was to decide which war material each firm could best provide. It was obvious that certain goods could best be made by the larger firms. Liberty engines, trucks, batteries, and gun carriages could most effectively be produced by automobile and carriage manufacturers. Shipyards, idle during the previous decade, were rapidly converted to the production of destroyers and cruisers. The clothing industry was able to produce not only uniforms, but tents and bandages. Smaller manufacturers, on the other hand, presented sensitive problems. Few could fulfill ambitious promises to turn out complex machinery and similar products. Thus, the WIB had to use its powers of persuasion to lead them into other, equally vital, areas. Dredging contractors who wished to enter airframe production were assigned to the excavation of berths in shipyards. Stove manufacturers were put to work producing guns and shell casings. Furniture makers became producers of airframes. In a remarkable show of ingenuity and adaptability, Baruch, Legge, and their aides led industry to institute large-scale labor retraining programs. Women were used in factories with great effectiveness, as were students and retired personnel.

Despite the existence of unused capacity at the beginning of the war, and notwithstanding the fact that the United States was, in 1914, the world leader in such areas as structural engineering, home building, railroad construction, and the manufacture of motor vehicles, shortages appeared early in the war. As the procurement program went into effect, the economy was unable to absorb the huge war purchases. By 1918, the army alone was taking more than the normal civilian production of woolen socks, blankets, steel, brass, aluminum, and zinc. The armed forces required three times as many gloves and twice as many blankets as the 1913 economy could have produced if run at capacity. In order to meet the needs of the armed forces, the government was obliged to take drastic action, and had to urge some major changes in several industries. In addition, mergers and combinations that might have been challenged by the Justice Department in 1913 were accepted and in some cases encouraged four and five years later in the name of industrial efficiency in wartime.

The American petroleum industry had such production problems, and the government took action to help solve them. In 1914, world production of crude oil stood at 407.5 million barrels, and of this figure, the United States produced 265.8 million barrels—more than two-thirds. Still, it was not enough for war needs. "Unless the European war comes to an end soon, or unless American oil refiners can find a way to get their product to waiting millions and hundreds of millions living on the borders of the seven seas, a large part of the world will have to go back to tallow dips or sit in darkness before the end of October." So wrote *National Petroleum News* in September 1914.

With the beginning of the European war, American refinery runs accelerated, but not nearly as fast as demand. By 1916, the nation produced 300.8 million barrels, while world production rose to 457.5 million barrels, due mainly to a sharp rise in Mexican production. In 1917 the WIB, together with petroleum executives, formed the Petroleum Advisory Committee and the National Petroleum War Service Committee, headed by Alfred C. Bedford, president of Standard Oil Company of New Jersey. Bedford enlisted the aid of presidents of other industry giants, and the companies instituted a large-scale search for new reserves and conducted research into more efficient methods of refining crude oil. Although there were no significant breakthroughs in technology during the war, the committee was able to raise output to 378.4 million barrels by 1919, while world production increased to 555.9 million barrels.

Shipbuilding involved a complex of problems, the most important of which were prices and supplies of plate, and the lack of adequate facilities. In April 1917, the Emergency Fleet Corporation was established by the government and private companies to solve these and related problems. The corporation mounted an advertising campaign to make the public aware of the situation. Slogans like "Ships will win the war" and "America must build a bridge to France" appeared on billboards in coastal cities. Charles M. Schwab, head of Bethlehem Steel, was named chairman of the corporation, and he promised that the ship shortage would be over within two years. The industry constructed three new shipyards, and one of these, the Hog Island Shipyard near Philadelphia, was finished within five months, due in large part to the cooperation of Assistant Secretary of the Navy Roosevelt and private speculator and banker Joseph Kennedy. The Hog Island facility was set up to handle seventy-eight ships at one time, making it the largest shipyard in the nation. Together with the other two yards, and improvements at existing facilities, the number of ships under construction rose to 934 in 1918 as compared to 256 in 1913.

At first the ships were constructed by conventional methods, and it took more than a year to turn out a destroyer. Since such schedules were harmful to the war effort, new methods of construction had to be found. A group of naval architects, led by a team from Bethlehem Steel, developed methods of prefabrication in ship construction by 1917. Although the method had been used prior to the war, it had never been utilized on larger ships or as a mass-production technique. By the end of the war, a prefabricated 7,500 ton ship could be launched at Hog Island within four days after the keel was laid. In late 1918, the United States had a fleet of more than 2,600 ships with a total tonnage of over 10 million. But despite the impressive showing and adaptability of the industry, the nation and the Allies suffered shortages of shipping throughout the war, and the construction program never reached its projected peak; more ships could have been launched in the six months after the armistice than in the eighteen months before. In addition, many of the ships that were launched could not be put into service for several months due to shortages in naval ordnance, fittings, and personnel. In all, then, the showing of the corporation was impressive but spotty.

The WIB's role in naval procurement was to hold down prices and assure a ready supply of steel shapes. When the steel producers proved unable to supply sufficient quantities of plate at what Baruch considered a fair price, he asked for and received Senate appropriations of $11 million for a government mill. Immediate protests were lodged by Bethlehem, Midvale, and U.S. Steel, which between them had a capacity of 32,000 tons of plate a year. Bethlehem offered to sell plate to the government at $395 a ton, a $30 reduction from the current price and $100 a ton lower than the price paid by the Allies. Bargaining was reopened, but due to the rapid inflation of 1917 and 1918, the price eventually agreed upon ranged from $420 to $485. Meanwhile, construction of the government mill proceeded. Then a further complication appeared. The British had overexpanded their plate facilities, and so were able to offer 14,000 fourteen-inch armor piercing shells at $356 each, against the $500 to $900 charged by American iron and steel companies. The offer was accepted, much to the chagrin of the American producers.

The WIB's firm stance led to industry concessions in September 1918, at which time steel company executives agreed that for the rest of the year, pig iron would be sold at $33 a ton and certain basic steel shapes at from $2.90 to $3.25 a hundredweight. The price of plate, which had stablized at $240 a ton that spring, now went to less than $80. These reductions cut profits to the bone at a time when U.S. Steel alone was spending $14 million a month on new facilities. The economies of scale, however, made such expenditures possible.

Even when private firms were willing to cooperate, they were often snubbed by the WIB. When du Pont and other powder manufacturers indicated that government demands for explosives could not be met, the director of United States explosives plants, D. C. Jackling, ordered the construction of government facilities. A plant was constructed at Nitro, West Virginia, which was turning out powder less than six months after ground was broken. A second plant, built at Nashville and called "Old Hickory," cost $90 million and was larger than any of the private plants. By the end of the war, the two plants were delivering more than 250 tons of explosives a day.

The WIB did not object to the means by which private industry acted, as long as maximum production was achieved. In 1916, Midvale Steel merged with Cambria Steel, giving that firm a dominant position in the specialty steel field. Bethlehem acquired Pennsylvania Steel Company the same year, making it the second largest factor in the industry. The Justice Department continued an old prosecution of U.S. Steel under the antitrust act, but charges were not brought against Cambria and Bethlehem for their actions.

During the war, business accepted federal regulation, while the government came to understand that bigness brought benefits, as well as problems. One of these benefits was standardization. Prior to the war, little had been done to rationalize industry, with the exception of the railroads. Regional compacts, the low state of management techniques, and sheer inactivity led to a seemingly endless duplication of facilities and proliferation of products. Legge and others reported that this condition hindered the war effort, and would have to be remedied. In farming supplies, there were more than 1,700 types of wagon gears, 326 models of plows, and 784 drills and other planting machines. With federal agencies indicating the benefits to be derived from rationalization, these numbers declined. By the end of the war, the number of plows stood at 76. The 232 kinds of buggy wheels were reduced to 4. There were 4 different colors of typewriter ribbon instead of the 150 of 1914. Auto tire sizes were reduced from 287 to 3. Like many other reforms, these were to prove a blessing to business and the consumer during the 1920s.

Not all companies or industries were able or willing to comply with the directives and laws controlling the economy. In general, industries with records of antitrust problems, usually consisting of several large producers of homogeneous items, had the best records for cooperation. Such firms were headed by men who were accustomed to sharing markets and avoiding cutthroat competition. Their sessions with Baruch or his aides were not too different from the Gary dinners, when shares were allocated in the steel markets and prices fixed, and the end result was not dissimilar: competition was lessened and firms could proceed with long-term plans without fear of major upheavals from within the industry itself.

Such was not the case with many industries noted for a multiplicity of producers and distributors and where products were not homogeneous. Manufacturers of women's quality clothing could not be controlled through allocations of material; they managed to locate the goods despite WIB attempts at regulation. Food processors posed a major problem, as some sought to avoid compliance and looked for ways around agreements. Herbert Hoover, who directed the food effort, noted that while most processors at least paid lip service to rules and regulations, some did not. Congressional enactments did little good, he noted, for many processors were not engaged in interstate commerce. Hoover balked at revoking licenses, a power which he could have used, for he felt such actions would be unduly harsh.

About 95 percent of patriotic processors and distributors were controlled by the co-operating committees of the trades and by the regulations contracted with them. But it developed that there were about 5 percent who refused to join in our trade-committee agreements and sought to gain special advantages for themselves. In time, we were compelled to license several entire trades in order to circumvent these poachers. Reluctantly, we had to undertake the huge burden of issuing more than 250,000 licenses. During the period in which the licenses were in force, our Enforcement Division had about 8,000 cases of violations. Most of them were not willful, and our officials simply reminded the offenders of the law and gave them a reprimand. In some cases of more gravity, we settled for a modest contribution to the Red Cross. In one case, a meat packer willfully violated his license three times for huge profits. . . . We actually cancelled only about 200 licenses out of 250,000, and those for willful or repeated violations. . . .

Hoover concluded that the "meager percentage of transgressors was a great tribute to the high level of integrity and patriotism of the American people."[4] His war experience reinforced his earlier belief that cooperation between businessmen was often beneficial, and that, though moral suasion, government could harmonize the various parts of the economy in times of distress. Just as one can find elements of Roosevelt's New Deal philosophies in his wartime experience, so the origins of much of the Hoover policies of the late 1920s and early 1930s derived from his work during the war.

Although the federal government was not the dominant factor in the economy in mid-1918, its agencies had mobilized business and agriculture into a formidable weapon in the war. The WIB had virtual control over almost all raw materials sources, while other agencies, both subordinate to the board and independent of it, dominated other industries. The United States Fuel Administration, for example, had complete control over the coal and petroleum industries; the railroads were nationalized in all but name insofar as day-to-day operations were concerned. The War Department had entered into more than 30,000

4. Herbert Hoover, *An American Epic* (Chicago, 1960), II, 55–56.

contracts with builders and producers by the end of the war, for amounts in excess of $7.5 billion. These contracts constituted the major consumption item in the national ledger.

Government contracts were let without bidding, due to the national emergency, and so Wilson once more saw his hopes of competition dashed by the need for massive industry in wartime. Since there were no bidders, prices could not be determined by the interplay of supply and demand. Instead, the War Department let contracts on the basis of cost-plus, a method which had been used infrequently in the past. Under the cost-plus arrangement, the government agreed to pay the producer all costs incurred in turning out the products needed, in addition to an agreed-upon percentage of the costs. As a result, most producers ignored cost problems in meeting War Department contracts, since the higher their costs, the greater their profits. Such contracts contributed to the general inflation of the war period and led to modifications of contracts later on. For example, contractors on jobs costing less than $100,000 were allowed a profit of 7 percent. Higher-priced contracts were written with sliding scales, to a minimum of 2.5 percent for work costing more than $9.65 million, with the provision that no single contract could result in a profit of more than $250,000. Finally, almost all contracts contained termination clauses, stipulating that the government could cancel work should the war end.

The American economy had reached a new peak just before the war ended. Thus, demobilization was bound to have a strong dampening effect on most firms. On November 9, two days before the official armistice news was released, production chiefs at the WIB and War Departments were notified to prepare for enforcement of cancellation clauses in contracts. As might have been expected under such circumstances, the government's role in the reconversion effort was marked by hesitation, mistakes, miscalculations, and lack of coordination.

On the morning of November 11, the chiefs of the major bureaus announced that Sunday and overtime work on government contracts would be halted at once. At the same time, the procurement agencies sent out notices to suspend the manufacture of munitions. The contradictions in the announcements and orders were soon worked out to enable a phasing-out process to take effect. Still, most manufacturers encountered problems in carrying out the orders. At the time, the War Department had some $6 billion worth of contracts outstanding, a third of which had been completed and were awaiting settlement. By December 5, more than $2.5 billion of the unfilled orders were cancelled. The United States Housing Corporation, formed early in the war to aid in the production of government housing, was ordered to halt work on all projects less than 70 percent completed. Soon after, the dismantling of the armed forces began; within six months more than two million servicemen received their discharges. The great influx of workers into an economy hit by mass cancellations seemed to indicate that World War I, like most other American wars in the past, would be followed by a depression.

Summary

During World War I the American businessman was obliged to work in close harmony with the government, usually as the junior partner. Although there were many problems arising from such arrangements, by and large they were carried off with success. One might say that the government-business partnerships of the war period paved the way for business influence in government during the 1920s, and the reverse in the New Deal period.

More specifically, American business was able to expand without fear of government opposition to market positions. While it was true that many felt hemmed in by regulations, price fixing, and the like, these restrictions were minor when compared to the opportunity presented to rationalize the economy and expand upon an already strong infrastructure. Further, foreign markets that previously had been dominated by the British and Continental powers were opened to American businessmen. The stage was set, then, for a rapid expansion upon a strong base.

CHAPTER II

The Glamour Industries of the 1920s

The first year after the peace saw a continuation of the wartime prosperity, which allayed the fears of those who claimed that the stoppage of military orders would lead to a major depression. Pent-up consumer demands, rapid demobilization, the end of war controls, and the need to continue relief work in Europe combined to produce a Gross National Product of $78.9 billion in 1919 against one of $78.7 billion the previous year. Then, late in 1919, the forces of deflation were felt. Consumer demand continued, but could not match production. Returning soldiers found it difficult to find jobs as the economy leveled off and mass discharges released a flood of workers on the market. In order to dampen the inflation, the Federal Reserve Board raised the discount rate in November. There followed a downward spiral, one of the steepest in American history, which affected almost all aspects of the economy, with the sharpest fall-offs in agriculture, mining, and housing. The 1919–1921 depression involved more than 30,000 bankruptcies, close to a 500,000 farm foreclosures, and 5 million jobless workers; the Gross National Product declined almost 10 percent.

Recovery from the postwar depression began in 1922, as the Federal Reserve reversed its tight money policy, demand caught up with supply, and the nation was no longer faced with large-scale lending abroad and could concentrate on the domestic economy. Tax cuts, cheaper money, and the need for a capital spending program to modernize plants, caused an upturn in 1922, which continued for seven years, with pauses and regressions in 1924 and 1927. In retrospect, this was one of American business's golden ages.

During the 1920s there was a remarkable expansion, reorganization, and reorientation in American business. The United States, only a few years earlier the world's leading debtor nation, was now its most important creditor. American business, long fearful of foreign competition, now embarked on a massive foreign expansion program, one which absorbed a good deal of domestic profits and was fueled by a bountiful capital market. And the domestic market grew as well. Stoked by credit and a rapid increase in real income (from $571 per annum in 1921 to $686 in 1929), nourished by the relatively new industry of public relations and advertising, sparked by the new giants in transportation and communications, and protected by friendly governments, expansion in almost all fields— the notable exceptions being mining and agriculture—seemed unlimited.

The expansion led to changes in business structure, as the unitary firm of prewar years proved incapable of meeting the complexities of the 1920s and was largely replaced by the decentralized holding company, which was better equipped to expand rationally and combine with other firms. As new markets, products, and demands appeared, old industries were transformed. Thus the concept of a transportation industry replaced that of a railroad industry, and the telegraph, vaudeville, and theater industries were combined, transformed, and augmented by new firms, which considered themselves to be in the communications or entertainment fields. And all seemed to work for the benefit of the entire nation; there was to be permanent prosperity in the business civilization of the 1920s. Further, it was a moral way of life. Bruce Barton, who was a pioneer in advertising, on the boards of directors of several leading firms, and a sometime congressman, summed up in his person the ideal of the age. To him, business was part of Jesus' divine plan of redemption for mankind. His favorite biblical quotation was,

"Wist ye not that I must be about my Father's business?" In his best-selling book, *The Man Nobody Knows,* Burton wrote of his boredom with Sunday school as a youth; at the time he did not understand what Jesus was trying to tell him. Later on he came to realize that "Jesus built the greatest organization of them all"; that He had "muscles so strong that when He drove the money-changers out, nobody dared to oppose him!" that Jesus "was the most popular dinner guest in Jerusalem!" and most importantly, "He picked up twelve men from the bottom ranks of business and forged them into an organization that conquered the world."[1] Although he did not say so directly, Barton implied that were He alive in 1924, Jesus would have the attributes to make a fine president of American Telephone & Telegraph, a good bond man at a Wall Street brokerage, or the president of a thriving Rotary Club. These words were not lost on the businessman of the 1920s, and gave moral support for his day-to-day activities.

If the businessman did not try to mold himself in the image of Jesus, but rather interpreted Christianity to suit his purposes, he did avoid competition and sought cooperation more than he had in the past. This was not a new attitude; it had been evolving for half a century before coming to fruition in the 1920s. The manufacturers of the late nineteenth century had learned that competition at a time of excess capacity could lead either to a kill-or-be-killed struggle or to cooperation in which all would share in the benefits. The trust movement was striking evidence that most big businessmen preferred the latter approach. The merger movement of the late nineteenth century was another example of the desire to lessen competition, while the antitrust movement, although it created more annoyance than actual dissolutions, put the businessman on guard against the kind of competition that might lead to industry-wide control by one or several manufacturers.

1. Bruce Barton, *The Man Nobody Knows* (New York, 1924), pp. iii–iv.

Then came the war, and while Bernard Baruch and others bedeviled and disturbed businessmen, profits rose, anxieties diminished, and rationalization brought added economies. The war experience led thousands of businessmen into an intimate relationship with the government, forced them to cooperate more than before, and resulted in a sophisticated realization of the wastes of competition. Further, all was done for a righteous cause; it was moral as well as profitable.

The postwar depression left mental scars on those who had failed and those who had suffered; at all costs such an experience would have to be avoided in the future. Finally, the businessman of the 1920s no longer had the direct proprietary interest in his firm that his predecessor had. Andrew Carnegie's attitude toward Carnegie Steel was quite different from that of an organization man who managed to rise to the top in the 1920s. The latter would give his all for the firm, but his rewards would take the form of increases in salary and perquisities, rather than the creation of a business empire or dynasty. The corporation was more impersonal than it had been even a few years before, in prewar America. The new businessman would be willing to fight for his firm, if the circumstances called for it and he was so inclined, but he would not "die for it." He saw more similarities than differences between his "team" and those of his nearest competitors, and job swapping made them even more interchangeable. Thus, he joined with the competition in many ventures so as to make life easier for all. He could reflect, too, that the consumer did not suffer from this, for due to advances in technology, cost would be lower than before, while wages would rise, although not as rapidly as increased profits would indicate.

The National Association of Manufacturers and the Chamber of Commerce were spokesmen for this type of businessman, and both organizations promoted interchanges between competitors and hoped for less competition while extolling the advantages of free enterprise. In a major speech on the subject in 1924, Chamber of Commerce President Julius H. Barnes claimed the organizational approach was ushering in a new era in the nation's history, and his theme was the virtue of cooperation, the cornerstone of Chamber of Commerce beliefs. As he saw it, the Chambers were not trying to lead a movement in that direction as much as they were reflecting the realities of a maturing industrial society. Without cooperation, Barnes said, there would be unemployment, anarchy, and the gradual decline of national unity.

> The men who administer the Chamber of Commerce of the United States have a sober responsibility and a solemn appreciation of the trust reposed in them by this position of leadership. They realize that every American home reflects, in its prosperity and contentment, the stimulated individual hopes and efforts that are secured by a social and political philosophy made effective in daily life through the processes of trade and industry; the American conception of equality and opportunity, and of government and individual fair play.[2]

Barnes concluded that "all enlightened businessmen" recognized this need for fairness, and he singled out the steel makers as prime examples of believers in enlightened free enterprise. The reality, however, was quite different from the Chamber's public morality. The U.S. Steel antitrust case was decided against the government in 1920. By a vote of four to three, the Supreme Court stated that the firm need not be dissolved, for although it had attempted to monopolize the industry, it had failed to do so. More important, however, was the attitude of U.S. Steel during the years between the initiation of the suit and its final disposition. Fears of dissolution and the rigors of fighting with Baruch had led Judge Gary to accept the status quo in steel; he no longer tried to overcome his competitors, but instead preached cooperation. Shortly thereafter the gov-

2. Julius H. Barnes, *The Genius of American Business* (New York, 1924), pp. 40–41.

ernment signaled its willingness to permit further concentration in the industry so long as U.S. Steel was not involved. The Webb Export Act of 1918 permitted cooperating firms to join in associations to market their products abroad. Trade associations, which were little more than gentlemen's agreements, were sanctioned by the Supreme Court in the Cement Manufacturers' Protective Association and Maple Flooring Manufacturers' Association cases. Finally, in 1924, the government's action against Aluminum Company of America—a firm that had monopoly position in the metal—was dropped.

The combination of U.S. Steel's forbearance and the friendly attitude of the government were necessary preconditions for the many mergers and consolidations in the steel industry. In 1922 Bethlehem Steel absorbed Lackawanna Steel and in the following year Midvale and Cambria were acquired. Pacific Coast Steel, which controlled Southern California Iron & Steel, was absorbed in 1929. In that year, Weirton Steel, Great Lakes Steel, and most of the business of M. A. Hanna Company were combined to form National Steel. Republic Steel was completely revamped by the additions of Central Alloy Steel, Donner Steel, and Bourne Fuller in 1930. The drive toward amalgamation seemed unstoppable and almost faddish; only the attempted merger of Youngstown Sheet & Tube into Bethlehem was foiled, this in 1929. By the end of the decade, the steel industry was the domain of giant holding companies.

As the new companies emerged, the need for restraint on the part of U.S. Steel and the government faded. The revamped firms could hold their own with the industry giant without government aid. This was due to two major changes in the industry. In the first place, U.S. Steel lagged behind in technological developments. American Rolling Mill Company became the leader in the continuous rolling process, the major advance of the decade. Republic's researches into alloy steels went far beyond those of the industry giant. Bethlehem took a commanding lead in structural shapes, while National concentrated on light steels. U.S. Steel, burdened with old facilities, could not move swiftly enough in these areas. Finally, the increased use of scrap negated the advantages U.S. Steel had previously enjoyed due to its plant locations, many of which were situated near prime ore areas. While U.S. Steel remained concentrated in the Pittsburgh area, the other firms built their new plants closer to the markets, and so enjoyed transportation advantages.

The second shift—the change in the product mix—was related to the first. U.S. Steel had led in the production of such heavy products as rails, plates, and structural shapes. But now the demand had shifted to sheet and strip steel, products that required new plants, such as those constructed by National and Republic, but which could not be produced easily at the older U.S. Steel works. U.S. Steel was seriously harmed by the change from railroads to automobiles during the 1920s.

Prior to the war, it had been the primary producer of steel for the railroad industry. Now Weirton (soon to become part of National) and Ford's captive facilities became the backbone for the growing automobile industry. As Pittsburgh declined, so did U.S. Steel; as Chicago and Detroit emerged, so did National and Ford. This is not to say that U.S. Steel was destined to become a minor factor in the industry. At the end of the decade, the firm had assets in excess of $2.4 billion and working capital of almost $500 million. Its sales in 1929 were nearly $1.5 billion. At the time, it owned 140 iron and steel works, more than one hundred blast furnaces, approximately 1,400 locomotives, and 55,000 freight cars, and employed more than 200,000 workers.

The change in steel was one of the many tranformations caused by the burgeoning automobile industry, which became the dominant force on the industrial scene in the 1920s. The statistics illuminate the magnitude of the industry. In 1913, the last prewar year, 462,000 vehicles were sold by all manufacturers. By 1919, the figure had risen to 1,658,000, and ten years later, 4,587,000 were sold. There were some 7,577,000 motor vehicles registered in 1919; in 1929, there were 26,705,000. By 1925, motor vehicles ranked first among all American industries in value of product. The fortunes of such diverse items as fabrics, steel, petroleum, asphalt, glass, and acid were intimately connected with those of the automobile.

The early motorcars were crude devices, almost entirely handmade, and sold to the wealthy as novelties and playthings. In 1908, Henry Ford introduced the Model T. At the time he was one of some 1,500 manufacturers of motor vehicles in the United States. By 1921, when he sold his five millionth Model T, Ford was the dominant factor in the industry. His philosophy regarding the market and the firm was simple: the public, which he considered homogeneous, should and would receive standardized, inexpensive transportation. As for Ford Motors, the founder would keep all power in his own hands through a high degree of centralization. Ford derided attempts to appeal to the growing middle class with model changes, often did not consider technological advances so long as the system in use seemed workable, and was adamant in refusing to accept any form of outside control. Ford summed up his philosophy of management in 1922 by stating that "the work and the work alone controls us." He believed the typical American worker was intelligent, ambitious, easily adapted to factory work, and democratic. For this reason he refused to have titles in his factories or for that matter assign specific responsibilities to all but a few workers; Ford thought that in this way he would encourage natural talent to rise. "Titles in business have been greatly overdone," he said, "and business has suffered."

> One of the bad features is the division of responsibility according to titles, which go so far as to amount to a removal altogether of responsibility. Where responsibility is broken up into small bits and divided among many departments, each department under its own titular head, who in turn is surrounded by a group bearing their nice sub-titles, it is difficult to find anyone who really feels

responsible. Everyone knows what "passing the buck" means. The game must have originated in industrial organizations where the departments simply shove responsibility along.[3]

In practice, Ford Motors did assign responsibility, but usually grudgingly. Ford's chief competitor, Alfred Sloan, Jr. (president of General Motors), followed a different philosophy. Believing the large corporation to be too complex to be run by a single man or even a committee, Sloan quickly decentralized operations, giving large grants of authority to divisional chiefs and asking results in exchange. Sloan spread authority thin at General Motors, pitting division against division, permitting what to some seemed wasteful competition between them, and allowing divisional vice-presidents to operate their own businesses to the extent of borrowing from the mother firm when they needed capital. Thus, Sloan combined the economies of mass production with the efficiencies of controlled competition. Further, he recognized, as had Baruch during the War Industries Board period, that once a firm reached a certain point, decentralization was necessary for the sake of progress.

Sloan represented a new type of business leader. He was scientific and methodical, with efficiency his goal and profits and losses his guide. Ford, on the other hand, was an intuitive genius, with an almost poetic view of the automobile. Ford has been called "the last populist," while Sloan gave little evidence of concern with social problems. Sloan cared little about his public image, believing it was his job to provide one for General Motors. Ford viewed his company as an extension of himself. In their own ways, both men succeeded. Ford became the symbol of the automobile, but his company declined. Sloan, a far more important figure in the 1920s and

3. Henry Ford (in collaboration with Samuel Crowther), *My Life and Work* (New York, 1923), pp. 93–95.

after, was a shadowy figure outside the industry, but General Motors had won its race with Ford by the end of the decade.

Sloan recognized that Ford's homogeneous American did not exist. Under his direction, General Motors produced a variety of automobiles, each designed to satisfy a different strata of society. Building upon the companies acquired by William C. Durant, his predecessor, Sloan covered the field.

> It is true . . . that Mr. Durant had established the pattern of variety in products expressed in the seven lines: Chevrolet (in two very different models with different engines, the "490" standard and a higher priced "FB"), Oakland (predecessor of the Pontiac), Olds, Scripps-Booth, Sheridan, Buick, and Cadillac. Of these, only Buick and Cadillac had clear divisional concepts. Buick with its high quality and fairly high volume in the high middle-price bracket, and Cadillac with its permanent endeavor to present the highest quality at a price consistent with a volume that would make it a substantial business; and in fact Cadillac and Buick had long been the industry leaders in their price classes.[4]

Sloan's view proved the more successful during the booming 1920s. In 1921, Ford's best year in terms of share of the market, the firm accounted for some 55 percent of unit sales, while General Motors' vehicles had 13 percent. In 1929, the new Model A and other Ford cars had only 31 percent of the market, while General Motors' share had risen to 32 percent.

Part of the reason for Ford's decline was the founder's unwillingness to take the market demands—the desire for model changes and different styles and colors—into account. Another reason was Ford's inability to assume the initiative in technological advances. Franklin introduced electric vaporizers in carburetors, Duesenberg pioneered in braking systems, and Packard used the first hypoid gears, and Stutz introduced safety glass in windshields. Walter P. Chrysler,

4. Alfred Sloan, Jr., *My Years With General Motors* (New York, 1964), pp. 58–59.

who helped found General Motors, then reinvigorated Willys, took over the Maxwell Company in 1924 and transformed it into Chrysler Motor Car Company. His Plymouth, introduced in 1928, provided additional competition for the Ford cars. By then, both Plymouth and Chevrolet were further advanced in styling and technology than the Ford.

> The Chevrolet in 1924 issued a handbill advertising its superiorities over "our nearest competitor." It boasted a water-pump cooling system; the Ford still had a thermo-syphon system, and its radiator still boiled under any engine strain. The Chevrolet had an oil-gauge on the dash and an Alemite lubricating system; the Ford was still lubricated by a primitive "splash system." The Chevrolet's Remy ignition system operated accurately; the Ford still had the old device of four spark coils and a "timer" which constantly needed attention. The Chevrolet had its gasoline tank in the rear, which was both safer and more convenient; the Ford gasoline tank was still in front. The Chevrolet had four springs, the Model T two. The Chevrolet had a foot accelerator, the Ford a hand accelerator. The steering system on the Chevrolet was superior. Even those most attached to the Model T admitted that it needed constant care; that its sparkplugs had to be cleaned every two hundred miles, that the greasy transmission bands required endless adjustment, and that the "vibrator" on the coils had to be checked. Most people now grew irritable over such jobs. They did not enjoy the carbon-knocks uphill and the connecting rod chatter downhill.[5]

Carbon knocks and related difficulties were of great concern to the petroleum industry, which underwent widespread changes as the automobile gained in popularity. Formerly devoted to the production of illumination, lubrication, and medicinal products, the petroleum companies became satellites of the automobile industry by the early 1920s. An example of this was the development of petroleum cracking, which had

5. Allan Nevins and Frank E. Hill, *Ford: Expansion and Challenge, 1915–1933* (New York, 1957), pp. 416–417.

been practiced prior to World War I, as the industry strove to extract more gasoline from each drop of crude. Then in 1916 Charles Kettering began his search for additives to meet the demands for more powerful fuels for larger engines. Kettering's self-starter, introduced a few years earlier, was powered by a battery ignition, which seemed to cause "knocks" in the engine. By 1920 it was discovered that the addition of tetraethyl lead to fuel eliminated the sounds. This additive, however, deposited lead on the cylinder walls and valves, fouling the engine in short order. In 1922, oil researchers learned that the addition of ethylene dibromide to the fuel eliminated the deposits. By 1923, Dow Chemical and Standard Oil of New Jersey were producing gasoline additives that enabled the more powerful General Motors cars to be marketed. Shortly thereafter, General Motors and Jersey Standard joined to form Ethyl Corporation, which became the world leader in the production of gasoline additives.

This was but one example of the impact of the car on the petroleum industry. During the 1920s, gasoline became big business in America. By 1925, petroleum exports led all others, with a net worth of $421 million, against $303 million for automobiles. Agricultural machinery and steel plates, two of the biggest exports of prewar America, accounted for only $163 million in exports that year.

But as important as the export market was, the growth of the domestic market accounted for most of the industry's gains. The oilmen were quick to grasp all the ramifications of the automobile revolution, and the scramble for industry position was both grim and exciting, leading to such episodes as the Teapot Dome scandal of the Harding administration and the struggle for new sources of crude, such as those in the Texas-Oklahoma and Mexican fields. Had the fight continued uninterrupted, price competition would have probably led to the industry's becoming dominated by two or possibly three huge refining and distributing companies, served by and servicing a host of exploration and specialist firms. But this did not occur. Instead the government, in the wake of Teapot Dome, established the Federal Oil Conservation Board in 1924. Its first president, P. S. Hurley of Gilliland Oil, said that the board would attempt to aid American firms in their marketing problems and work for the conservation of petroleum resources and against wildcatters who practiced uneconomical, wasteful methods of oil recovery. In practice, however, the board acted primarily to ensure that price wars and duplications of effort were ended. In 1926, Jersey Standard erected price umbrellas for many of its most important products, and other firms in the Standard group followed suit. By the end of the year, almost every major firm had entered into price and territorial agreements.

Two years later the American Petroleum Institute undertook to add a code of ethics which would rationalize previous agreements. The code, proposed in December 1928, recommended the discontinuation of those marketing practices that encouraged intensive price and nonprice competition, including rebates, concessions, gifts to customers, and the hiring of employees by one firm from another. The Federal Trade Commission approved the code in July 1929, after which it was submitted to the industry for approval. This was given by most producers, so that by August 1929 it was adopted in all states except California and Texas.[6]

The agreement had immediate results. In 1930, Jersey Standard announced that 80 percent of the American petroleum companies had joined to control the future of the hydrogenation process, by which larger gasoline yields were obtained from crude. Figures for that year showed that Jersey Standard produced 102.5 million barrels of oil, with Gulf Oil second with 75.8 million barrels. Rounding out the "big five" were Indiana

6. Harold Williamson, Ralph Andreano, Arnold Daum, and Gilbert Klose, *The American Petroleum Industry: The Age of Energy, 1899–1959* (Evanston, 1963), p. 504.

Standard (63 million barrels), the Texas Company (42.3 million barrels), and California Standard (41.3 million barrels). These firms also dominated the service station and distribution networks. Together with other large refiners and marketers, they tried to avoid price competition, concentrating instead o advertising appeals and regional domination. Since gasoline, unlike the automobile, was a homogeneous product, this seemed the only possible alternative to the cutthroat tactics sometimes practiced prior to 1925.

The trend toward cooperation and controlled competition in the drive to exploit the mass market could also be seen in the radio and motion picture industries, both of which expanded rapidly during the twenties, and were considered the "glamour" sector of the economy.

Although public screenings of motion pictures were held as early as 1895, and the first motion picture theater was opened in 1902, the outlines of the industry were not clear until the next decade. At that time the field was dominated by firms that manufactured equipment and then produced films so that their customers would have something to show on their projectors. Edison's Kinetoscope and Biograph, for example, both became producers for this reason, selling projection equipment to theaters and then offering film for from $10 to $25 a show, depending on the length of the strip.

As the number of theaters grew, this method of distribution became inadequate. Schedules of leases, duplicate prints, and cost lists became too complex for the equipment manufacturers. In 1902, Harry Miles opened the first distribution center that was not affiliated with the producers. Miles would arrange schedules, move films from one theater to another, and make duplicates. He made handsome profits on all these operations, while at the same time lowering the unit costs for exhibitors. Within a few years, when the producers realized that large profits were to be made from distribution, they acted against Miles. In 1908, the seven leading producers organized the

Motion Picture Patents Company, to protect themselves from infringements of patents and to combat the independent distributors. Despite this, unaffiliated producers continued to infringe upon protected patents and lease film to the independents. Recognizing this situation, the Patents Company, in 1910, organized the General Film Company to distribute films made by the seven film and equipment producing and distributing firms and to prosecute unaffiliated dealers who violated the patents.

Within three years General Film was able to destroy or purchase fifty-seven of the fifty-eight independents. The sole survivor, William Fox, decided to fight back, and as a result of his efforts, the federal courts ordered General Film dissolved for having violated the antitrust act. With this, the industry was once again forced to face the basic problems of distribution and pricing on the one hand and production on the other.

During World War I, two clearly defined operations were evident in the industry: production and distribution. There were innumerable producers, most of whom operated on shoestrings, and hundreds of independent theater owners, with a few minor chains such as Gorden in Boston, Mark in New York, and Kunsky in Detroit. Since it was evident that cartel arrangements such as General Film would not be permitted, many producers and distributors planned for industry domination by their firms. The problems here were artistic as well as commercial; firms tried to compete by constructing better theaters and producing more salable, popular films, usually through the use of celebrities or "star" actors and actresses. First National Exhibitors Circuit, a cooperative distribution concern, entered into agreements with independent producers to form First National Pictures, thus becoming the earliest to attempt industry-wide domination. Carl Laemmle, who was a leading distributor and had joined Fox in the fight against the Film Company and General Film, formed Universal Pictures to gain a production unit. Later on other distributors and producers would attempt to gain monopoly or oligopoly powers in this way.

More important, however, were the mergers that led to joint firms. The capital requirements for expansion were heavy, and mergers seemed more sensible in any case. Thus, Famous Players-Lasky, organized as a production firm by Adolph Zukor in 1912, merged with Paramount Pictures, a distribution company in 1916 to form Paramount Famous Lasky Corporation, which for a while dominated the industry. Pathe Exchange, a significant distributor with the wherewithal for expansion, chose to conserve its resources and merged instead with DeMille Studios and acquired the businesses of Producers Distributing Corporation and the Cinema Corporation of America.

The new concerns attempted to enjoy the benefits of partial monopolies. As the star system developed, and as the product lines became highly differentiated, this seemed possible. Thus, Paramount would charge what seemed exorbitant prices for the right to show its product; Zukor took advantage of his position to require theaters to show all of his films or none. In order to fight Zukor's "block booking," exhibitors combined into circuits, thus countering one partial monopoly with another. First National expanded from 26 theaters in 1917 to 639 in 1920, and other chains, though not as large, appeared in many parts of the country.

The battle of the giants was avoided by the organization in 1922 of the Motion Picture Producers and Distributors of America. This was a trade association of producers and distributors which, together with the exhibitors, attempted self-regulation, partially to stabilize the market and avoid industry-wide combat, and partially to obviate the need for government regulation and censorship. Industry peace also brought an end to the bitter fights for domination of both aspects of the business. Now Paramount was content to concentrate on production. In 1922, the firm owned or controlled 203 theaters; by

1924, the number had dropped to 181. First National cut down on productions, and by 1923 had more than 3,600 theaters under its franchise. At the same time, the Fox and Loew's chains experienced rapid growth as exhibitors.

The relative industry peace was shattered by the advent of sound. The need for sharply increased capital expenditures—for equipment, new production schedules, and advertisement—brought producers and exhibitors into closer contact with investment houses than had previously been the case. Loew's financed operations through Liberty National Bank and General Motors, Paramount formed an alliance with Kuhn, Loeb, & Company, and Chase National Bank backed the rapidly growing production company of Twentieth Century-Fox.

A second result of sound was the emergence of new or revitalized companies. Since American Telephone and Telegraph owned patents on sound equipment and had signed long-term leases and agreements with the industry giants, Radio Corporation of America, which also had sound patents, had to search elsewhere for outlets and sales. Harkening back to a previous generation, when equipment manufacturers released films to gain markets, RCA founded Radio Keith-Orpheum Corporation through a merger with Booking Office Pictures and the Keith-Albee-Orpheum circuit of theaters. Almost immediately, RKO was a major factor in the industry. Similarly, A.T.&T. backed Warner Brothers, then a minor firm, and maintained licensing arrangements with Paramount and other older concerns.

The formation of RKO and the new role of A.T.&T. illustrated still another aspect of the motion picture business in the late twenties: the emergence of a new type of communications and entertainment industry, which would be closely allied with the electric equipment industry. RCA was controlled by General Electric and Westinghouse, and it in turn controlled RKO and the National Broadcasting Company. American

Telephone and Telegraph owned Bell Laboratories and Western Electric Company, and found outlets for their talents and products in both motion pictures and radio. General Motors, the giant of the automobile industry, had a passing interest in films as well. As one commentator wrote:

> The entertainment of the future, carried from a central point by radio to the eyes and ears of millions of persons in thousands of theatres all over the country, and perhaps throughout the civilized world, took a step toward actuality ... with the announcement of the formation of Radio-Keith-Orpheum Corporation.
>
> Keith-Albee-Orpheum provides a nucleus of 700 theatres as a starter. Film Booking Office provides motion picture producing facilities. The National Broadcasting Company, through its concert bureau and jointly with Keith-Albee-Orpheum, offers unusual program making facilities and experience.
>
> Talking pictures by the Photophone process will be the primary basis of the new development. Later those will probably be broadcast by radio. Television entertainment is an ultimate possibility.[7]

The origins of the radio industry can be traced to the incorporation of the American Marconi Company in New Jersey in 1899. The firm was controlled by British interests, which were eager to exploit the wireless discoveries of Guglielmo Marconi, a farm boy who failed in Italy but succeeded in developing his inventions in London. The firm grew rapidly, gaining prominence for its role in attempting to save the survivors of the *Titanic* in 1912. Two years later American Marconi had sixty-five sending stations on land and hundreds of transmitters on seagoing vessels. Wireless came into its own during World War I.

As wireless succeeded a feeling grew that American Marconi should be owned by Americans. The British were reluctant to sell, but the desire to keep American goodwill, and the fact that General Electric refused to provide the firm with

7. *New York World*, October 23, 1928.

some important equipment until it was controlled by Americans, led the founders to relinquish ownership in 1919. Shortly thereafter American Marconi was reorganized and enriched with new personnel and money, and emerged as Radio Corporation of America. As arranged, General Electric supplied the firm with patent rights plus a $3 million line of credit, receiving in return 25.7 percent of RCA's common stock plus a block of preferred as well. In 1920, RCA gained patent rights from A.T.&T. in return for 4.1 percent of its stock. United Fruit Company transferred some wireless installations to RCA for 3.7 percent ownership. Through cross-licensing arrangements, Westinghouse Electric & Manufacturing had gained important patents and licenses; these were granted to RCA in return for 20.6 percent of the common stock. Thus, RCA was dominated by several large American firms, while the former American Marconi owners were placed in a minority position.

At the time it appeared that the major commercial possibilities of radio lay in marine and business transmissions, but some industry leaders, including David Sarnoff, then commercial manager of RCA, expected radio to be used primarily as home entertainment and a "magazine of the air." In other words, the radio would resemble the motion picture more than it would the telephone. Its impact, however, would be greater than that of the movies. Whereas films could not be shown at home due to the expenses involved, radio sets could be made for less than $100. As prices declined, almost every family could afford a receiving set. Thus, the major difference between movies and radio, from a business point of view, was that distributors and exhibitors would be replaced by station managers and advertisers. Equipment manufacturers, the men who actually began the motion picture industry, became a minor force by 1920, since a limited number of cameras and projectors were needed. But the demand for radios was limitless, and the set producers soon came to dominate the industry.

Westinghouse was one of the first to see important possibilities in the sale of receiving sets. In order to promote these sales, Westinghouse established station 8XK, playing phonograph records and mentioning the name of the music store that donated them as a matter of courtesy, but not yet thinking in terms of commercial messages. In November 1920, station KDKA was established in Pittsburgh, just in time to broadcast the results of the Harding-Cox election. Westinghouse executives were pleased: radio sales rose sharply in 1920 and 1921.

The immediate success of KDKA forced radio leaders to face several problems, many of which were similar to those of the motion pictures. Just as movie executives had been obliged to divide the industry into equipment and film producers and exhibitors and then tried to dominate both aspects, so the radio men saw possibilities in set manufacture and programming. A major difference, however, lay in the fact that government regulations affected radio far more than movies, and the radio firms were large enough to meet the capital demands of the industry, thus limiting the number of competitors and enabling a few gaints to emerge early in the industry's history.

General Electric, American Telephone, and Westinghouse were the "big three" in station management in the early years. Westinghouse had KDKA and WJZ in New York, and outlets in other major cities. General Electric owned WGY in Schenectady and KOA in Denver, among others. A.T.&T.'s major station was WEAF in New York, and the firm also licensed its equipment to some forty stations which were almost completely controlled by the industry giant. There was infighting between these three groups, and between them and the independents.

Westinghouse did not make a major drive in broadcasting, mainly because of its great success in set manufacture, where it concentrated its activities. Accordingly, it sold WJZ to RCA, which replaced Westinghouse as a big three member. RCA and A.T.&T. began a "broadcast war" in New York, with WEAF and WJZ competing for rights to air important events. By then each recognized that substantial fees could be charged for advertising. WEAF led the way, selling "spots" in 1922. Secretary of Commerce Herbert Hoover strongly opposed these commercials.

> I believe the quickest way to kill broadcasting would be to use it for direct advertising. The reader of a newspaper has an option whether he will read an ad or not, but if a speech by the President is to be used as the meat in a sandwich of two patent medicine advertisements, there will be no radio left. To what extent it may be employed for what we now call indirect advertising I do not know and only experience with the reactions of listeners can tell. The listeners will finally decide in any event.[8]

By 1924 advertising had replaced set sales as the major incentive for establishing stations, and many more independents were attracted to the field. To counter this, and at the same time further exploit radio's commercial possibilities, American Telephone combined its stations with some independents in October 1924 to establish the Red Network, which included WEAF, WEEI in Boston, WGR in Buffalo, WJAR in Providence, and WCAE in Pittsburgh. The network's purpose was to lower programming costs and make a stronger appeal to nonregional advertisers. It was also expected that the high qualities of programming either would force other stations to leave the air or oblige them to join the Red Network on American Telephone's terms.

RCA counterattacked by suggesting a second network, to embrace RCA, General Electric, and the remaining Westinghouse stations. The new network would use Western Union and Postal Telegraph lines and avoid any connections with A.T.&T. The RCA plan also included the establishment of

8. *New York Times,* October 5, 1924.

a Broadcasting Foundation of America, which would be made up of the new network and important set manufacturers. In this way, RCA attempted to gain a position in radio similar to Paramount's in motion pictures.

Although the plan did not materialize, it did serve to crystallize matters between the two rivals. American Telephone had already sold its RCA stock in 1923. General Electric and Westinghouse had come to terms with RCA in 1920, with the former firm retaining rights to manufacture sets using RCA patents but with RCA having the right to sell them. In 1925, one out of every three sets sold was an RCA Radiola, manufactured jointly by General Electric and Westinghouse.

American Telephone bowed in 1926. It had the resources, but not the patents or interest to dominate radio. The firm sold WEAF to RCA for $1 million, and agreed to stop certain legal actions against RCA. In return RCA contracted to use American Telephone's lines and dropped its agreements with Western Union and Postal Telegraph. Then, with General Electric and Westinghouse, RCA formed the National Broadcasting Company. NBC set up two networks: the original Red, which was expanded and centered around WEAF, and the Blue Network, revolving around WJZ. By 1931, the two networks had seventy-four stations. Its only significant competitor at that time was the Columbia Broadcasting System.

CBS was an outgrowth of the embryonic United Independent Broadcasters, which was the brainchild of George A. Coats, a salesman for a roadbuilding firm. He had an interest in radio, and strongly resented NBC's agreement with the American Society of Composers, Authors, and Performers (ASCAP) which kept much music off independent stations. Together with Arthur Judson, manager of the Philadelphia Symphony Orchestra, Coats organized the Judson Radio Program Corporation, which planned to syndicate shows. After being brushed off by Sarnoff, who resented their intrusions, Coats and Judson formed United Independent Broadcasters, and searched for financial backing. Coats was turned down by Paramount, radio set manufacturer Atwater Kent, and Victor Talking Machine Company. He had success at Columbia Phonograph Company, however, since Columbia viewed the new network as a counterattack against RCA's entry into the phonograph and radio set business. If radio succeeded, the Columbia executives reasoned, then the phonograph would decline as parlor entertainment. In order to remain in business, then, Columbia would have to meet RCA on its own grounds. Lewis Sterling of Columbia negotiated an arrangement with Coats whereby Columbia would back the new firm, whose name would be changed to the Columbia Phonograph Broadcasting System (later shortened to the Columbia Broadcasting System). The new firm's true beginning, however, came in 1928, when William Paley, a cigar executive who had become interested in radio after sponsoring several programs, purchased control of the company. Recognizing the need for outside capital and expertise, Paley arranged for the sale of 49 percent of CBS stock to Paramount in 1929. By encouraging new concepts in programming, Paley was able to establish CBS as an important firm, but it still ranked a poor second behind RCA in the late twenties and early 1930s.

CBS's union with Paramount (which was dissolved in 1932) was matched by RCA's purchase of RKO stock and its takeover of Victor Talking Machine Company. In addition, the music publishing firms of Leo Feist and Carl Fischer were soon added to the RCA constellation. In 1932, a Justice Department suit resulted in the termination of the General Electric-Westinghouse ownership of RCA stock. By then, RCA and CBS were both independent of outside control or interests, and each was a factor not only in the radio industry, but in the emerging communications and entertainment industries as well.

The set manufacturers—again dominated by RCA—underwent a period of sustained demand throughout the decade.

In early 1922 there were little more than 60,000 families with sets in the United States; by the end of 1924, the number had risen to approximately 1,250,000, as hundreds of firms entered the promising field. Technological change and price competition led to the demise of many, a situation which resembled the automobile industry prior to World War I. Financial as well as technological problems plagued the new firms. The demand for radios was seasonal, with sales increasing in the fall and winter. Firms that could not finance their accounts receivable often found themselves in bankruptcy. In order to eliminate some of these pitfalls, the larger firms—RCA, Atwater Kent, Kolster, and Crosley—sold their sets through licensed or carefully chosen jobbers, who then distributed them to retail outlets. Medium- and smaller-size firms, including Stromberg-Carlson and Freshmen, could not afford or did not need the jobbers, and sold directly to the retailers. Some tried to develop their own small retail outlets, but the economy could not support such specialization, and the experiment was soon abandoned. In all cases, the set producers resorted to extensive use of advertising.

Pierre Boucheron, RCA's advertising manager in the late 1920s noted that the industry's rapid growth was due, in part at least, to a campaign directed toward an increasing acceptance of its products. Around 1920 the idea of radio had been made known, and at this time equipment manufacturers either established their own experimental stations or encouraged others to do so. Then they began to advertise in fan magazines, such as *Radio News* and *Wireless Age*, in an attempt to sell receiving sets to amateur engineers and "hams." By 1922 the idea had trickled down to the more general public, and the companies directed their efforts at existing retail outlets, while at the same time mounting campaigns in such popular magazines as the *Saturday Evening Post*. According to Boucheron, all of this had been accomplished by 1923, at which time public demand

for receivers outstripped the manufacturers' capabilities to produce them, marking the beginning of the radio boom.

By the end of 1923, so many mushroom manufacturers had entered
the radio field that the seller's market turned into a buyer's market.
The public began to discriminate in their purchase of radio. No
longer did they buy simply because it was radio, but instead began
to look for performance and the reputation of the maker.[9]

Then came the winnowing process, as hundreds of small manufacturers fell by the wayside leaving a handful of large manufacturers and several dozen marginal firms, who between them
were able to offer radio sets for all pocketbooks and tastes.

By the end of the decade radio was as ubiquitous as the
automobile and the motion picture theater. Together these three
not only dominated the growth sectors of the economy, but
were revamping American life and tastes as well. The nation's
horizons were broadened, its tastes were stimulated and sharp-
ened, and the old prewar ethic of production was replaced
by a desire for greater consumption. According to Robert and
Helen Lynd, as early as 1924 the "typical" American was
beginning to view himself and his world through the medium
of radio. The comments they received from Middletown
(Muncie, Indiana) residents to their questions were revealing.

"I use time evenings listening in that I used to spend in reading."
"The radio is hurting movie going, especially Sunday evening."
(From a leading movie exhibitor.)
"I don't use my car so much any more. The heavy traffic makes
it less fun. But I spend seven nights a week on my radio. We
hear fine music from Boston." (From a shabby man of fifty.)
"Sundays I take the boy to Sunday School and come straight

9. Graduate School of Business Administration, George F. Baker Foundation, Harvard University, *The Radio Industry: The Story of Its Development*
(New York, 1928), pp. 261–270.

home and tune in. I get first an eastern service, then a Cincinnati one. Then there's nothing to do till about two-thirty, when I pick up an eastern service again and follow 'em across the country till I wind up with California about ten-thirty. Last night I heard a ripping sermon from Westminster Church somewhere in California. We've no preachers here that can compare with any of them.''

"One of the bad features of radio," according to a teacher, "is that children stay up late at night and are not fit for school the next day."

"We've spent close on to $100 on our radio, and we built it ourselves at that," commented one of the worker's wives. "Where'd we get the money? Oh, out of savings, like everybody else."[10]

In time the worker's wife, "like everybody else," would make such purchases on a time payment plan. Radio, motion pictures, and automobiles would build up a consumer ethic that would not wait on savings, and prompted by advertising, would create a new kind of economy, one that came to a sudden end in 1929.

Summary

Lessons learned during the antitrust period and the era of forced cooperation during World War I were applied in several important industries during the 1920s. The firms engaged in radio, motion picture, and automobile production took large risks in the battle for market position, but took them eagerly since the prizes were equally great. Bitter competition led to the formation of several large firms in radio and motion pictures, and an oligopoly situation existed by the end of the decade. In automobiles, Ford and General Motors—despite the slippage of the former firm—dominated the field, followed by a host of other firms, most of which were on the verge of failure,

10. Robert S. Lynd and Helen M. Lynd, *Middletown: A Study in Modern American Culture* (New York, 1956 ed.), pp. 269–271.

but some of which were on the way toward capturing a small but significant share of the market. Similarly, the undifferentiated nature of the petroleum industry led the top half-dozen firms into cooperation, and the creation of an oligarchical situation. In steel, the restraint of U. S. Steel and the rise, usually through mergers, of other giants, created a controlled competition which enabled all to survive.

CHAPTER III

An Age of Power, Consolidation, and Mass Distribution

In the spring of 1929, the Committee on Recent Economic Changes of President Herbert Hoover's Conference on Unemployment published a massive study of the American economy, based on extensive field work and drawing upon the best academic minds in the nation. Among its many conclusions, the committee stated that "acceleration, rather than structural change, is the key to an understanding of our recent economic development." To justify this statement, the committee offered two basic sets of data: the first was the result of a questionnaire to businessmen, asking them to list the most important new products of the past ten years, while the second consisted of statistics regarding the growth of power and production. The new products included cellophane, celluloid, ethylene glycol (antifreeze), dry milk, oleomargarine, several new steel alloys, bakelite, panchromatic motion picture film, rayon, and "dry ice." The list contained many products that proved commercially important, but none represented discoveries or products that would bring immediate sweeping changes to any important segment of the economy. The economy of the 1920s, then, was noted for the development of new management forms and the exploitation of earlier discoveries and inventions, but not for radically new products.

To these was added the key element of power. While the population increased 62 percent from 1899 to 1929 and wage earners 67 percent, production rose 295 percent and power production 331 percent. By 1929 per capita production of the

American worker was 60 percent higher than it had been in 1900. All this was taken into consideration by the committee, which also attempted to discover the reasons for this radical transformation. After citing the development of new management techniques, the market's expansion through advertising and credit sales, the impact of new industries and technological breakthroughs, the members cited the extraordinary rise in power production. "Paralleling these developments is the rapid growth of power producing plants, driven by steam, oil, or water, and greatly increasing the output per person."

From 1919 to 1927 the number of electric motors in use in the United States rose from 9.2 million to 19.1 million, and the percentage of electric power machinery in use in factories went from 31.7 percent to 49 percent. In this period the number of kilowatt-hours per capita rose from 425 to 860. The effect on industry was tremendous. In 1929, 95.7 percent of machinery manufacturing was carried out by electricity. The same increase took place in almost every major industry classification, down to 47.2 percent in the lumber industry.[1]

Most of the electricity came from coal (35.1 million short tons consumed by electric power plants in 1919, 41.9 million in 1927) and natural gas (21.4 thousand cubic feet in 1919, 62.9 thousand in 1927). Although the use of these fuels rose dramatically, the efficiency of electric power generation was such that the number of pounds of coal it took to produce a kilowatt-hour of electricity fell from 3.20 in 1919 to 1.84 in 1927. Thus, power generation did not bring great booms to the coal industry. Indeed, the replacement of coal by petroleum and natural gas and the development of highly mechanized means of mining led to depression in that industry.

The United States produced more electric power than the

1. U.S., *Recent Economic Changes in the United States: Report of the Committee on Recent Economic Changes of the President's Conference on Unemployment* (New York, 1929), pp. 93–95.

rest of the world combined in 1929, and power generation had become a major American industry. Most of the electric power was produced by the 4,000 or so operating systems, 96 percent of which were privately owned and publicly regulated. Since some 70 percent of American homes in 1929 were electrified, and many used gas for heating and cooking, electric utilities often became distributors and at times producers of natural gas. Brooklyn Union Gas, Pacific Gas and Electric, and Public Service Corporation of New Jersey were a few of these combined firms.

Although the utility firms sold an undifferentiated product, and despite regulation by local, state, and federal agencies, concentration occurred in utilities to an even greater extent than in most other sectors of the economy. By 1930, the United Corporation group, dominated by J. P. Morgan & Company, controlled firms that produced some 23 percent of the nation's electricity. Included was Commonwealth and Southern Corporation, which was second in size to Consolidated Gas Company of New York in terms of assets. Others of the United group were Niagara Hudson Power, Public Service Corporation of New Jersey, Columbia Gas and Electric, and many minor firms. Electric Bond and Share, backed by Chase National Bank, was second in size, controlling firms producing 17 percent of the nation's electricity. The Insull group, which was made up of two giant holding companies and several major operating companies, including Commonwealth Edison and Middle West Utilities, produced 11 percent of the nation's electric power and dominated the Midwest. All were united in gentlemen's agreements and interlocking directorships, although they clashed over several disputed territories, and all were controlled or dominated by investment bankers. Considering the heavy capital requirements of the industry, no other way seemed possible. S. Z. Mitchell of Electric Bond and Share, a significant factor in the industry, stated the reason succinctly in a 1920 speech.

We all know that in the past our business has had an average growth of say about 10 percent per annum—many companies have materially exceeded this—and we know that, averaged over a long time and at pre-war prices, it has taken from $4 to $6 capital investment to produce $1 per annum gross revenue. We also know that a growth of about 10 per cent per annum compounded as it has in practice will double their gross receipts every seven years. Many companies have doubled their gross in from four to five years. We also know the approximate amount of additional capital required per person net increase in population and in a general way what the growth of the communities served is likely to be. To adequately provide light and power service, experience teaches us that we must be continually providing from $30 to $80 more new capital for every individual increase in population.[2]

Mitchell went on to say that from 60 to 70 percent of the new capital needed by business—and especially by utilities—would come from the sale of bonds, with the rest from retained earnings and the sale of common and preferred stock. "The day of enlarging plants of public utilities even in part through reinvestment of earnings is gone," he believed. "The days of building plants through sale of bonds alone, if ever there were such days, have gone never to return." Thus, Mitchell tied the fate of his industry to the ability of the se curities markets to absorb new stock issues, while implying that the profits of operating companies also would have to rise. At the time public service commissions used as their guidelines a 6 or 7 percent return on investment; some utilities were earning as much as 20 percent, as both they and the government ignored the inept commissions. Yet even these highly profitable firms were obliged to go to the securities markets with common and preferred stock issues to finance expansion.

Plant expansion was a necessary part of the drive to electrify

2. S. A. Mitchell. *S. Z. Mitchell and the Electrical Industry* (New York, 1960), pp. 117–119.

the nation. The motion picture and radio industries would have been crippled, if not made impossible, without the electrification of homes and theaters. Just as radio and movies grew out of the electrical industry, so other businesses expanded rapidly to meet the needs of the new power complexes. The value of insulated wire and cable produced in America rose from $128.6 million to more than $210 million from 1919 to 1927. Telephone and telegraph apparatus production went from $50.9 million to $119.3 million in the same period, while transformer production rose from $37 million to $66.7 million.

These materials and products were used to bring electric power and its benefits to the vast majority of American homes, and to make possible the development of the appliance industry. Sales of electric irons, coffee makers, toasters, cooking ranges, and other appliances increased rapidly in the decade's early years, and at a slightly lower rate after 1926. The sales of home appliances in 1922 was $178 million; five years later the figure reached $361 million. Most of these appliances were "sold" rather than "bought," as advertising was used to intensify demands and credit buying was utilized to finance the purchases.

Credit buying increased in good years and declined sharply in poor ones. From 1925 to 1926, the volume of financing increased $512 million. Then, during the mild recession of 1927, it declined $540 million. It was evident that the manufacturers and loan companies would have to counteract such declines in order to use plants at full capacity. Instead of taking the conservative suggestion that plants be cut back, operate at low levels of capacity, and then expand gradually to meet demand as it developed, the appliance manufacturers sought to maximize sales, hoping to create demand in bad years as well as good and thus to lower their unit costs. Manufacturers argued that it was their way of flattening out the business cycle. Wesley C. Mitchell, the noted economist, thought that such uses of production facilities combined with advertising might help meet the slack demand. Writing of the subject in 1927, he said that advertising served a useful, though at times abused, function.

> The picture given by so many economic treatises of buyers coming to market with their minds already made up about what goods they wish, and what price they are willing to pay for successive units of each kind, is an undeserved compliment to the mental energies of mankind. Even to canvass the market's offerings thoroughly takes more time and thought than the average shopper will devote to the task. So people follow an easier course, buying what they have bought before, what they see others using, or what advertisements and salesmen urge them to buy. The psychological categories important to the understanding of consumers' demand are habit, imitation and suggestion—not reflective choice. In particular new products are seldom called for by consumers conscious of ungratified wants; they are pushed upon consumers by business enterprises, which often spend large sums in "educating the market" or "creating demand."[3]

Thus, manufacturers found it necessary to expand plants, produce new goods, and then advertise them hoping for sales. Mitchell believed this all but ensured plant overcapacity, since not all products were successful and the plants would necessarily be cut back and perhaps even abandoned. "This task of stimulating demand is never done; for the march of technical improvement is ever increasing our capacity to produce, and before we have learned to distribute and to use what has just been added to our output, new advances have been scored."[4] Mitchell saw no solution to this problem and wondered whether or not it was indeed something to be concerned about.

Of the more than $1.5 billion spent on advertising in 1927, the largest portion—$690 million—went to newspapers. Magazines accounted for $210 million, billboards another $75

3. Wesley C. Mitchell, *Business Cycles: The Problem and Its Setting* (New York, 1927), pp. 164–165.
4. Ibid., p. 166.

million, and radio $7 million. Direct mailings and announce-
ments accounted for $400 million, with the rest distributed
to trade journals, streetcar signs, premiums, and others.
Growth for all types of advertised products was impressive,
or at least so it seemed at the time, and advertising budgets
rose steadily and sharply throughout the decade. As might
have been expected, the field came to be dominated by new
products (especially electric appliances and automobiles) and
the new media showed the greatest advances. For example,
magazine advertising for radios rose from less than $80,000
in 1922 to $3.4 million in 1927. Equally dramatic was the rise
in magazine advertising for food and related products in
this period. The public saw more appeals to buy canned
goods ($3.4 million to $8 million); cereal products ($2.5 million
to $5.4 million); tea and coffee ($386,000 to $1.3 million); and
candy and gum ($609,000 to $2.2 million) than ever before.
Automobile products accounted for the largest amount of
magazine advertising in 1927 (19.3 percent), but toilet articles
(17.9 percent) and foods (13.1 percent) were not far behind.

The attempt to sell essentially undifferentiated products to
unsophisticated consumers and to enlarge production at an
ever-increasing tempo was the primary reason for the growth
of advertising in the 1920s. The existence of national markets
and the presence of means of communication made the growth
possible; the development of large-scale merchandising units
made advertising of low-price goods economically feasible.

The development of mass merchandising was both the cause
and effect of these forces. During the 1920s, more small "mom
and pop" stores were opened than chain units, but their closing
rate was about the same as the opening rate, while the chain
units' closings were roughly one-quarter that of the openings.
By the end of the decade, it was clear to almost all industry
observers that the small store was doomed. The economies
of scale, the ability of a chain to absorb losses for a while,
and the availability of special skills and resources to the chain

made the persistence of small units doubtful. Some observers thought that although the chains might destroy the independent units, in time they would falter as well.

> It seems to be a characteristic of new types of distributive enterprise that in the first stage of their development they gain a foothold primarily by means of low prices, in the second stage they "trade up" the quality of the merchandise carried, and in the third stage they compete by offering services. Companies in this third stage, unless they are managed with exceptional ability, not uncommonly encounter an increasing cost of doing business, a rising ratio of fixed investment to total investment, and a decline in the rate of return on capital. There are reasons for thinking that this broad generalization has some application to the chain grocery business, and that if chain grocery companies are able to avoid these contingencies they will do so primarily by effecting and continuing to maintain substantial economies in their costs of doing business.[5]

In practice, however, the chains could afford smaller profit margins than family stores, since their volume was so much greater. Further, the chains enjoyed bargaining advantages with producers, made larger profits from private label brands, and gained through standardization. In the end, the smaller independent unit was forced to cut prices, so that its return on investment was almost nil, or go out of business. More often than not, it chose the latter course of action.

Some hoped the way to survive might be found through the merchandising of unique items, or through offering superior service, in effect turning the small grocery into a specialty shop. But advertising appeals by larger units, along with the entire drift of the distribution networks of the period, dictated that the future lay with undifferentiated goods. As M. S. Rukeyser wrote in *The Nation* in 1923,

> Many, of course, have been involuntary philanthropists, working

5. M. P. McNair, *Expenses and Profits in the Chain Store Business* (Cambridge, 1929), p. 21.

without net return, being rewarded only with insolvency. Others who keep going are in many instances earning little more than wages for themselves and the members of their families who contribute all the labor needed. They mistakenly believe they are amassing profits; adequate bookkeeping would reveal that they have only been earning wages. Only a small minority of the independents are talented merchants who make handsome profits.

The food industry helped set the pattern for other lines. Generally speaking, food chains would expand into areas adjacent to already existing outlets, so as to enjoy distribution and advertising benefits, as well as to assure customer familiarity with the store name. Thus, the Great Atlantic & Pacific Tea Company (A&P) was concentrated in the East, while Kroger Grocery & Baking Company was in the Midwest. A&P sold more than a billion dollars worth of food in 1930, while Kroger sales were $270 million. Other regional giants were Safeway Stores (East), $220 million; American Stores (central states), $142 million; and First National (New England), $109 million.

Chain units, employing all the advantages of their species, were not limited to groceries. Candy stores did not develop as rapidly, since there was less need for them, but during the 1920s such firms as Schrafft's, Loft, Happiness, Page & Shaw, Mary Lee, and Fanny Farmer became regional chains. Unlike the grocery chains, these candy stores usually concentrated their retail units near candy factories, and in practice acted as outlets for sales by captive factories. Whereas only a small proportion of the grocery sales by A&P were of the captive Ann Page label, all of Loft's sales were of Loft candy. This made for higher profit margins, which were needed in an industry that might suffer during periods of recession.

Another difference was the close collaboration of candy and tobacco merchants. Happiness Candy was allied with United Cigar Stories, and Huyler's candy stores were controlled by D. A. Schulte, a leading tobacconist. In addition, Schulte and

United joined to form Schulte-United 5 cents to $1 Stores, thus entering the lucrative variety store field.

The variety store of the 1920s was a far cry from its ancestor, the dry goods store. Like the smaller unit, it specialized in low-cost, nonperishable, household goods; unlike the dry goods store, it offered a wide line of other products, from candy to pet supplies. The largest of the chain variety stores, F. W. Woolworth Company, expanded rapidly in the 1920s, usually at the expense of family-owned dry-goods and hardware stores. From 1,182 units in 1922 the chain grew to 1,581 in 1927. In the same period total sales went from $167 million to $273 million. Woolworth's nearest competitor, S. S. Kresge Company, established stores selling low-priced items and in addition experimented with units selling goods for prices up to one dollar. But Kresge started later than Woolworth and lacked the older company's reputation. Its sales increased rapidly, however, going from $65 million in 1922 to $134 million in 1927. Other firms in the same and related fields were S. H. Kress & Company, the McCrory Stores Corporation, and W. T. Grant Company. These chains, like Kresge, attempted to imitate the Woolworth model, while at the same time trying to upgrade their prices. Generally speaking, the chains were in competition, with one another, but not as much as the food markets. Each variety chain tried to create a different image for itself. Woolworth liked to be known as old-fashioned and inexpensive, for example, while W. T. Grant cultivated an urbane approach. Kresge and Kress both tried to emulate Woolworth in the lower priced stores, and that plus the similarity in names tended to confuse customers. Despite these differences in corporate strategy, there was no serious threat to the leader, since Woolworth was too firmly entrenched to be successfully attacked. Instead, the competing chains had agreements not to engage in significant price wars, in effect sharing the market as did most of the oligopolies discussed earlier.

The growth of variety stores had an adverse effect on department stores insofar as low-priced items were concerned. On the other hand, department stores were almost always located in prime downtown areas of large cities, while variety stores catered to local neighborhood trade. In addition, the great growth of department stores occurred prior to World War I, and by 1920 they had begun to stagnate, as prime markets were covered and traffic congestion made shopping more difficult. Some stores, such as R. H. Macy & Company in New York, managed to add considerably to their sales, as a result of expert management and merchandising, but they were exceptions. From 1922 to 1927 the number of department stores with annual sales of over one million dollars increased from 151 to 180. The growth was uneven as well as slow in comparision to other retail stores; in 1925 there were three more department stores in that category than in 1927.

Another reason for the decline in department store growth was the rapid development of the old mail order houses. These firms, the most important of which were Montgomery Ward & Company and Sears-Roebuck & Company, suffered sharp declines in sales as a result of the postwar depression. As prices in retail outlets declined, those in mail order catalogs, which were issued every six months, seemed too high, and many sales were lost to department and variety stores in this period. The mail-order houses acted to correct the inroads made by other stores by 1924; they opened their own department stores. Sears-Roebuck began selling goods from its warehouses in 1925, and by 1928 the firm had thirty-seven department stores and 155 small stores, most of which were located on the outskirts of medium-to-large cities, where traffic would not be too much of a problem. In 1926, Montgomery Ward began opening stores in towns with populations of from 3,000 to 6,000 and by 1928, it had 230 such stores in addition to eighteen department stores in larger centers. Sears reported sales of $390 million in 1930, while Montgomery Ward's sales approached $273 million. J. C. Penney, which operated a chain of department stores similar to Sears and Montgomery Ward, had more than 1,450 stores with sales of nearly $200 million. W. T. Grant had nearly 300 stores in 1929, Hahn Department Stores had twenty-two large units, and there were more than a dozen other chains with less than twenty stores.

But the expansion of chain department stores and mail order houses was dwarfed by that of the grocery and variety chains. The latter grew more than 300 percent from 1919 to 1929, while the former did not increase by more than 50 percent. Still, the growth in all branches of retailing was impressive. The 29,000 units in chain operations in 1918 had expanded to 160,000 ten years later.

By 1929, the retailers had added producing units as well. Practically all the food chains had their own brands, usually purchased on contract from established manufacturers or processors. A&P owned bakeries, canneries, and other production facilities, and sold its products under the Ann Page label. Sears and Montgomery Ward had made small beginnings in private label brands, although the variety stores found that it did not pay for them to follow this lead. Penney had long experience in merchandising goods it produced, as did the candy chains. Drug, Incorporated, a large holding company, owned some 10,000 Rexall drugstores, more than 700 Liggett Stores and the West Coast Owl chain, which sold Vicks, Bayer aspirin, and Bristol-Myers products, all produced by Drug, Inc. factories.

While the retailers were dominated by chains, forcing the smaller units into submission or bankruptcy, the wholesalers, particularly those in the always precarious agricultural fields, formed combinations. In 1915 there were fewer than 6,000 farm cooperatives; by 1926, there were more than 12,000, while the volume of business handled by cooperatives increased more than 1,000 percent and exceeded $2.8 billion.

No two cooperatives were alike, as each had to adapt itself to the nature of the product and its markets. For example, the Dairymen's League Co-operative Association was formed by farmers to furnish milk to metropolitan New York. The Wisconsin Cheese Producers' Federation, with 299 members in Wisconsin and Minnesota in 1929, marketed its nonperishable product in all parts of the nation. Land O'Lakes Creameries, centered in Minnesota, was the nation's leading butter producer. The California Fruit Growers' Exchange, the Florida Citrus Fruit Exchange, the California Prune and Apricot Growers' Association, and the California Associated Raisin Co. were formed to gain marketing advantages, stability, and increased markets. The cooperatives enabled many small farmers to survive against larger units, but the price paid was a relinquishing of individual control over production and prices.

The familiar pattern of concentration into an oligopoly situation prevailed in other sectors of the food industry. Meat packing was dominated by Swift & Company, Armour & Company, Wilson & Company, and Cudahy & Company. By the end of the decade, the "big four" had effective control over beef prices, refrigerator cars, and markets. Despite federal prosecution under the antitrust acts, the big four continued their domination throughout the decade, with smaller firms such as John Morrell & Company and Adolph Gobel, existing under their protection and with their forebearance. Although the government claimed conspiracy, and to an extent showed that the big four acted together in setting prices and dividing markets, the industry leaders claimed that this situation actually benefited all. Profit margins in meat packing were among the lowest of any American industry. Meat packing led all others in the introduction of labor-saving equipment, the development of by-products, and packaging. Given this situation, only firms capable of undertaking huge capital investments and able to support large volumes of sales could survive.

The first meat-packing pool was organized in 1902, when Armour and Morris created the National Packing Company, which acquired other firms and attempted to control all the packing houses in the Midwest. This trust was destroyed when the government's charges of rigged, artifically high prices were substantiated. The gentlemen's agreements of the 1920s were of a different order; the firms combined and cooperated in such a way as to make market forecasting possible and preserve rather than expand the profit ratio. From 1919 to 1925, productivity per worker in the industry increased some 30 percent, while the wage bill declined the same amount, as did unit costs. On the other hand, production remained stagnant, with extensive capital charges made by all of the packers. This heavy capital investment was necessary in order to keep the product price low, and was paid by cutting back on labor costs. Only large firms could do this, which made oligopoly natural in the meat-packing industry.

The development of oligopolies could be seen in other areas of the food industry. Continental, General, and Ward dominated the baking industry, each with regional markets that overlapped. Packaged crackers and biscuits were led by National Biscuit, United Biscuit, General Mills, and Pillsbury Flour Mills. The last two were also giants in the flour milling industry, and competed in cereals with Standard Brands, Quaker Oats, and General Foods. National Dairy, Borden Company, Nestle's, Carnation, and Helvetia were the giants in almost every aspect of the creamery industry, although local firms still had large shares of the markets.

In every year of the decade, more regional and small firms either failed or were absorbed by the giants, whose sales and territories were always increasing. Price competition became a secondary aspect of the food markets, although costs remained stable and often declined due to economies of scale. Advertising and packaging replaced word of mouth and price as prime selling tools. In order to cater to the expanding tastes of the urban American, new products were continually being presented for his palate—a cereal could be considered "old and established" if its package had not been changed for more than two years. Foods, like automobiles, had "model changes" to please a market used to such features. Only large firms, with the personnel, distribution networks, factories, and capital for such markets could hope to survive. By the end of the decade there were few major soaps, canned goods, coffees, breakfast cereals, and crackers that did not have national distribution. Gold Dust, Carnation canned milk, Maxwell House, Shredded Wheat, and Uneeda were known in San Francisco as well as New York, in Chicago as well as New Orleans.

In some industries near-monopoly situations, usually a legacy from prewar America, remained. International Salt was the leading factor in its field. Its nearest competitors, Worcester, Leslie-California, and Diamond Crystal, were far behind in sales and market coverage. The International brands were old, established, and well known. In such a field, a newcomer whose product and price was identical to International's, but not as well known, could not easily compete. Thus, other firms did not try to enter the market. Corn Products Refining Company, which processed some three-quarters of the nation's glucose, had the technological skill, market contacts, and personnel to dissuade all who might try to compete. Such firms as Penick and Ford and International Milling Company, were able to take positions in specialized sectors of the market, but never attempted to challenge Corn Products head-on. United Fruit had no real competition in the banana and tropical fruits fields, due to its commanding position in Latin America. American Sugar Refining Company, like International Salt, dominated an industry that contained several smaller firms—National Sugar, Spreckels Sugar, and Great Western Company—which existed through its sufferance and unwillingness to destroy them through price wars.

Throughout the decade antitrust advocates called for the destruction of the monopolies and oligopolies in food, charging that the public suffered by paying high prices, while the farmers were forced to take whatever was offered for their products. Evidence was introduced to prove these allegations, while the companies responded by observing that prices were falling (but much more slowly than costs) and that farm prices often fluctuated in such a way as to benefit the farmer, not the processors. In addition, they said, monopolies and oligopolies in their fields were natural; destroy them, and they would reappear in some new form. The example they cited to prove their point was that of tobacco.

Prior to 1911, almost the entire tobacco industry was dominated by two firms; American Tobacco Company and Continental Tobacco Company, each controlled by the same group, Consolidated Tobacco Company, which owned most of the stock of the two operating firms. A government antitrust suit led to the dissolution of the monopoly in 1911, and the formation of four successor companies: American, Lorillard, Liggett & Myers, and R. J. Reynolds, as well as a host of smaller, more specialized firms. At first there was price competition between the four large firms, and the remaining independents. This proved ruinous, and the firms created new products in an attempt be dominant in the market, especially the rapidly developing ready-made cigarette field. Reynolds proved the most adventurous here, introducing a new cigarette, Camels, consisting of blended tobaccos, including burley, which was sweeter than the straight Turkish and earlier blends. Reynolds lowered the price of a package of twenty cigarettes from fifteen to ten cents, employed a soft package rather than the cardboard slide packs then used for most brands, and made up extra costs by abandoning the practice of including coupons for gifts with each package sold. Reynolds hoped to increase profits, despite the reduction in price, through greatly expanded sales volume. To do this, the company employed the new medias of advertising. "Don't look for premiums or coupons as the cost of the tobaccos blended in Camel cigarettes prohibits the use of them," was one slogan.

At first the campaign seemed to fail, and the Reynolds executives prepared to return to the older methods of packaging and promotion. Then came the war, and shortages in other brands led many to purchase Camels. The public preferred the burley blend, and sales shot up rapidly. By 1917, Camels accounted for 35 percent of all American sales of cigarettes; by 1923, the figure had reached 45 percent.

The other firms retaliated. American Tobacco concentrated on Lucky Strike, while Liggett & Myers advertised Chesterfield. Both were packaged, blended, promoted, and priced in the Camel pattern. The new brands met with success, and by the end of the decade accounted for more than 80 percent of all cigarette sales. Lorillard, which lagged behind and continued its line of Turkish blends, was the last to join in the movement, introducing Old Gold in 1926.

The transition was complete by 1929 with four firms occupying an oligopoly position in tobacco, charging identical prices for their leading brands, mounting similar advertising campaigns, and blending their cigarettes in substantially the same way. The tobacco trust had been liquidated in the hope of developing a more competitive atmosphere in the industry. As a result, there were far fewer brands in use, and the four best-selling brands were almost identical. The industry leaders were content with this situation, and none asked, "In what way was the public interest served by the 1911 dissolution?" The antitrust laws, written before the age of mass distribution, communication, and advertising, did not seem workable, or desirable, by the end of the decade. Was competition the desideratum of those who would destroy the huge trusts? If so, it existed in tobacco. The big four would compete with each other in purchasing leaf, packaging, and advertising, but this did not lead to better products, or make entry into the industry any less difficult than it had been prior to 1911.

In 1912, a year after the Consolidated Tobacco dissolution, the Justice Department initiated prosecution of Aluminum Company of America under the Sherman Anti-Trust Act. Alcoa was under the control of the Mellon family of Pittsburgh, which ran the firm through Arthur Vining Davis and with the estate of Charles Martin Hall, who was responsible for many of the leading technological breakthroughs in the industry. Andrew Mellon had organized the Pittsburgh Reduction Company in 1888 for the purpose of initiating the first commercial production of aluminum in America. During the years that followed, Pittsburgh Reduction attempted to gain control of the few important bauxite ore bodies in the nation, a drive that ended with the 1905 purchase of General Bauxite Company from General Chemical Company, and the 1909 acquisition of the bauxite properties of Republic Mining & Manufacturing Company. With this, the Aluminum Company of America had a monopoly over production of the light metal.

Alcoa skillfully gained control over all new deposits of bauxite, leading the world in exploration for the ore and gaining possession of more than 90 percent of the commercially usable bodies. In addition, the firm spent a great deal of money on research and promotion to expand the use of aluminum and gain it wider acceptance. Practicing vertical integration effectively, Alcoa established subsidiaries in every stage of production, from raw materials to consumer products. Having a monopoly, it was able to set the price of ingot as high or as low as it deemed wise. Throughout the decade aluminum prices fell, as Alcoa hoped lower costs would encourage greater usage. At the same time, the company made certain that the price of fabricated products was not much more than that of the ingots, so as to discourage other firms from purchasing ingots and using them to develop rival fabricating firms. Persistent pressure combined with vast resources kept competitors away from aluminum.

The combination of monopoly or near-monopoly with vertical integration also existed in the nickel industry. The giant here was International Nickel Company of Canada, which was organized through a merger of several Canadian copper firms, and was incorporated in 1916. International had substantial American interests and was strong enough to survive the sharp decline in nickel consumption and prices after World War I, using the slump to take over defunct mines and gain a commanding position. In the next few years the firm concentrated on stabilizing prices, advancing research, and encouraging the increased use of nickel. In 1925, the firm merged with Mond Nickel, which gave it industry leadership. Although other firms continued to exist, International Nickel so dominated the field that the rival firms remained small until World War II.

Like Alcoa, International Nickel made certain that it gained control of significant ore bodies. Since the primary use for nickel was in alloys rather than extrusions, as was the case with aluminum, International did not concern itself with the profit spread between ingot and shapes, concentrating instead on the development of new alloys that would find commercial markets.

Copper, on the other hand, was under oligopoly control. Anaconda Copper Mining Company mined twice as much ore as its nearest competitor, Kennecott Copper Corporation, while such smaller firms as Phelps Dodge Corporation and Calumet & Arizona trailed far behind. Between them, Anaconda and Kennecott smelted more than 40 percent of the nation's copper on 1929. These firms did not dominate the refining of the red metal, but in that field as well there was substantial concentration, with American Smelting & Refining, Nichols Copper Company (controlled by Phelps Dodge and Calumet & Arizona), and Raritan Copper Works refining more than 70 percent of the nation's output. Anaconda and Kennecott used their own captive refiners, in addition to the facilities of the independents.

Like aluminum and nickel, the trend in copper was toward vertical integration. This was accelerated due to the general oversupply of the metal in the early years of the decade, as war orders stopped and many firms were caught with excess capacity. Anaconda and Phelps Dodge responded by attempting to dominate geographic markets and control outlets, while all major producers sought mergers with fabricators. Kennecott acquired Chase Brass Company in 1929 and six years later merged with American Electrical Works, which became Kennecott Wire and Cable Company. Taunton-New Bedford Copper Company, finding itself crushed by the giants, joined with five other small firms to form Revere Copper and Brass Corporation, and then integrated backwards to ore fields. All the large firms entered and competed in the expanding and lucrative field of electric wire, each hoping to gain contracts from the rapidly expanding utilities and motor manufacturers. Another major market was brass, and the larger firms all entered this field as well. The wire and brass companies were eager for such mergers, as competition in their area was equally keen and subject to cyclical influences. Thus, Anaconda merged with American Brass Company in 1922. John D. Ryan, a founder of Anaconda and a prime figure behind the merger, explained it this way:

> The time has come when we cannot compete in the industry if we control only one stage of the business. Anaconda is not now able to operate its mines at a steady and economical rate. We have had high prices during periods of scarcity and low prices during periods of depression. The American Brass Company has not been able to pledge steady production and employment to its workers because it has not been able to book orders far in advance, not knowing what the cost of raw material would be. This is a faulty condition, and we believe that great benefits will arise by reason of the proposed merger.
>
> The raw material supply will be assured at steady prices, and the manufacturer can then book his orders with the certainty of obtaining material at reasonable costs. In this way, from the mine to the consumer, there can be one just and fair profit, and the industry will be stabilized.[6]

6. Isaac F. Marcosson, *Anaconda* (New York, 1957), pp. 175–176.

A growth of concentration and vertical integration occurred in almost all raw materials industries, where competition was either discouraged or merged or destroyed.

Perhaps the major exception to this trend could be found in the chemical industry, primarily due to several unique circumstances. Prior to World War I, America lagged behind the rest of the world in most areas of chemistry. During the war, the industry expanded as the armies needed munitions and the home markets demanded replacements for lost imports. This led to the rapid growth of old firms, such as E. I. du Pont & Company, which revived after antitrust prosecution in the immediate prewar period.

A second factor was the seizure of alien property in the United States, and its disposition to American firms. This was particularly true in the dyestuff industry, where 4,500 German patents were seized. American firms organized the Chemical Foundation, Incorporated, through which they purchased these patents and properties, thus initiating an almost completely new area of interest for American firms.

Allied with this was the growth of research. Within the next few years industrial research increased tremendously, but nowhere as much as in the chemical industry. By 1925, more than half the industrial researchers in the nation worked for chemical firms.

Diversification followed rapidly as each firm attempted to gain a dominant position in the new products and take advantage of new discoveries. An instance of this was Allied Chemical & Dye Corporation, formed in 1920 through a merger of five firms, each in a different branch of the chemical industry. General Chemical was a leading acid manufacturer; Solvay Process was the nation's oldest alkali firm; Barrett Company was well known for its coal tar derivatives; Semet-Solvay made coke and had experimented with by-products; and National Analine & Chemical Company was a leading dye manufacturer.

The rapidly expanding industry made it possible for each firm to concentrate on several areas of interest and perhaps gain dominance through patent, marketing, or price factors, but no single company or group of companies was able to blanket the entire field. Thus, Texas Gulf Sulphur and Freeport Sulphur dominated sulphuric acid, Allied Chemical was a leader in alkali products, du Pont was a leader in fabrics and plastics, Union Carbide pioneered in batteries, American Cyanamid was well known for its fertilizer products, a field in which two firms—American Agricultural Chemical and Virginia-Carolina Chemical—had dominant positions. Of course, all of these firms attempted to expand from their bases into other related fields, usually through mergers.

The natural concomitant of the rapid growth of giant firms was the disappearance of small businesses. Merger and acquisition was a significant part of big business growth, with a peak being reached just prior to the great depression. Of the 7,259 firms merged or acquired from 1919 to 1928, 1,259 disappeared in 1928 alone. Usually, the small firm was forced to submit, either through lack of capital, personnel, or ability to adapt to new circumstances, or through the destructive competition from the giants. Sometimes all of these factors combined in destroying a firm. Each had its own story; few are recorded by historians, but one is known: Smith & Griggs Manufacturing Company of Waterbury, Connecticut. Smith & Griggs was a minor factor in the brass industry, with sales never exceeding half a million dollars. The firm had been dependent upon a few large customers, which it had retained through personal contacts and price competition. In the 1920s it lost several key men and found it could not compete with the larger companies. Too, the firm was unable to finance the purchase of new equipment early in the decade and later on refused to do so in fear of increasing an already burdensome debt structure. To this was added old-fashioned marketing techniques in the age of advertisement. Unable to make the adjustment to the new business climate, the firm went under.[7]

It was many times more difficult to survive in industries that, unlike brass, had rapidly changing technologies, heavy capital requirements, and the need for increased research and development. It was virtually impossible to survive in areas where large advertising and promotional expenses were required. The future appeared bright, however, for the giant survivors, both in the glamour industries and the rejuvenated older industries. Viewing the age of power, consolidation, and mass distribution, business leaders were optimistic. Wesley Mitchell, writing for the Committee on Recent Economic Changes in mid-1929, feared what might happen if demand for goods did not constantly increase. In such a case the nation might face an inventory crisis of major proportions, one that could lead to an economic slump or worse.

> Whether the present rate of progress in the arts of industry and business can be maintained is another uncertainty. Past experience suggests that the pace will slacken presently, and that years may pass before we see another well-maintained advance. But that is a matter in which experience is not a trustworthy guide.

Still, he believed that nation's businessmen had the resources and intelligence to survive and prosper. "All that is certain is that whatever progress in efficiency we continue to make must be won by the same type of bold and intelligent work that earned our recent success."[8]

Summary

The American economy during the 1920s was marked by the rise of several major industries and the acceleration of pre-

7. Theodore F. Marburg, *Small Business in Brass Fabricating: The Smith & Greggs Manufacturing Co. of Waterbury* (New York, 1956).
8. *Recent Economic Changes in the United States* U.S., Department of Commerce, pp. 909–10.

viously existing trends in others. The key element was usually electrification, with consolidation following close behind. Power generation increased more in this decade than at any time before or since, serving the burgeoning new consumer demands for electrified products. In addition, the new industries used large amounts of power, either directly or indirectly, as they helped create greater marketing areas served by rapidly expanding chain stores, which, in turn, were supplied by newly organized cooperatives. By the end of the decade, the small, self-sufficient unit had declined considerably, to be replaced by large monopolies or oligopolies, which practiced vertical integration wherever applicable.

CHAPTER IV

The Failure of Finance Capitalism

Before World War I, most corporations relied upon commercial banks for capital needed for current operations and minor expansion. Dividends were paid as earned, leaving little free cash for self-financing. Important capital improvements were usually financed through long- and short-term credits, although some firms made a practice of issuing additional common stock. These operations were carried on through the investment departments of commercial banks and the investment banks, which sometimes marketed the securities and at other times kept the paper so as to control the firm, or at least influence it in its major decisions. The result was banker-domination of many industries. J. P. Morgan, the symbol of the period, was the single most powerful American from the time of Abraham Lincoln to that of Woodrow Wilson.

This situation changed drastically during the 1920s. Many firms instituted the practice of paying regular dividends from monies left over after provisions for expansion and sinking funds were made. The great prosperity of the period was highlighted by the spectacular performance of the stock market, and when firms realized that their securities would rise even though large dividends were not paid, they retained more cash than ever before, using it for reinvestment, and in some cases making loans in such a way as to become quasibanks themselves. Thus, the role of the commercial bank as a source of corporation credit was seemingly in decline.

During the decade of the twenties, bank credit was of little importance for large manufacturing corporations; bank debt, measured by notes payable, was reduced sharply throughout that period. In 1929, the year before "free" cash began to accumulate, 27 companies out of our sample of 45 large manufacturing corporations had no notes payable. Therefore, when these concerns became liquid the paying off of bank debt did not provide an outlet for their excess funds. Total notes payable of the other 18 companies in 1929 amounted to 2.6 percent of their combined total assets. By 1931, the payable of 8 of these companies had been reduced to zero, and those of the remaining 10, to 0.7 percent. By 1931 the absolute amount of notes payable for the entire group of corporations had declined to 21 percent of the 1929 level. Thus the great liquidity which corporations built up after 1929 was accompanied by an almost complete disappearance of bank debt.[1]

The change was unexpected and caught many commercial banks unaware. Some recovered in time to find profitable investments elsewhere. Real estate loans became important in the 1920s, going from $2.1 billion in 1921 to $5 billion by 1929. Another growing investment was in bonds and stocks, which rose from $8.4 billion to $13.2 billion in the same period. In order to fuel the overheating stock market, commercial banks increased their brokers' loans, most of which went to purchasers of securities on margin. These loans increased from $800 million to $2.6 billion from 1921 to 1929, and made up a significant part of the money flowing into Wall Street toward the end of the decade.

In this same period, as investments rose from $24.9 billion to $34.6 billion, demand deposits increased slightly, from $18 billion to $22.7 billion. Time deposits, which provided only $12.2 billion for investment in 1921, increased to almost $20 billion by the end of the decade, and were a major source

---

1. Freiderich A. Lutz, *Corporate Cash Balances, 1914–1943* (New York, 1945), p. 52.

of new funds for commercial banks as well as a sign of the general prosperity of the period.

The increase in long-term commitments and the decline in the volume of short-term business loans meant a loss of liquidity for commercial banks, which made it difficult for all but the strongest to maneuver through periods of uneasiness. At the same time, the decline of business loans led many small banks to close their doors. These two factors combined to cause 5,209 banks to fail or suspend operations in the 1920s; approximately one out of every six banks in existence in 1921 no longer operated on the eve of the Great Crash. Most of these were small local or regional banks, and only one-fifth were members of the Federal Reseve System.

Trust companies dominated the area of trust services prior to World War I. Although the Federal Reserve Act allowed commercial banks to enter the field, little was done until after the war. Then the banks began to explore the entire area of investments, and within a few years many either merged with trust companies or opened small trusts departments. In addition, the investment bank affiliates of commercial banks, which had become important during the Morgan era, expanded rapidly. The National City Company, First Securities Company, Guaranty Trust Company, and other older firms, along with the established investment banks, remained the major source for corporation securities in the 1920s. But despite their rapid growth, they could not handle the enormous amount of equity underwriting that took place toward the end of the decade, and the commercial banks' investment affiliates grew steadily. From less than 10 percent of the underwriting in 1921, commercial bank investment affiliates took more than 41 percent of the business in 1929. Competition for rich shares in underwritings was keen, for the profits were great at a time when customers would pay premium prices for almost any type of security. As a result, many large urban commercial banks concentrated more on their investment affiliates than on the older lines of business. By 1929, for many of these banks, the investment affiliate tail wagged the commercial bank dog.

Another area of interest for commercial banks in this period was that of time deposits. Although commercial banks had accepted interest-paying deposits for generations, these had a particular interest for bankers in the 1920s. There was more money available for savings than before, and the bankers wished to avail themselves of its use; investment opportunities in land, brokers' loans, and investment affiliates demanded more money, and time deposits were one way to get it. Finally, since time deposits were more stable than demand deposits, the reserve ratio set by the Federal Reserve was far lower, meaning a smaller percentage of the money had to be retained in reserve for time deposits than for demand deposits.

As competition for funds grew, it was natural that the large city banks would seek mergers and expansion. The McFadden Banking Bill of 1927, passed by a friendly Congress, permitted national banks to establish branches within their municipal confines if allowed by state laws. With this, the drive to absorb smaller banks and then continue them as branches, grew. By the end of the decade, many large banks, such as Chase National and National City, had branches throughout their home cities. These two giants not only absorbed eight competitors between them, but they extended their reaches into foreign banking to a greater extent than before, while offering a variety of new services. In 1929, 744 commercial banks were operating 3,496 branches, and it apppeared that more mergers were in the planning stages, and that expansion would, if anything, accelerate.

The drive toward oligopoly appeared in banking as in other large industries. Some institutions went one step further: they attempted to combine banks, nonbanking operations, and stock speculation in single operations. The most famous of these institutions and bankers were Bank of America and A. P. Giannini, its president, the nucleus and driving force for the huge Transamerica complex. In 1928 Giannini announced the incorporation of Transamerica, formed from Bank of Italy and Bancitaly Corporation, themselves holding companies for National Bancitaly Corporation, California Joint Stock Land Bank, Bancitaly Agricultural Credit Corporation, Bancitaly Mortgage Company, Americommercial Corporation, Pacific National Fire Insurance Company, and the Capital Company. This new firm was capitalized at 8.7 million shares, valued at $217.5 million.

Giannini formed Bank of America in much the same way. It included Merchant's National Trust and Savings Bank of Los Angeles and the United Security Bank and Trust Company of San Francisco, among others. It had 145 branches, total resources of $410 million, and invested capital of $50 million. Among its affiliates were Corporation of America, Merchant's National Realty Corporation of Los Angeles, and other trust, real estate, insurance, and financial and development firms, all of which in short time would come under the Transamerica umbrella.

Giannini was the most spectacular banker of his day, and the Transamerica Corporation might have become the model for other banking combinations had not the depression intervened. Few small or even medium-size banks could compete with such giants in customer services. Banking, like so many other industries that had become oligopolistic in the 1920s, dealt in an undifferentiated product, and many bankers seemed to believe that customers and depositors would shift from one unit to another if the terms were only slightly better. While this was true in soap and, to an extent, even in automobiles, it was less true in banking. Somehow fears and customs kept most depositors and commercial houses loyal to old, established banks.

The financial institutions were deeply concerned with regulatory agencies in this period. The American banker of the 1920s considered himself the victim of excessive government regulation. All states had banking laws, and membership in the Federal Reserve System brought additional controls from Washington. The bankers longed for a return to the pre-Federal Reserve days, forgetting that in that period self-regulation was often as strict, and that the Federal Reserve had been formulated by bankers or their representatives, and in general acted more for the benefit of bankers than for any other group.

During World War I, the Federal Reserve worked together with the Treasury Department to help finance the government's increased spending programs. Like most other industries, banking allowed itself to be mobilized for the war effort, and private bankers usually cooperated fully. This situation changed with the end of the war. Since corporation borrowings declined sharply, many banks no longer found it necessary to call upon the Federal Reserve for rediscounting, and so drew away from the central bank, and in some cases went so far as to drop membership.

This situation was compounded by the shifts in interest at the central bank. Unwilling to admit the loss of power, the Federal Reserve concentrated on acting as a rudder in the financial seas. In October 1922 the Treasury established an Open Market Committee, consisting of the governors of the New York, Philadelphia, Chicago, and Boston banks, which would act to supervise open market operations of the system. In addition, the Federal Reserve started to manipulate the rediscount rate so as to encourage and discourage demands for loans at times when such policies were appropriate. The rediscount rate in the spring of 1921 was 6.5 percent; it was lowered steadily so as to encourage expansion in the postwar period and prevent a serious depression, and by the summer of 1924 it had fallen to 3 percent. Then, from 1924 to 1928, the Federal Reserve raised, lowered, raised, lowered, and again raised the rate in an attempt to contain the rapidly expanding economy, which by that time had already shown signs of excessive speculation.

Another important interest of the central bank was international finance. In the aftermath of war, the United States had emerged as the strongest financial power in the world, while Great Britain, whose pound still financed a large number of international transactions, was in stagnation and decline. Benjamin Strong, head of the Reserve Bank of New York, and the most powerful figure among the governors, felt it essential to aid Britain in maintaining its financial integrity. To do this, he worked closely with Montagu Norman, governor of the Bank of England, to prevent gold losses from London to New York. The task was difficult, and of questionable value. The pound was overvalued, and periodic liquidations took place during the decade. Norman had embarked on a program of aid to British industry that required low interest rates and was inflationary. In order to prevent gold losses, it was vital that interest rates in other countries be in line with those of London. Strong agreed to use his influence to keep American money rates low, even if this resulted in excessive borrowing in America. If the Federal Reserve had used its influence to halt the over-heating American economy by raising the rediscount rate, it would have resulted in a flight from the pound, and a possible London panic that would quickly spread throughout Europe. Partly to avoid this, Strong became an apostle of cheap money. To his way of thinking, this was the best way to insure continued prosperity and growth. Some critics and not a few friends warned him that cheap money had become the engine for speculation by 1926, and that the Federal Reserve might not be able to bring excesses to a halt as easily as Strong thought it could. The banker shrugged off these thoughts, believing the Federal Reserve capable of handling any problem that might come along. Furthermore, he held to the view that speculation could be crippled, not through raising the rediscount rate, but rather through a further lowering of it. Writing in February 1927, he said:

> If we lost control of the market, that is to say, if money rates ease so appreciably, due to the accumulation of surplus balances

in New York, these could be mopped up by gradual liquidation of our security holdings. On the other hand, at some point, I recognize that a real liquidation might result which would have some effect upon general business, and if the minute evidences of it appeared, it would then be desirable for us to purchase securities and so lay the foundation, if necessary, for a lower discount rate.[2]

Indeed on August 5, 1927, the rate was lowered from 4.0 to 3.5 percent. The primary impetus for this move came from overseas again, however, as the central bank acted to support the Bank of England's move from 5 percent to 4.5 percent in April.

The lowering of the American rediscount rate served to further stimulate the rampaging stock market, already fueled by brokers' loans. Money rates rose in New York, not so much to dampen the boom, but rather because the private bankers found that the demand would support increases. Recognizing, finally, that the speculation would have to be curbed, Strong was reluctantly obliged to raise the rediscount rate. In February 1928 the rate was raised to 4 percent, in May to 4.5 percent, in July to 5 percent. Finally, on August 9, 1929, the rate was raised to 6 percent, the high point of the boom, a point not touched since mid-1921. Roy Young, who had replaced Strong as the Federal Reserve's leader (Strong died in 1928), issued warnings against excess speculation and called upon the banks to cooperate. But the banks, long free of strong Federal Reserve control, ignored his pleas. Instead, they led a revolt against Washington. Charles A. Mitchell, head of the National City Bank and a Class A Director of the New York Federal Reserve Bank, announced that National City would advance $25 million to traders on Wall Street to take up any withdrawal of Federal Reserve funds. Professor Joseph Lawrence of Princeton University called upon Wall Street to defy Washington.

2. Lester V. Chandler, *Benjamin Strong: Central Banker* (Washington, 1958), pp. 436–437.

The central bank has broken faith. . . . and undertaken a punitive excursion against the stock market without adequate provocation and in contravention of every principle of justice. Wall Street should patronize only banks without the system. As a community, it has ample financial strength to be independent of a central bank which has demonstrated its unenlightened and militant provincialism. The state of New York will charter institutions to provide for the banking needs of the financial community. Although the provinces dominate in politics there is no reason why that domination should extend into the field of finance. That independence may be and should be achieved without the blare of trumpets or the clash of cymbals. It is within the reach of Wall Street and should be embraced.[3]

But the private bankers' revolt was more apparent than real; the Federal Reserve would raise rates, to be sure, but it refused to back its desires with force against noncooperating institutions. When several New York bankers indicated a willingness to work with the central bank in order to keep rates from rising further, the Federal Reserve Board refused the offer, thus allowing men like Mitchell to continue without opposition. Congress refrained from taking action to curb private bankers. President Hoover, who had opposed Strong's cheap money policy throughout the 1920s, said that he lacked the authority to act. Since the private banks and the New York Stock Exchange were incorporated under New York State Law, only the governor of that state could force the bankers to adjust their rates. And Governor Franklin D. Roosevelt remained silent.

The story of the stock market collapse in October 1929, the brief rally of November and December, and the sharp decline that followed, is one of the most familiar in American history. Gross national product declined from approximately $104 billion in 1929 to $56 billion in 1933. Unemployment rose

3. Joseph Lawrence, *Wall Street and Washington* (Princeton, 1929), pp. 365–366.

from 1.5 million to 12.8 million in the same period. Corporate profits, which reached a high of $9.6 billion in 1929, fell rapidly, and in 1932 American corporations reported losses of $3 billion. Commercial banks, many of which were caught with little liquid capital, faced crises throughout the period, heightened by periodic runs on the banks and defalcations.

At first most banks seemed capable of weathering the storm. Then, in 1930, more than 800 banks declared bankruptcy. Thousands of others followed in the next three years. The veins and arteries of the nation had petrified. Bethlehem Steel, Continental Can, American Telephone & Telegraph, and other large firms, all of which had planned bond issues to gain funds for expansion, were obliged to cut back on operations, which led to more unemployment and further business declines due to decreased consumption. The merger movement was halted abruptly. Some 1,100 firms had disappeared through mergers or acquisitions in 1929; the figure for 1933 was 107, with only twelve disappearing in the fourth quarter of the year. National City Bank and the Corn Exchange Bank called off their planned merger, as did many other financial institutions.

Hastening to alleviate the situation, the Federal Reserve tried to make money cheap so as to encourage business expansion once more. By December 1930 the rate was 2 percent, the lowest in the history of the system. Still, businessmen were loath to commit themselves to new capital spending. The depression had changed a business atmosphere of unbridled optimism to one of unqualified gloom. From what had seemed the apogee of American business, the nation had gone to the nadir of the businessman.

The business decline of 1930 was rapid, as an inexorable chain of events took form. Bank insolvencies led to corporate difficulties and resulted in the firing of employees who, as consumers, cut down on spending. This led to a further cutback in production and more firings, followed by still greater declines in consumption. And so the cycle continued throughout the year. By the winter of 1930, employment had dropped 25 percent, and wages, showing the impact of overtime losses, had fallen almost 35 percent. Business activity was down more than 30 percent due to lack of purchasing power and other constrictions, as well as a rush of failures.

At first the President and business leaders seemed unaware of the nature of the crash. Leading government figures, such as Treasury Secretary Andrew Mellon, said that the crash was primarily financial, and that the Wall Street speculators were being punished for the recklessness. In time they would be destroyed, and then sounder heads would preside over the business of putting the finances of the nation back on its feet. President Hoover believed that spending excesses had been partly responsible for the panic, and thought that by balancing the budget he could regain public confidence in the economy. Relief and aid would be offered, but wherever possible it would be provided by local and state governments, and private organizations. Hoover held several White House conferences with business leaders hoping to win their agreement to maintain employment and production until the crisis passed. At the same time, he increased expenditures for needed public works, gaining the cooperation of some governors, who added workers to state rolls for such improvements.

Many leading businessmen reacted more like Mellon than like Hoover. The National Association of Manufacturers observed that panics and depressions were not new to America; there had been at least seventeen of them since 1800. The business cycle could no more be stopped than man could be made immortal. Some badly managed large concerns, and many smaller businesses, would doubtless be liquidated, and Wall Street speculators and the banks encouraging them would be forced into bankruptcy, but after the panic subsided, reorganization would lead to greater efficiencies and a sounder economy.

An indication of this myopic view could be found in the tariff discussions of 1930. During his campaign, Hoover had promised to seek rate increases on imported farm products, so as to encourage American farm prices to move upward. Accordingly, a tariff bill was introduced into the House in 1929. But during the debates, it became clear that business leaders, fearful of foreign competition during the depression, would insist on higher duties on manufactured goods. Operating through Senator Joseph Grundy of Pennsylvania, big business —especially heavy industry—insisted on raising duties on most manufactured goods. Grundy's argument was that high tariffs would prevent cheap foreign goods from competing with their American counterparts in an already crippled market. Although Hoover had committed himself to international cooperation to end the depression, he accepted the Hawley-Smoot Tariff, which on the average increased duties 40 percent. The academic community called upon Hoover to veto the measure, claiming it would only deepen the depression. In a petition signed by more than a thousand economists, Hawley-Smoot opponents claimed higher duties "would operate, in general, to increase the prices which domestic consumers would have to pay. By raising prices, they would encourage concerns with higher costs to undertake production, thus compelling the consumer to subsidize waste and inefficiency in industry." Every facet of the domestic economy, from farmers to miners, from businessmen to the unemployed, would suffer in one way or another under the new tariff, which would also lead to retaliation, a new trade war, and a further decline in trade and international goodwill. [4]

Although Hoover had called the Hawley-Smoot Bill "vicious, extortionate, and obnoxious," he signed it on June 17, 1930, stating that he hoped the tariff commission would

4. *New York Times,* May 5, 1930.

act slowly to reduce rates. This hope, feeble though it was, was dashed; within a year, twenty-five nations had responded to the American action by either raising their own tariffs or threatening to do so.

By early January 1931, it appeared the optimists were correct, as business statistics showed a turn in the cycle. Factory payrolls, construction contracts, and industrial production all increased sharply, as did prices of common stocks. Factory employment and department store sales leveled out and began to show signs of turning upward. There was talk of cutting back on emergency programs and returning to the pre-1929 situation; those who spoke of fundamental difficulties in the economy were either ignored or castigated.

But the difficulties were fundamental. The banking situation remained weak, with many institutions on the brink of insolvency. In April 1931, the Kredit-Anstalt Bank of Austria failed, bringing down many central European banks in its wake. President Hoover responded to a threatened world panic by proposing a moratorium on major international debts. The French, whose help might have prevented the failure of the Kredit-Anstalt, again hesitated, and by the time that nation agreed to the moratorium, the panic had spread out of control. Germany was forced to freeze foreign accounts; Great Britain suspended foreign gold sales on September 21; and panic set in among American bankers. The European crisis affected every American bank with foreign holdings, but most could have survived even this had it not been for a second panic on Wall Street. The combination of blocked European accounts and the loss of portfolio values led to a new wave of bank failures, which began in spring 1931 and continued through winter 1932. In this period, more than 2,000 banks with liabilities in excess of $1.7 billion failed. Business failures increased, reaching 2,000 a month in the spring of 1932, then rising to 3,500 a month a year later. The gross national product for 1932 was approximately half that of 1929, and there seemed no way to stem the collapse.

By late 1931, few businessmen dared talk about the beneficial nature of periodic purges of the economy; it was clear that the depression they faced was far more severe than any in American history. Some suggested that it might spell the end of American free enterprise and ultimately end in communism. Others thought that the key to ending the depression lay in an extension of the government–business cooperation that had existed since World War I, together with joint actions by businessmen through trade and other associations. This idea was particularly attractive to businessmen who had participated in the economic conscription of World War I. One of them, Gerard Swope, had become president of General Electric after working with Baruch's War Industries Board. On September 16, 1931, Swope spoke of his program for recovery before the National Electrical Manufacturers Association, in an address entitled "The Stabilization of Industry." In it he discussed his belief that the function of industry was to provide a higher standard of living for the nation, not merely to produce higher profits for the individual firm. Clearly such was not the case in 1931, and Swope doubted that government on any level was capable of halting the depression or returning the nation to some semblance of prosperity. Industry had made possible the great economic advances of the past, he said, and industry should take the lead in 1931, without waiting for governmental sanctions of one kind or another. Toward this end, Swope put forth a five-point program which he hoped would be accepted by the electrical manufacturers first, and then by the rest of the business community.

1. Every effort should be made to stabilize industry and thereby stabilize employment to give the worker regularity, and continuity of employment, and when this is impracticable, unemployment insurance should be provided.

2. Organized industry should take the lead, recognizing its responsibility to the employees, to the public, and to its stockholders—rather than that democratic society should act through its government. If the various States act, industry will be confronted with different solutions, lacking uniformity and imposing varying burdens, making competition on a national scale difficult. If either the individual States or the Federal Government act, the power of taxation has no economic restraints.

3. There should be standarized forms of reports so that stockholders may be properly informed. As a result of the steady increase in number and size of corporations and number of shareholders, there has been much discussion of the uniformity, frequency, and regularity of reports of corporate activities, and considerable criticism of the forms of these reports; some too conservative, some not sufficiently complete; while others are considered to be fair and complete, but even so there is lack of uniformity among the different companies.

4. Products and consumption should be coordinated on a broader and more intelligent basis, thus tending to regularize employment and removing fear from the minds of workers as to continuity of employment, as to their surviving dependents in case of death, and as to old age. This should be done preferably by the joint participation and joint administration of management and employes. These things cannot be done by an individual unit—organized industry must do them.

5. If organized industry is to undertake this work, every effort should be made to preserve the benefits of individual originality, initiative and enterprise, and to see that the public is assured that its interests will be protected, and this can be done most effectively by working through the agency of the Federal Government.[5]

The plan drew instant responses from all segments of the business community as well as government. Some thought it would destroy free enterprise and create a fascistic state. Generally speaking, this reaction was prevalent among businesses not active in the trade association movement and among smaller businessmen, who had little experience with working with government. Although it was not put in this way at the time, Swope proposed to bring the federal government into the trade associations, and the trade associations into the government; he would unite the experiences of World War I with those of the 1920s. The first step would be to jettison ideas of monopoly and competition prevalent among reformers prior to the war, and to forget the idea of limited government. Henry I. Harriman, president of the Chamber of Commerce, was one of the few who recognized the ramifications of the Swope program. As head of New England Power Company, he had long experience with government regulation and had no fear of it; as a participant in the WIB, he knew that such controls brought benefits as well as restrictions. "Business

5. *New York Times,* September 17, 1931.

prosperity and employment will be best maintained by an intelligently planned business structure," he said. "We have left the period of extreme individualism," he concluded in a report to the Chamber of Commerce. The antitrust laws, "suitable as they may have been for economic conditions of another day," should be discarded or at least modified drastically. As for businessmen, they must join in organizations that will limit competition, enforce prices, and insure profits. On the other hand, businesses must also set aside a portion of their profits for sickness and old age insurance for employees. As for businessmen who would not join in such organizations, "they'll be roped, branded, and made to run with the herd," said Harriman. In 1931, a majority of the members of the Chamber of Commerce accepted this report.

President Hoover was opposed to the Swope plan, which went against every tenet of "rugged individualism." In a memorandum of the period, he wrote:

> This plan provides for the consolidation of all industries into trade associations, which are legalized by the government and authorized to "stabilize prices." There is no stabilization of prices without price-fixing, and this feature at once becomes the organization of gigantic trusts such as have never been dreamed of in the history of the world. This is the creation of a series of complete monopolies over the American people. It means the repeal of the entire Sherman and Clayton Acts, and all other restrictions on combinations and monopoly. In fact, if such a thing were ever done, it means the decay of American industry from the day this scheme is born, because one cannot stabilize prices without protecting obsolete plants and inferior managements. It is the most gigantic proposal of monopoly ever made in history.[6]

Thus, Herbert Hoover evoked the progressive attitudes of prewar America to respond to the challenges of the depression.

6. William Starr Myers and Walter H. Newton, *The Hoover Administration: A Documented Narrative* (New York, 1936), p. 119.

In so speaking he earned the enmity of a large portion of the business community, which had not trusted him in the first place. On the other hand, the liberal intellectuals, who considered him the last spokesman of a corrupt plutocracy, also remained cool toward the President. Herbert Hoover was caught between the attacks of both business and its critics.

In 1931, after the Swope plan was introduced, the President unveiled his own program of ending the depression. While reiterating his belief that the domestic depression had been cured when foreign difficulties created a new depression, Hoover did admit that self-help and volunteerism had not worked as well as he had hoped. Reluctantly, he turned to new measures.

Hoover was convinced that the key to recovery lay in a restoration of the banking system. During the first half of 1931, he asked the banking community to draw up plans to aid failing banks. None were forthcoming. As a result, Hoover called financial leaders to Washington early in October to tell them that the federal government would fill the vacuum of leadership. He proposed the establishment of a National Credit Corporation, which would be capitalized at $500 million, this amount to be raised by the banks. The NCC would rediscount paper ineligible for acceptance at Federal Reserve Banks and would make loans to banks on the verge of dissolution due to insolvency.

From the first it was recognized that stronger measures would be necessary. Nonetheless, the NCC loaned $153 million to 575 banks during its three months of existence. Although this was hardly sufficient to stem the crisis, whatever value the agency had was almost destroyed as a result of a provision by which a borrowing bank had to make public its difficulties. Such publicity usually did more harm than could be remedied by loans. On January 4, 1932, Hoover sent a special message to Congress asking for strong measures. Among the eight points of his new program were calls for the creation of a system of home loan discount banks to assist homeowners in retaining their property and to stimulate the construction industry, the strengthening of the Federal Land Banks to aid farmers, the removal of all rediscounting restrictions regarding Federal Reserve activities, "revision of banking laws in order to better safeguard depositors," and a balancing of the federal budget. The key proposal, however, was Hoover's request for "the creation of a Reconstruction Finance Corporation to furnish during the period of the depression credits otherwise unobtainable under existing circumstances in order to give confidence to agriculture, industry and labor against further paralyzing influences."[7]

The Reconstruction Finance Corporation, the heart of the Hoover program, passed both houses of Congress on January 16 and was signed into law on January 22. President Hoover announced the selection of Eugene Meyer of the Federal Reserve as chairman of the RFC, and Charles G. Dawes, who had been vice-president in Calvin Coolidge's administration and was an important member of the banking fraternity, as its president.

The RFC was capitalized at $2 billion, $500 million of which was subscribed to by the Treasury. The remainder was to be taken up by private interests, or failing that, by the government. The money was to be loaned to banks, insurance companies, building and loan associations, and other financial institutions in difficulty. By March 1933, when Hoover left the White House, the RFC had authorized $2.9 billion in loans and had disbursed $2.2 billion, of which $368 million had been repaid. Nonetheless, the organization was not able to stem the depression.

The RFC faltered for several reasons. In the first place, the banks were unable to support the loans, since they were in such poor financial shape that increases in their indebtedness

7. *New York Times*, January 5, 1932.

often did more harm than good. In addition, most of the important loans went to a relatively few large banks, while the smaller institutions were unable to get needed help. Shortly after Dawes resigned his post in June 1932, it was learned that the Central Republic Bank, of which he was the chairman, had received an RFC loan of $90 million. Finally, the Democrat-controlled Congress insisted that all loans be made public. This led to the same difficulty that had plagued the NCC: once the depositors learned that an institution needed a loan, they would begin a run, which would lead to its downfall. By 1933 few banks were willing to risk using the facilities of the RFC.

The rationale and operation of the RFC indicated that Hoover was prepared to offer business a partnership with government in saving the nation, while at the same time allowing businessmen their dominant positions in the economy. Business' unwillingness to cooperate fully with Hoover and its insistence that any government interference was ipso facto evil demonstrated the business community's essential unwillingness to recognize the social and economic threats posed by the depression.

By the time the two national political parties gathered in convention in the summer of 1932, the businessman's reputation had fallen to a low point. Those who supported the Swope plan and called for expansion of the RFC were called fascists by reformers, and those who defended the theory that a periodic purge was good for the economy were castigated as being heartless. Ivar Kreuger, the "Match King" who had been considered an international version of men like Andrew Carnegie, committed suicide. Samuel Insull, the utilities tycoon of Chicago, was indicted for embezzlement and fled the country. Jobless workers marched on Henry Ford's River Rouge plant in Detroit and were cut down by Ford's private police force and the Dearborn police; four were killed in the skirmish. The Bonus Expeditionary Force gathered in Washington to demand support for a bonus bill then before Congress. Revolution seemed to be in the air, and the businessmen seemed to have no stomach for the fight. There were no defenses of free enterprise capitalism such as those that filled the newspapers in 1930, and few predicted a quick end to the depression. Indeed, big businessmen not only refrained from defending the administration, they showed their lack of faith by participating in a wild flight from the dollar. Approximately $100 million a week in gold was sent to Swiss and Dutch banks in anticipation of American insolvency. A vacuum of power existed, and it was clear that it would have to be filled if the economic system as it had existed prior to 1929 were to be rescued.

The Democratic party's candidate for the presidency, Franklin D. Roosevelt, realized that his victory was almost assured, since the American people could be counted on to give a no-confidence vote to Hoover. Accordingly, Roosevelt spoke vaguely of lower tariffs, cutting government expenditures, and balancing budgets, and concentrated his attacks on Hoover's weakest points. There were few criticisms of the business community at large in most of his speeches, for such was not necessary. Instead, Roosevelt showed some sympathy for business, and spoke of the need for a new role for the businessman in the New Deal he hoped to create. This new role was sketched in a speech before the Commonwealth Club in San Francisco on September 23. After reviewing the history of government–business relations during the early part of the nation's history, Roosevelt spoke of the rapid growth of industry in the late nineteenth century, when industry benefited from government aid while at the same time speaking for laissez-faire. Similarly, supposedly staunch believers in free enterprise hastened to use the RFC soon after that agency had been established. It was time, said Roosevelt, for business to better align its words with its actions and recognize that government had a role—an important one—to play in the economic arena. America was entering a new age, one in which there were no new frontiers, in which immigration was no longer a major factor, and in which economic concentration had reached new levels.

> This implication is, briefly, that the responsible heads of finance and industry instead of acting each for himself, must work together to achieve the common end. They must, where necessary, sacrifice this or that private advantage; and in reciprocal self-denial must seek a general advantage. It is here that formal Government—political Government, as you choose—comes in. Whenever in the pursuit of this objective the lone wolf, the unethical competitor, the reckless promoter, the Ishmael or Insull whose hand is against every man's, declines to join in achieving an end recognized as being for the public welfare, and threatens to drag the industry back to a state of anarchy, the Government may properly be asked to apply restraint. Likewise, should the group ever use its collective power contrary to the public welfare, the Government must be swift to enter and protect the public interest.[8]

Despite disclaimers in the middle of the speech, and hope expressed toward the end, the Commonwealth Club address was essentially pessimistic. It reflected ideas associated with A. A. Berle, Jr., then a member of the Brain Trust, and an advocate of a stronger government role in the economy. It also seemed related to Swope's idea; later on Roosevelt and Swope corresponded, and the General Electric executive was looked upon as one of the President's emissaries to the business world.

The Commonwealth Club speech drew criticism from both left and right. One school of reformers demanded that Roosevelt advocate a strong antitrust program, punishing business for its role in causing the depression. A substantial part of the business community opposed any further government entry into the economy, arguing that such interference might

8. Samuel Rosenman, ed., *The Public Papers and Addresses of Franklin D. Roosevelt*, I: *The Genesis of the New Deal, 1928–1932* (New York, 1938), pp. 742–56.

prolong the depression and in the process destroy the economic system. President Hoover spoke forcefully on the latter point. If the New Deal were implemented, it would kill rather than cure the patient. As serious as the depression was, it did not call for actions as drastic as those Roosevelt suggested. A combination of self-help with government aid, Hoover believed, was the best policy. Speaking in New York on October 31, he said:

> This campaign is more than a contest between two men. It is more than a contest between parties. It is a contest between two philosophies of government. . . . Even if the government conduct of business could give us the maximum of efficiency instead of least efficiency, it would be purchased at the cost of freedom. It would increase rather than decrease abuse and corruption, stifle initiative and invention, undermine development of leadership, cripple mental and spiritual energies of our people, extinguish equality of opportunity, and dry up the spirit of liberty and progress. Men who are going about this country announcing that they are liberals, are not liberals, they are reactionaries of the United States.[9]

Government–business relations as Roosevelt would have them and Hoover thought they existed were not vital in the election of 1932; poverty, unemployment, and stagnation were. Accordingly, the electorate cast a massive vote against Hoover. Roosevelt received a popular vote of 27.8 million and an electoral vote of 472. Hoover received a popular vote of 15.8 million, and succeeded in carrying only six states, with an electoral vote of 59. Roosevelt took office on March 4, 1933, at a time when every bank in the nation was closed, and the depression at its low point. He had a mandate for change which he meant to use. The New Deal would bring drastic changes to almost every aspect of American life. For business, it meant the end

9. *New York Times,* November 1, 1933.

of the era of modified laissez-faire, and the beginning of one in which the government's attitude would have to be considered in every major decision.

Summary

After World War I, American banks consolidated and expanded into new areas of investment, while at the same time breaking loose from some of the restraints imposed by the Federal Reserve System. As a result, much of the banking excesses of the 1920s went unchecked. On the surface, it appeared that banking was as secure as ever; in reality, the banking practices of the period, based as they were upon the promise of continued prosperity, helped contribute to the collapse of 1929.

President Hoover attempted to check the depression by encouraging business to help itself, using federal power only when such help was not forthcoming. Some businessmen, led by Gerard Swope, suggested a return to government-business cooperation, stating that only in such a way could a massive effort be mounted. During the election campaign of 1932, Franklin Roosevelt tried to refrain from committing himself to any single policy, but did indicate that controls over and through business would have to be considered. Meanwhile the business community as a whole could offer no meaningful solutions after the panic of 1931. It was evident that laissez-faire capitalism, as the term was then commonly understood by businessmen, was to be sharply changed.

CHAPTER V

Business and Government During the New Deal

In all of American history there has never been a period in which the government was not involved in the workings of the economy, and during which businessmen could proceed with their affairs without taking the attitudes and actions of government into account. This was true in the period of the Virginia Company, of the colonial governments, the Confederation, and the national era. It was manifested in the form of bounties, money and land grants, franchises, tariffs, currency legislation, judicial decisions, and taxes. During the early twentieth century, moral suasion, manipulation of public opinion, and other more sophisticated methods were used. Businessmen were used to such things, and during the 1920s did not think of them as being interventions in their affairs. But the New Deal was different. The 1929 crash and the depression that followed made businessmen more concerned with their positions than they had been in the past, and certainly more aware of the relations they had with government.

This had happened before; it could be seen during the panics of 1893 and 1907, for example. But in the past, it was the businessmen who aided government, rather than vice versa. Grover Cleveland in 1893 and Theodore Roosevelt in 1907 deferred to J. P. Morgan when the economy was shocked, and the bankers did not fail to stem the crises. There was no Morgan in the business community in 1929. The postwar business world was noted for its corporate character, not for its individualism. In the developed capitalism of the twenties, men like Morgan were no longer needed. Individual entrepreneurs, such as Sarnoff in radio, Sloan in automobiles, Lasky in motion pictures, and Davis in aluminum, had some difficulties in defining the nature of their businesses, much less transcending their boundaries to give national leadership. Reluctantly, and only after urging business to produce a group of new Morgans, did President Hoover step into the breach and offer national leadership in the crisis. But Hoover was unfitted by temperament to fill the vacuum successfully. Not even the business community seemed to believe that rugged individualism could lead the way back to prosperity in 1932. Some spoke of the need for a truly national bank when asked for concrete proposals. None were willing to go further than this, however, in terms of government actions to end the depression. On the eve of the New Deal, only those businessmen who supported the Swope plan and a few individualists demanded an enlarged role for the federal government in the economy.

There have been many hypotheses as to the underlying philosophy of the New Deal. Some see it as a continuation of Wilson's New Freedom; some as an implementation of Theodore Roosevelt's New Nationalism; one school of historians considers it a three-phase movement, with Roosevelt shifting ground to meet new challenges as old programs became outmoded or failed; others see the period as a series of pragmatic responses to practical problems, with ideology playing a secondary role throughout. All of these positions, as well as several others, can be supported by patterning the evidence and quoting leading New Deal figures. In fact, the period was marked by contradictions, inconsistencies, personal clashes, and wide-ranging experimentation, all of which was presided over by the magisterial, charismatic figure of the President, who took credit for, or was credited with, the work and ideas of aides of sharply differing temperaments and philosophies, and who rarely bothered to attempt a rationalization of the New Deal.

Insofar as the business community was concerned, Roosevelt seemed pro-business in his belief that the economic order must remain undisturbed in its true essentials. On the other hand, he was willing to make any changes he or his advisors deemed necessary to do away with abuses. In the beginning, he concentrated on eliminating features that caused misery, or that he thought responsible for the depression. The visionaries in his administration were disappointed in his moderation, finding, with the exception of the Tennessee Valley Administration, little to cheer. Then, as the depression seemed on the way to solution, and with the failure of several programs, Roosevelt shifted to a more reformist stance. Finally, after the depression of 1937, he began an all-out attack on business concentration.

The business community regarded Roosevelt with suspicion at first. The fact that he was a Democrat and an unknown quality had a good deal to do with this distrust in 1933; the tendency of businessmen to confuse reforms with revolution was more important later on. In retrospect, Roosevelt's major accomplishment during the New Deal was to preserve American capitalism by reforming it. Business critics of Roosevelt usually disregarded the first part of this phrase and concentrated on the second. Having created a caricature, they proceeded to attack it with vigor during the rest of the decade. What they failed to realize was that Roosevelt, more than Hoover, recognized the nature of their problems and was attempting realistic solutions. Hoover's "rugged individualism" speeches of 1932 harkened back to nineteenth-century ideals; Roosevelt's actions after 1933 more often than not responded to immediate problems but showed little sign of a coherent philosophy. Hoover had a tendency to measure reality by the yardstick of his ideological commitments; Roosevelt, less the intellectual than his predecessor, was more concerned with problem solving. It would appear that these two presidents each concentrated on a different aspect of what could also be found in businessmen of the period. Hoover's rhetoric was that of the Chamber of Commerce and National Association of Manufacturers, while Roosevelt's actions were akin to the pragmatic methods businessmen used in day-to-day dealings.

The key elements of the early New Deal, insofar as the businessman was concerned, were bills relating to the financial complex and the National Industrial Recovery Act. The former was aimed at correcting the abuses that many claimed had caused the depression, while the NIRA was an attempt to reform business-government relations so as to secure stability in the economy and insure closer relations between the political and economic forces in the nation.

On March 5 Roosevelt issued a proclamation declaring a four-day bank holiday. Four days later Congress passed, and the President signed, the Emergency Banking Act, which gave Roosevelt the power to close banks in the Federal Reserve System and to control the export and hoarding of precious metals. This legislation was intended to take care of immediate problems in banking; the Glass-Steagall Banking Act, ratified on June 16, represented the major drive to reform banking in America. Under the terms of this legislation, commercial and investment banking were divorced, and national banks were permitted to establish branches in states which allowed such practices among the state banks. In addition, the act established the Federal Deposit Insurance Corporation.

During the next few months, the banking complex was dismantled by its controllers. J. P. Morgan & Company, for example, chose to remain in commercial banking, and separate from its investment affiliate by forming Morgan Stanley & Company. Edward B. Smith & Company merged with the investment affiliate of the Guaranty Trust Company of New York and eventually became Smith Barney & Company. Harriman Ripley & Company was formed through the dissolution of the National City Bank's prominent affiliate, National City Company, and the disaffiliation of the investment functions of Brown

Brothers, Harriman & Company. Supplementary legislation in 1935 completed the change to distinct banking systems. On the other hand, legislation could not erase the important personal ties that existed in the financial community, and the investment bankers worked together with their former commercial partners whenever possible.

Until the new systems could establish themselves, a reinvigorated and reshaped Reconstruction Finance Corporation engaged in what formerly had been thought of as banking functions. The RFC had been considered a vehicle for aid to large financial institutions and a psychological weapon by the Hoover administration. The first RFC chairman of the New Deal, Jesse Jones, hoped to use it to aid all segments of business and to end the deflationary spiral that had existed since 1929. Under the terms of the Emergency Banking Act of March 9, the agency's powers were extended, and Jones meant to use these powers to the utmost. Approximately $2 billion—or one-third of RFC's funds—went to banks, but Jones used most of this money to purchase preferred stock and debentures in shaky institutions rather than making loans. The banks needed more equity capital and accepted the funds, which were instrumental in saving dozens of large and medium-size institutions. Furthermore, Jones acted to revive those institutions in bankruptcy; $700 million was extended to closed banks and disbursed to holders of blocked accounts. The money then reentered the nation's financial stream, thus acting to stimulate consumption and employment. By the end of 1935, the RFC had loaned or invested over $3.7 billion to and in banks, which amounted to more than half the nation's reported banking capital for that year. Of this sum, nearly $1.7 billion had been repaid, a tribute to Jones' sagacity and vigor. By then, the Roosevelt "revolution" in banking was essentially completed.

As important as the banking legislation and the RFC were in the first period of the New Deal, the National Recovery Administration had more widespread implications for the businessman. Its coming was no surprise. Theodore Roosevelt had talked of such an agency, and Swope had proposed one several times since 1931. Speaking before the United States Chamber of Commerce on May 4, the President called for an end to unfair and destructive competition in business. On May 17, in a recommendation to the special session of Congress, he spoke of the need for changes in the antitrust laws. By then, the President had several drafts of proposed legislation designed to mobilize the business community for recovery. These came from a number of sources, but two stood out as being more important than the rest. General Hugh Johnson, who had participated in the War Industries Board, offered a program, similar to that used by Baruch, in which the government would control the economy, work with businessmen, and dictate policies to them. Undersecretary of Commerce John Dickinson, working with members of the business community, called for industrial self-regulation guided and aided by the federal government. As was his custom, Roosevelt asked both groups to merge their ideas, although each was based on a different hypothesis. Despite much acrimony, compromises were reached. The resulting proposal allowed businesses to join together in industrial groupings to write codes of fair conduct, but gave the government the power to accept or reject them, and to administer the codes.

The idea behind the National Recovery Administration seemed simple enough. Title I of the NRA would organize industries, maintain employment and wages, and set standards. Title II established the Public Works Administration, which would undertake needed projects and so add to the nation's purchasing power. General Johnson, who headed the NRA, saw both as being interrelated; the failure of one would result in the crippling of the other. In explaining NRA to the public—and the businessmen—Roosevelt showed his mastery of language and his ability to simplify complex problems.

The law I have just signed was passed *to put people back to work,* and let them buy more of the products of farms and factories and start our business at a living rate again. This task is in two stages; first, to get many hundreds of thousands of the unemployed back on the payroll by snowfall and, second, to plan for a better future in the long pull. While we shall not neglect the second, the first stage is an emergency job. It has the right of way.... Between these twin efforts—public works and industrial re-employment—it is not too much to expect that a great many men and women can be taken from the ranks of the unemployed before winter comes. It is the most important attempt of this kind in history. As in the great crisis of the World War, it puts a whole people to the simple but vital test: —*"Must we go on in many groping, disorganized, separate units to defeat or shall we move as one great team to victory?"*[1]

Translating the NRA's plans into actions was not as simple as FDR supposed it would be; nor was it viewed with unquestioned favor by the public and the business community. General Johnson proved mercurial, dynamic, and at times appeared a caricature of Theodore Roosevelt; he was inspiring, but he was a poor administrator and an inept coordinator. Three factions vied for power within the NRA, and Johnson seemed incapable of resolving their differences. First there were those who believed that businessmen and business interests should dominate the agency. They were opposed by old-line Wilsonians who dreamed of a commonwealth of small competing units. A third group hoped the NRA would sponsor cooperation among the various units, but itself act as a check on the power of any single one.[2]

The men in control during the first months of the program were generally of the first group: businessmen—usually with

1. Samuel I. Rosenman, ed., *The Public Papers and Addresses of Franklin D. Roosevelt;* II: *The Year of Crisis, 1933* (New York, 1938), pp. 251–256.
2. E. W. Hawley, *The New Deal and the Problem of Monopoly* (New York, 1966), p. 35.

experience in the WIB or related agencies—who thought in terms of industrial self-regulation. Under their leadership, dozens of codes emerged from Johnson's office weekly. Business leaders cooperated with the New Deal in this period, and many looked upon Roosevelt as the savior of American capitalism. They noted that he said nothing about such code hallmarks as high price fixing and attempts to find loopholes in the minimum wage provisions. This brought criticisms from the unions and antibusiness reformers in the Roosevelt camp, as well as the two opposing groups within the NRA. In addition, overconfident businessmen suggested that the government withdraw from the agency, and allow it to function as a completely private, voluntary organ. Gerard Swope thought the Chamber of Commerce could do the job as well as Johnson. This gave more fuel to the anti-Johnson forces, who claimed that NRA was becoming little more than a vehicle for American fascism. Business had been responsible for the depression, they claimed, and now Roosevelt was rewarding the culprits with more power than they had obtained during the Coolidge Administration. Finally, Johnson was not able to bear the strain of the work. He drank more heavily than before, and began to make what some considered dictatorial speeches, in which he referred with favor to Mussolini and the corporate state.

In March 1934, Roosevelt appointed an investigatory board, headed by Clarence Darrow, to study the NRA. Darrow, whose socialist views were well known, presented a damaging picture of an agency dedicated to serving big business through the creation of de facto monopolies. Donald Richberg, who had been a devoted follower of Theodore Roosevelt and was now a bitter opponent of the general, spoke of the need for stronger government supervision of the agency. Johnson was unable to stand the pressure; he submitted his resignation on September 24, 1934.

Despite Johnson's departure, Roosevelt attempted to maintain his close relations with the business community. A

National Industrial Recovery Board was named to administer the NRA. The board would consist of two businessmen, two academics, and one labor leader. The businessmen—S. Clay Williams of Reynolds Tobacco and Arthur Whiteside of Dun and Bradstreet—were both Democrats, supporters of the New Deal, and believers in the essentials of the Johnson program. The remaining members were Leon Marshall and Walton Hamilton, both college professors, and Sidney Hillman, president of the Amalgamated Clothing Workers Union. Others were named to act in an advisory capacity.

From the start, the board divided into three groups. Williams and Whiteside were the moderates, Marshall and Hamilton were in the "middle of the road," and Hillman was on the political left. During the struggle, Richberg emerged as the pro-business candidate, a switch from his earlier position, while Hillman supported Robert Hutchins, president of the University of Chicago, in the fight for the chairmanship. Secretary of the Interior Harold Ickes, who distrusted businessmen instinctively, backed Hutchins, while Richberg, realizing he could not hope for the post himself, preferred S. Clay Williams. The fight for domination of this key agency was intense.

In the end, Williams, not Hutchins, got the appointment, a further indication of the growing power of the cooperationists and the decline of antibusiness forces in the NRA. In 1934 and 1935, the National Industrial Recovery Board rarely acted against business wishes, and accepted most of the codes written by business. There were some attacks on the price-fixing mechanism, led mostly by Leon Henderson, a lawyer-economist who became a leader of the antibusiness faction, and who thought the primary function of the NRA should be recovery and not reform. These did not get far, despite some changes made in late 1934 and early 1935. At the same time, small business constantly complained of being harrassed and controlled by a board that favored large operators. This was particularly true in industries dominated by small units, such as neighborhood retailers, beauty shops, candy stores, and the like. Chairman Williams proved to be openly favorable to large enterprise, and won the opposition of defenders of small units—the trustbusters—as well as almost every other antibusiness element in the Roosevelt administration. Roosevelt responded by putting the same pressures on Williams he had previously placed on Johnson. The chairman resigned, but this did not change the essential big-business orientation of NRA, as his place was taken by Richberg. The new chairman was greeted with enthusiasm by men like Swope, but some businessmen feared that Richberg would bring dynamic change to NRA and transform it into a fascistic agency controlling their every action.

On February 20, 1935, Roosevelt asked Congress to extend NRA for two years. To fail to do so, he said, would be to return business to a state of chaos. With this, a full-scale debate on the agency was opened. Old-time progressives argued against extension, some New Dealers thought the government should be given more power over business, and many Republicans thought industry should govern itself once more. There seemed to be general agreement that NRA, or something like it, would be needed, but there was no clear majority in favor of any one philosophy or program. Finally Congressman Robert Doughton introduced a measure to extend the life of the agency for two years, calling upon it to act only in areas involved in interstate commerce, to combat monopoly, and to aid in conservation efforts. A vote on the Doughton Bill was scheduled for May 28. On May 27, the Supreme Court found the NIRA to be unconstitutional. The decision was welcomed by those businessmen who were convinced Roosevelt meant to dominate their companies, by old-line Wilsonians who had always opposed the agency, and by dissident NRA officials who were unhappy with the agency's leadership.

The death of the NRA reopened the debate on the proper relationship of government to business. Many businessmen still hoped that NRA-type codes, drawn up by businessmen without government interference, and in violation of the anti-trust acts, would be encouraged. Few wanted the government to continue joint projects. Fear of an antibusiness totalitarianism, sparked more by radicals such as Huey Long of Louisiana, Upton Sinclair of California, and Floyd Olson of the strong Farmer-Labor party of the Midwest, than by Roosevelt, led to a revival of laissez-faire talk in the business community. Forgetting that they had been enthusiastic supporters of the early NRA, such men joined organizations like the Liberty League to protest government controls of all sorts. They thought business was admirably equipped to fill the gap through the oligopolistic system that had existed prior to the depression. Price leadership, "understandings," cartels, and interlocking directorates assumed a new importance.

By 1935, business was prepared for a return to the cooperative institutions of the mid-1920s. Herbert Hoover, castigated by the business community in 1928 as a reformer and in 1931 as a timid soul, again became the hero of the group. The type of industrial self-government he had called for during and before his administration was also endorsed by several prominent supporters of the Wilsonian philosophy of pre–World War days. Like the businessmen, such liberals feared the growth of big government, and called for an end, or at least major changes, in the New Deal. One of them, David Lawrence, thought he saw changes of this nature in the administration.

> The most important principle recognized in Washington as essential to the operation of the whole plan is that self-government in business and industry through the trade association must be encouraged as the ultimate objective. The trade associations, however, have not been in every instance representative of the businesses they cover. And some of those which are representative were not particularly well-managed. Also there was no opportunity in many of these trade associations for any interest to be considered except that of the members. . . . Industry with its trade associations

had not developed codes of ethics of self-discipline such as we find in the professions of law and medicine. Still the principle is just the same. Through the code authorities we may expect to see limitations imposed by industry itself through trade associations sitting in council with representatives of the government. In the last analysis, however, it will be the suggestion and opinion of the majority of each trade association or group which will become the law of that group or industry.[3]

Few New Dealers were willing to abandon the idea of planning, however. Many of these were found in the Department of Agriculture, where the Agricultural Adjustment Administration was attempting, without too much success, to bring prosperity to the farmers and at the same time assure a plentiful food supply. The leaders of this group—Secretary Henry Wallace, Rexford Tugwell, and Jerome Frank—differed as to the means but all agreed that business could not be allowed to operate without strong government controls. These planners held that competition had disappeared long before the New Deal and had been replaced by systems of business control. There was no hope for any antitrust crusade, for such would do more harm that good. Instead, the planners proposed that the federal government establish overall plans for the entire economy, into which each business would be integrated. One of their number, Mordecai Ezekiel, put forth several of their ideas in a program called "industrial expansion."

Each major industry would ... figure out how much more product it could sell with a 14 percent increase in the national income. This estimate would be worked out by each Industry Authority after investigation and discussion. In industries where rapid technical progress or full-volume operation made lower prices possible under the program, the effect of those reduced prices in further stimulating sales would also be allowed for in estimating the probable market. After each industry had worked out its figures, they

3. David Lawrence, *Beyond the New Deal* (New York, 1934), pp. 103–105.

would be checked one against the other. The increase in production under the cement program, for example, would be checked against the increases worked out for housing construction, road building, and factory construction. The increase in each kind of goods to be sold to consumers would also be checked against what consumers would probably buy with their increased income. When these cross-checks showed gaps or inconsistencies between the different programs, modifications would have to be made in the preliminary industry estimates until they all fitted together, and added up to the proposed increase in national production and in national income.[4]

Often allied with men like Ezekiel were economists who argued that business power had grown in America without any force to oppose it. During the 1920s, they said, the United States became a business civilization, without effective opposition to bring restraint and a proper sense of responsibility to the businessman. The depression offered an opportunity for government not only to bring recovery, but also to erect effective safeguards against future spreads of business power. The bible for this group was the book by Adolf Berle and Gardiner Means, *The Modern Corporation and Private Property,* in which the authors argued that the modern corporation was no longer controlled by stockholders, but rather by a managerial class that had power but little responsibility. Stockholders had traded their right of control for dividends and capital gains and cared little how the corporation gave them these things. The modern corporation, they claimed, had become a semistate and required more regulation than in the past.

The rise of the modern corporation has brought a concentration of economic power which can compete on equal terms with the modern state—economic power versus political power, each strong in its own field. The state seeks in some aspects to regulate the corporation, while the corporation, steadily becoming more power-

4. Mordecai Ezekiel, *Jobs for All Through Industrial Expansion* (New York, 1939), pp. 79–81.

ful, makes every effort to avoid such regulation. Where its own interests are concerned, it even attempts to dominate the state. The future may see the economic organism, now typified by the corporation, not only on an equal plane with the state, but possibly even superceding it as the dominant form of social organization. The law of corporations, accordingly, might well be considered as a potential constitutional law for the new economic state, while business practice is increasingly assuming the aspect of economic statesmanship.[5]

Berle and Means took care not to draw out every implication of the change they described, leaving this job to the reformers. One implication, that in the future corporations should have greater power, was rejected out of hand. The second, that government must take steps to control corporations, was seen during the NRA and in reform programs that followed. The third, which called for a massive attack on the part of organized political power (the state) against organized economic power (the corporation), proved to be the next answer of the Roosevelt administration.

There had been cries for a revival of the antitrust movement since the early days of the depression. Felix Frankfurter, considered by conservatives the "Rasputin of the New Deal" for his supposed influence on Roosevelt, was thought the leader of the antitrusters, which included Benjamin Cohen and Thomas Corcoran, young lawyers close to Frankfurter and Thurman Arnold of Yale. These men reasoned that the depression had been caused by excess of bigness, which could be corrected only by a return to the Wilsonian program of trust-busting and encouragement of small business. Such men seemed to think that once the curse of bigness was removed, the economy would right itself automatically. By 1936, however, such thoughts seemed simplistic; the removal of abuses without a program for increased consumption was unacceptable to Roosevelt. Just as Title I of the NRA was coordinated

5. Adolf A. Berle, Jr. and Gardiner C. Means, *The Modern Corporation and Private Property* (New York, 1932), pp. 356–367.

with Title II, so an antitrust program had to be connected in some way with a program for recovery. This link was found, primarily by economist Paul Douglas and Marriner Eccles of the Federal Reserve, in applications of Keynesian economics. By the end of the year, men like Arnold, Douglas, and Eccles were in the ascendant. After the 1937 recession their views gained still wider currency. Arnold was named Assistant Attorney General and charged with a sweeping antitrust program, while Eccles and his friends gained a broader audience than ever before. Of the three, Arnold was the most famous. Through his book, *The Folklore of Capitalism* (1937), and his many speeches, he became the scourge of big business. Speaking on the subject, "Competition Requires a Referee," he told the Economics Club of New York that only through competition could the economy recover.

> The antitrust laws represent one of our oldest economic traditions. They represent the ideal of a society which produces and distributes through free independent competitive enterprise. They also represent a recognition of the fact that the maintenance of competitive conditions is impossible unless firm action is taken against the tendency of private groups to restrain competition in their own interest. I know of no important political group which desires to abandon this ideal. Indeed such is its strength that any economic adjustment must be made in conformity to this principle.[6]

Douglas, who at the time was considered more a technician than a social reformer, observed that the discouragement of competition did not necessarily lead to a more productive economy. Such was the lesson of the NRA. In its place, Douglas suggested, the government should adopt Keynesian ideas through a more vigorous fiscal program. In chiding the "old-fashioned" presidential advisors, he warned against the impact of the policy of restraint and budget balancing Roosevelt seemed intent on carrying through.

6. Thurman W. Arnold, "Competition Requires a Referee," *Vital Speeches* (March 1, 1939), p. 290.

Such a program, of course, calls for the curtailment of government expenditures during a depression. For revenues from income, inheritance, property and excise taxes would all be diminishing, and if a deficit were to be prevented expenditures would have to be cut. This would mean stopping some services outright and curtailing others. This would cause an increase in the number of unemployed and a decrease in the quantity of monetary purchasing power distributed. Matters would thus be made worse than better. Such a program for balancing the budget in a period of depression has been well labeled by J. M. Keynes as "a campaign for the intensification of unemployment." All this curtailment, moreover, would happen at a time when the relief needs of the people would be vastly increasing so that if it were strictly adhered to widespread starvation and revolution would result.[7]

By 1938 it appeared the New Deal had accepted the antitrust philosophy of Arnold and the Keynesian concepts popularized by Douglas. Roosevelt was forced to abandon his dream of a balanced budget and search for other ways to bring recovery. On April 14, 1938, he indicated clearly that he had accepted the Arnold-Douglas views: Roosevelt asked Congress to pass a $3 billion relief and works program. "Let us unanimously recognize the fact that the Federal debt, whether it be twenty-five billions or fifty billions, can only be paid off if the Nation obtains a vastly increased citizen income," he said. During that week, presidential confidant Harry Hopkins told the Senate Special Committee to Investigate Unemployment that the depression could be ended through two programs, "government contribution to purchase power" and a renewed competition "on a scale we have not known for many years."

In the days that followed, businessmen learned what the new program would mean to them. Despite conciliatory statements by Secretary of Agriculture Wallace and Secretary of Commerce Daniel Roper, both of whom told business groups that the President did not mean to attack them, it was clear

7. Paul H. Douglas, *Controlling Depressions* (New York, 1935), pp. 134–135.

that the antitrusters had become Roosevelt's chief advisors. On April 29 the President told Congress that the nation was controlled by a clique of private individuals who dominated every branch of the economy. To change the situation, he asked for more funds for antitrust prosecutions, further banking legislation, and $500,000 for a "study of the concentration of economic power."

Congress was generally favorable to the first two items, but had reservations about a presidential inquiry into economic concentration. In the aftermath of clashes between executive and legislative leaders, Congress was wary about delegating more powers to Roosevelt. Instead, some suggested that such a probe be made by a joint congressional committee. The leader of this group, Senator Joseph O'Mahoney of Wyoming met with administration spokesmen to iron out differences. The result was the establishment of the Temporary National Economic Committee whose membership included senators and representatives, as well as such administration leaders as Arnold and Leon Henderson. The TNEC was to investigate economic concentration in the United States and then recommend legislation to control industry abuses.

From the beginning, the desires of the administration were evident, as were the economic ideas of those senators who would defend business and hold down spending. The first witness, Commissioner of Labor Statistics Isador Lubin, reviewed the losses of the depression, and then recommended Keynesian measures to alleviate suffering and increase production. Senator William King of Utah questioned him sharply on this point.

> DR. LUBIN: I think it is very significant that although the amount of Federal expenditures for relief is increasing, it is still small as compared to the total income of private industry. In other words, the percentage of the total national income payments that went to direct relief, payments to veterans and things of that sort, has been relatively small.

THE CHAIRMAN: In other words, all that the Federal Government has expended by way of work relief and P.W.A. and payments to veterans, is actually but a drop in the bucket compared with the national income which we need to restore even the 1929 degree of prosperity.

SENATOR KING: Isn't it a fact that if you should make a proper appraisal of the amount which is coming out of the Federal Treasury directly for relief through the P.W.A. and the Works Progress and through cities and counties and States, and then further appropriations by the Federal Government for the Army and for the Navy and for increased shipyards, and what not, it would be a very large part of the national income?

DR. LUBIN: Well, of course, "large" is a relative term. It is a significant amount, very definitely. The question is, not only how significant it is in terms of dollars, but also how significant it is in creating jobs, and profits and dividends. That to me is the measure of its real significance. If it has a stimulating effect and helps keep things going, then I would say that the amount isn't so very great, if, as a result of every dollar you spend, you increase the income of our workers two or three times. I think that is the only criterion we can use in judging whether or not these expenditures should be made.

SENATOR KING: If you adopt a policy under the terms of which 30 to 40 percent of the gross income of all the people of the United States is taken by the Government, to be expended as Congress and the Executive may determine, is it not a fact—I don't want to be argumentative—that you are drying up the fountains of private industry which would give employment to a large number of people?

DR. LUBIN: I will say this: If by spending 30 billion dollars you increase the national income by 40 billions, you've made a swell investment. . . .

SENATOR KING: Do I understand you to mean the more the Federal Government takes from the people and spends, the better is it for the people?

DR. LUBIN: It depends on the conditions. If everybody is working, and such expenditures mean that the Government comes in and competes with private industry for labor and materials, I would say no, but if there are people unemployed and the factories unused and if by spending money the Government can create jobs in those factories so that not only will wages be more plentiful, but profits and dividends larger, I'd say yes.

SENATOR KING: You are not assuming that the larger the expenditure by the Federal Government, the larger will be the expenditure by entrepreneurs and by those who are engaged in manufacture?

DR. LUBIN: It depends entirely upon what conditions are under which the expenditures are made, the extent to which you have unemployment, unused capacity, and things of that sort.

SENATOR KING: We are entering a field of speculation and argument now rather than objective study.[8]

The TNEC met—with interruptions—until April 26, 1940. In the seventeen months of its existence, it heard 552 witnesses, who filled thirty-one volumes with testimony and exhibits. The economists retained by the committee submitted an additional forty-three special studies, which were published separately. The reports and studies constitute the most comprehensive study of the American economy ever made.

The committee began its work in an atmosphere dominated by fear and dislike of big business. While the committee met, the Antitrust Division of the Justice Department filed 183 cases, which covered many industries, including automobiles, insurance, publishing, and dairy. The vigor and dedication of Thurman Arnold and his staff dwarfed the efforts of the Theodore Roosevelt and Woodrow Wilson administrations, yet Arnold was able to effect structural changes and increase competition in only a few fields. As a result of U.S. v. Paramount Pictures, motion picture producers were obliged to leave the field of distribution. The decision in U.S. v. Pullman Company resulted in that firm's concentrating on the production of sleeping cars and withdrawing from the provision of services. But

8. U.S., Congress, Temporary National Economic Committee, *Hearings before the Temporary National Economic Committee*, Part 1: *Economic Prologue* (Washington, 1939), pp. 72–73.

cases attempting to divorce the several processes in the refining and distribution of petroleum products were postponed as were those asking for divestitures brought against automobile manufacturers. Toward the end of the period, Roosevelt indicated a loss of interest in the antitrust campaign, although he took pains to maintain Arnold's budget and staff.

The experience of the TNEC was similar. At first, many businessmen feared that the O'Mahoney Committee wanted to introduce legislation that would either establish American fascism or promote small, inefficient firms at the expense of larger ones. The committee spent a good deal of time on the question of industry patents, and it appeared that some change in the law would be demanded so as to enable small competitors to enter the market against the giants. But this was soon dropped, especially after Edsel Ford's testimony that Ford Motors would be willing to license almost all its patents, since its position in the industry was maintained through other means. The investigation of the trade associations seemed to promise new legislation also; many administration leaders believed them to be conspiracies in restraint of trade. But here too the committee report was moderate.

> As to the basic issues, it appears that two paths are open. The first is to sharpen and strengthen the antitrust laws in the effort to approach more closely to the idea of perfect competition. In such a program the functions of trade associations would be further limited and restricted. The second path is to relax the antitrust laws, opening the way for industries to endeavor to deal with specific problems by group action, under the supervision of some appropriate Government agency. Many individuals have urged the desirability of some agency whose duties would not be overwhelmingly those of prosecution and law enforcement but which could contribute toward the operation of a more flexible policy with respect to business practice and performance. In such a program trade associations would be the natural vehicles in the business structure for approaching the problems of particular industries, and their present activity would undoubtedly be further

extended. Further consideration may indicate that these two programs are not necessarily antithetical except in logic. The best immediate step might be to sharpen the antitrust laws in their definitions of acts in restraint of trade while at the same time opening the way for more flexible treatment of industry's problems in those situations where the processes of free competition appear to lead to social waste and instability.[9]

In the end, the committee presented no recommendations for major changes in the antitrust laws. Like the Arnold program in the Justice Department, the TNEC seemed to lose energy in 1940, and its hopes seemed antiquated in 1941.

There were several reasons for the failure of this ambitious antibusiness movement. In the first place, Roosevelt had less political power toward the end of the New Deal than he had in the dark days of 1933, when he seemed the only person able to save the nation from collapse. Despite the recession of 1937, the American business structure was far more secure in 1940 than it had been in 1933. Ironically, Roosevelt's antibusiness ideas of the late 1930s were combated by the businessmen he had saved in the early part of his administration.

In addition, the TNEC program was opposed by many reformers who thought it was too severe, as well as the type of reformer who had supported cooperation with business in 1933. Donald Richberg, for example, said that Arnold prosecutions and the TNEC hearings were undermining business confidence and could easily lead to a new depression. Hugh Johnson considered the TNEC a reactionary movement aimed at destroying American industry and returning to a nineteenth-century economy. Raymond Moley, head of the Brain Trust, said that businesses should be encouraged to expand, rather than attacked for whatever successes they may have had. Many

9. U.S., Congress, Temporary National Economic Committee, *Investigation of Concentration of Economic Power:* Monograph No. 18 *Trade Association Survey* (Washington, 1941), p. 358.

others observed that the investigations had failed to uncover any new information which might lead to a reassessment of business-government regulations.

Most important, however, was the fact that the investigations had begun during a recession in a nation at peace, and ended at the beginning of an economic boom made possible by war preparations in Europe and America. Woodrow Wilson had been obliged to cut short his antibusiness crusade when World War I made it clear that businessmen would be needed to provide war materials and industrial leadership. Now Franklin Roosevelt found himself in a similar situation. It would be bizarre, to say the least, for one branch of government—the Justice Department—to insist that a particular industry conform to the letter of the Sherman Act, while another—the War Production Board—granted firms in that industry immunity from prosecution. The great debate as to proper government-business relations was suspended, never again to be discussed so fiercely. For although agencies like NRA and committees like TNEC debated the problem and developed rival philosophies, the entire New Deal experience resulted in the intrusion of government into business activities on a greater scale than ever before in the nation's history. This happened not as a result of a concerted effort on the part of the New Deal to dominate business, but rather when businessmen refused to take responsibility and assume leadership of the economy in the last years of the Hoover administration and the first months of the Roosevelt administration. Only then did the New Deal formulate plans for massive intervention in the economy. By the time business had regained its nerve, it was too late to return to the relative independence of the 1920s.

Summary

The business community, which had provided national leadership during previous depressions, was unable and unwilling to assume responsibility during the Great Depression. As a result, the federal government expanded its role considerably in the period from 1929 to 1940. Under President Hoover several attempts to draw the businessman into close cooperation were made, and in general failed. During the Roosevelt administration, government attempted several programs, based on different philosophies. First, government–business partnerships under the NRA were attempted. Although business supported NRA when it began, in time many industrial leaders came to fear big government and demanded a return to the laissez-faire system of the 1920s. Reformers also protested, and after several political setbacks and a further drop in the economy in 1937, Roosevelt adopted an antitrust program combined with Keynesian economics, both of which were strongly opposed by the businessman. This joint attack was ended with the coming of World War II, which ushered in a new period in the government-business relationship.

CHAPTER VI

Elements of Growth During the Depression

Although most Americans think of the 1930s as a decade of economic stagnation, the period was far from being one of unalloyed decline. Indeed, in some respects the depression was a time of remarkable technological growth. This was particularly true of the large-scale, oligopolistic industries that were rationalized during the 1920s, such as petroleum, chemicals, automobiles, steel, aircraft, and food distribution. Faced with declining sales, the giant companies were forced to look to technological advances and efficiencies to maintain their profit margins and shares of the market. The American firms, many of which were more interested in the domestic market than in foreign sales during the lush years, now became more aggressive in seeking new markets, both domestic and foreign. Not even the quasi-cartels of the National Reconstruction Administration period and the growing economic nationalism in all parts of the world could blunt these forces. The growth of union power in the New Deal period, while opposed by most businessmen (in some cases violently), also served as a stimulus to growth and efficiency, as well as to technological change.

Most of these developments were triggered by the depression, but they could not have occurred without the firm foundations put down during the previous decade. Although it was common to castigate business practices during the 1920s, it should be noted that few of the large firms of that period were in serious economic difficulty during the depression, and their ability to continue to function without the aid of the investment bankers and the relatively easy money that had made them possible was a tribute to the men who had formed them in the first place. The investment bankers had organized firms able to withstand the severe storms that came in the wake of a financial collapse that took many of them under.

During the first half of 1929, 744 firms disappeared through mergers, most of which were handled by investment bankers. The figure for the period from 1933 to 1939, inclusive, was only 769. This sharp drop in merger activity can be traced to two factors. In the first place, the financial machinery for mergers was crippled, not to be rebuilt effectively until the late 1930s. Mergers through exchanges of securities did not seem attractive when the securities were worth so little when compared to the values of the earlier decade. Second, there was less reason for mergers during the 1930s, since many large firms had completed their basic structures by the eve of the stock market crash.

An investigation of individual firms shows that while many small- and medium-size companies in highly competitive fields suffered during the depression, the large, oligopolistic companies made rapid recoveries from the bottoms of 1933 and actually profited in the years that followed. Sales, profits, profit margins, and other significant gauges of performance showed significant increases in the 1930s. This may be seen by comparing performances in 1934, the first full year of the Roosevelt administration, when the gross national product was $65 billion, to those of 1937, when the first leg of recovery was completed, and the gross national product stood at $90.8 billion. The figures in Table 1 indicate that as great as the recovery was for the economy as a whole, it was magnified for the giant firms of the period.

Table 1

Figures for Selected Firms, 1934 and 1937

Company	Sales (000's) 1934	Sales (000's) 1937	Net Income (000's) 1934	Net Income (000's) 1937
Allegheny Ludlum Steel	21,800	49,527	1,364	3,886
Allied Stores	77,547	100,976	1,775	4,659
Allis Chalmers Manufacturing	20,332	87,311	6,518	28,979
American Home Products	16,091	25,711	2,472	3,662
American Locomotive	14,312	50,477	(1,966)	6,782
American Tobacco	222,648	242,645	26,702	31,365
Atlantic Refining	96,118	131,217	7,100	11,420
Bristol-Myers	9,754	15,974	2,459	2,963
Burroughs Adding Machine	24,588	38,395	3,842	10,065
J. I. Case	8,586	27,429	(700)	4,826
Chicago Pneumatic Tool	7,103	13,566	611	2,206
Chrysler	371,657	769,808	13,723	63,031
E. I. Du Pont	179,933	286,043	52,494	99,298
Eastman Kodak	96,829	136,115	17,677	27,933
General Electric	225,663	468,027	24,052	78,207
General Motors	882,094	1,635,141	110,353	246,853
Goodyear Tire & Rubber	136,801	216,175	8,502	11,942
Hudson Motor Car	52,568	74,502	(3,135)	1,092
International Business Machines	20,949	31,787	7,570	10,605
International Harvester	138,312	351,928	8,899	43,945
Lone Star Cement	13,649	21,252	1,863	4,565
Maytag Company	14,717	16,985	2,305	2,718
Minneapolis Honeywell Regulator	5,390	15,810	1,146	3,579
National Cash Register	23,846	42,280	1,732	5,462
Packard Motor Car	21,855	109,572	(7,267)	3,665
Phillips Petroleum	77,520	118,722	8,078	26,804
Radio Corporation of America	77,303	111,853	5,631	11,444
Remington Rand	34,726	51,104	2,975	6,140
Schenley Distillers	40,275	83,899	8,643	9,833
Socony-Vacuum Oil	456,016	552,785	34,838	73,333
Standard Oil Company (Cal.)	130,986	192,146	20,000	45,568
Standard Oil Company (Indiana)	278,180	365,521	20,833	65,373
The Texas Corporation	272,619	376,238	12,397	65,291

Table 1 *continued*

Company	Sales (000's) 1934	1937	Net Income (000's) 1934	1937
United States Rubber	105,477	186,253	3,546	12,800
United States Steel	591,609	1,395,550	(11,078)	129,653
Wright Aeronautical	9,340	16,654	1,059	2,608

SOURCE: US, Congress Temporary National Economic Committee, *Investigations of Concentration of Economic Power Part 31-A. Supplemental Data Submitted to the Temporary National Economic Committee* (Washington, 1941), pp. 18213–18440.

One company that did flourish during the 1930s was Gulf Oil Company, which in 1920 had assets in excess of $196 million, produced 35 million barrels of petroleum, and showed an income of $159.6 million. Gulf expanded its operations in the 1920s, seeking foreign markets and sources of crude. In addition, it searched for mergers and cooperative ventures. The company was refinanced in 1922 to facilitate such deals. Small acquisitions were made during the next three years, and in 1926 the firm acquired a quarter interest in the Nobel-Andre-Good group of petroleum marketers, followed in the next year by a contract giving Texas Gulf Sulphur rights to mine on Gulf properties in return for half the profits from the mining.

Assets reached $430 million in 1929, income $246 million, and production 90 million barrels. The firm was well integrated and financially strong. Gulf service stations were in all parts of the nation, and its petroleum sources, both domestic and foreign, were more than adequate for its refinery runs. Thus, the company was able to absorb a $23 million operating loss in 1931 and continue research and exploration activities even though sales, production, and prices had declined. The firm reorganized and decentralized operations in 1932, refinanced its debt so as to take advantage of lower interest rates, and increased its advertising budget.

Gulf's income did not reach its 1929 level again until 1937, and production did not recover until 1940. Still, the firm was able to increase its foreign operations, gain a foothold in the rich Kuwait fields, and expand research operations. In 1939 Gulf announced the development of an airborne magnetometer, which enabled the company to make underwater explorations for crude deposits. Most of this would have been impossible were it not for the firm's strong position on the eve of the depression. It indicates that large companies could expand during the depression; it was the small- and medium-size firms, usually in highly competitive industries, that declined and became insolvent. Not until the TNEC investigations did the New Deal give clear indications of attacking such concentrations of power, and the government never acted on the findings of the committee. If the New Deal did not actually aid big business in the 1930s, it did little to hinder its growth.

Of course, each industry presented its own problems, and what was true for petroleum may not have applied in the case of other businesses. The petroleum industry had been reluctant at times to deal with conservation of resources, and was finally pushed toward the working out of codes of behavior by the NRA. But instead of hindering operations and lowering return on capital and profits, the compacts stimulated technology, called upon unused resources, and in the end worked toward increasing margins. In 1929, 30 percent of all drillings resulted in dry holes; by 1937, the figure had dropped to 22 percent. In the same period the price of crude went from $1.27 a barrel to $1.18, after reaching a low of $.67 in 1933. More important was the development of a national pipeline system for distribution of petroleum products and crude, and the technological developments in refining. As a result of the first, transportation costs declined; as technology added to production, market costs were further lowered.

In 1929 almost 1.5 million barrels a day were refined, with the largest percentage of it (29 percent) processed by the tube and tank method, which resulted in the production of a relatively small amount of gasoline. In order to gain more gasoline from crude, the major companies embarked on research programs in the 1920s that came to fruition in the 1930s. Eugene Houdry, a French engineer, had shown as early as 1925 that better methods were possible, if not economically feasible. Most major companies sent representatives to speak to Houdry, and in 1930 Vacuum Oil set up a laboratory for him in New Jersey. Three years later, after Vacuum withdrew support, Sun Oil picked up Houdry's costs. In 1937 Houdry demonstrated that his process was commercially feasible, produced more gasoline than any other, and produced gasoline of a higher octane. Almost 7 percent of production came from the Houdry process in 1941 while the tube and tank method had declined to 18.2 percent. By then, Standard Oil of New Jersey and other giant firms had developed processes similar to or based on Houdry's, and the efficiencies of the new methods were translated into profits.

The price of gasoline did not decline in the 1930s, in spite of the use of new refining techniques. The weight of evidence indicates that notwithstanding new economies, capital costs were so high as to dictate an increase in prices, not a decrease. In 1927, refineries required approximately $240 in capital investment per barrel of capacity; the figure had risen to more than $320 by 1935. The new facilities cost considerably more than the less complex thermal refineries erected in the 1920s. Although the new refineries required less labor, the investment per worker was among the highest in America. At the end of the decade, the refineries employed $38,700 of capital per worker against $3,700 for all manufacturing industries. In addition, a good deal of the investment was in plants which, due to rapidly changing technology, would become obsolete in short order. In 1938, 120 refineries were idle due to obsolescence, although most were less than ten years old.

Such rapid increases in capital costs could not have been handled were it not for the ability of the major companies to support enormous cash flows, due in large part to the developments made in the 1920s. Such was the situation at Humble Oil and Refining, a subsidiary of Standard of New Jersey. After suffering through a bad year in 1931, Humble turned around, and throughout the decade showed considerable profits, most of which came from the exploration and production departments. This growth would not have been possible were it not for steady increases in the need for petroleum products. The demand for automobile fuel did not rise as rapidly in the 1930s as it had in the 1920s, but it did not decline in any year save 1932. Although the automobile industry was in the doldrums in the 1930s, the number of passenger cars and trucks on the road increased steadily from 1932 on, as did the production of gasoline. In 1929, American refineries produced 445 million barrels of gasoline; by 1939, the figure had risen to over 600 million.

The rapid growth of aviation added to demands on the refineries. From 1929 to 1939, sales of aviation fuel rose from 753 thousand barrels to 1,883 thousand barrels. Both automobiles and airplanes required higher octane fuels at the end of the decade than they had at the beginning, and this served as a major stimulant to the search for the Houdry process and other similar methods of gaining more powerful fuels. The requirements of these two industries also sparked the search for better lubricants; the demand for highways and runways led to increased sales of asphalt, most of which was produced by the petroleum companies. Thus, developments in oil were intimately connected with those of a strong mature industry—automobiles—and a rapidly growing newer one—airplanes.

In 1928, the automobile industry posted record profits, as sales of cars and trucks easily passed the 4.3 million units figure. The next year was even better, with sales increasing by almost 1 million units. Then came the depression, and the automobile industry was among the hardest hit in the nation.

The 1929 sales of 5.3 million declined to 1.3 million in 1932, the lowest figure since 1918. Such a decline was bound to cause a shakeout in so heavily capitalized an industry. In 1930 and 1931 such established firms as Moon, Kissel, Locomobile, Elcar, Jordan, Gardner, and Stearns disappeared, with Marmon soon to follow. All of these firms either were producers of specialized vehicles, lacked imaginative leadership, or had weak capitalization. Some suffered from two or even all three of these problems. Elcar and Jordan collapsed without an attempt at salvaging the firms. Moon and Gardner consolidated their sales and engineering staffs, and soon after joined with Kissel. But all three were bankrupt by the end of 1930. Franklin, which sold cars with air-cooled motors, could survive in an era of prosperity when such novelties were desired. It could not compete in the difficult markets of the depression and failed in 1934. Marmon thought the luxury market would remain stable, concentrated its resources on the production of a large, sixteen-cylinder sedan, and reorganized itself to form Marmon-Herrington. The gamble failed, and the company went bankrupt in 1933. Stutz and Cord had better fortune with their specialty cars, but they too went under in the 1930s. Peerless Motor Car Company, recognizing that it could no longer compete, sold its assets, its Cleveland plant was converted to the production of Carling ale.

Some independents were able to survive. Packard, the producer of "the American Rolls-Royce" was more successful in the luxury field than Marmon. Under the capable leadership of Alvan Macauley, the company was able to sustain repeated deficits in the early 1930s and came out of the red in 1935. Sales, which had fallen to $22 million in 1934, were back to $110 million in 1937. Nash Motors experienced similar deficits, but was saved when Charles Nash, the founder, merged his company with Kelvinator Corporation, a manufacturer of refrigerators, whose profits carried the new Nash-Kelvinator until better times. Hudson Motors, which posted its first deficit in 1930, remained in the red until 1935, having lost $17 million in the years between. Hudson never fully recovered from the depression but was able to survive due to the excellent leadership of Roy Chapin and the introduction of streamlined low-cost models which found favor with the public for a while.

Studebaker, which had merged with Pierce-Arrow just before the depression, found that its luxury car affiliate was a white elephant in a period of economic decline. President Albert Erskine, who hoped to compete with General Motors and Ford, refused to retrench, and the company found itself with mounting deficits. Not even a 1932 merger with White Motors, undertaken to gain working capital, was able to stem the mounting financial difficulties. In that year, the firm was forced into receivership, and was saved only through the heroic efforts of Paul Hoffman, who became chairman of the board after Erskine killed himself. Hoffman sold off the Pierce-Arrow and White holdings, retrenched, and, through capable management, aided by business recovery in 1934, he was able to post a profit. Studebaker lost money again in 1935, but through the rest of the decade showed modest profits and returns on capital. Willys-Overland, which had never fully recovered from the 1920 business slump, was saved temporarily when founder John Willys resigned his post as ambassador to Poland to take control again. The company was reorganized in 1936, recapitalized, and like Studebaker, maintained a marginal position in the industry. REO Motor Car Company was in a similar situation. Founder Ransom E. Olds clashed with other company leaders who opposed his program of aggressive advertising and technological change, which he thought would lead to increased sales in spite of the depression. Internal discord, competition from the large firms, weak financing, and unimaginative models led to Olds' resignation and new attempts to seek ways to stay alive. In 1934 the board of directors considered a merger with Graham-Paige or Hupp, but nothing came of it. Cooperation with Graham-Paige was initiated in 1935, however, with

REO permitting that company to use certain dies in return for a royalty fee. But this was insufficient to permit the firm to survive in the passenger field, which it abandoned late that year.

No doubt the nature of the automobile business—the need for large capital investments, marketing facilities, advertising costs, complex production networks, etc.—would have led to a thinning out of the field even if there had not been a depression. Indeed, hundreds of small companies had vanished or merged in the two decades prior to the depression. But the firms that left the industry between 1930 and 1936 had been considered secure in 1929. Under better conditions, some might have survived as producers of specialty vehicles. As it was, by the end of the depression only eight companies—Crosley, Graham-Paige, Hudson, Hupp, Nash, Packard, Studebaker, and Willys-Whippet—remained to challenge the Big Three; between them they shared only 10 percent of the market. The next generation would see the survival of only two independents, Studebaker-Packard and American Motors (Nash and Hudson), both the results of mergers. Only American Motors remained by 1970, and that firm was in none too secure a position.

The disappearance of the independents had widespread effects on the Big Three. In the first place, it enabled them to gain larger shares of the declining market, and so cushion the blow of falling sales to a degree. Too, it enabled the larger firms to offer more models as they moved to capture markets left vacant when the independents failed. Finally, the depression offered a major challenge to what had become a key American industry, and one which all three were prepared to meet.

General Motors remained the dominant force in the industry, and in some ways actually benefited from the depression. Alone among the firms in the industry, General Motors had excellent leadership, strong financial resources, and a wide range of vehicles and other products covering the entire market. As for the first, Alfred Sloan, who had led the firm to first place over Ford, remained president until 1937, at which time he moved to the position of chairman of the board and was succeeded by William Knudsen, who had come to General Motors from Ford in 1922 to take charge of Chevrolet operations. At that time, the duPont interests had lost all hope of catching up with the Model T, and considered closing down the division. Knudsen led the fight to maintain the competition, and in 1927 he won the battle, passing Ford's sales for the first time. Knudsen was an admirable successor to Sloan; he inheritied a well-run concern, and was able to expand its range even further.

The General Motors product line remained the broadest in the field, running from the Chevrolet, which competed successfully with the Model A, to the Cadillac, which outsold the Packard. Frigidaire sales expanded, as did the lucrative parts operations. General Motors Acceptance Corporation, which financed the bulk of the firm's sales, was also profitable. In 1930 General Motors purchased Winton Engine Company and the Electro-Motive Corporation on the advice of Charles Kettering, the engineering genius. Both firms had talent and experence in the field of diesel locomotion. Backed by the GM research staff and money, the two new acquisitions developed engines for trains which soon drove the old steam engines off the tracks, and at the same time added profits to the mother company's coffers. General Motors' older lines did well too. In 1929, the firm had sold 1,799,427 automobiles in the United States. Sales dropped to 506,928 in 1932, but full recovery was reached soon after, and in 1936, General Motors topped the 1929 figures, selling 1,803,275 units. In that year, profits were almost a quarter of a billion dollars. Sloan gave the reasons for this record in his autobiography:

> What accounts for this exceptional record in a period in which many durable-goods producers failed or came close to bankruptcy? It would be unfair to claim any particular prescience on our part; no more than anyone else did we see the depression coming. I

think the story I have told shows that we had simply learned how to react quickly. This was perhaps the greatest payoff of our system of financial and operating controls.[1]

One would have predicted similar experiences for Ford Motor Company. The Model A was the resounding automobile success of 1929, outselling Chevrolet by more than three to one. A still-vigorous Henry Ford expanded production in spite of the stock market panic, and predicted continued success against Chevrolet and Chrysler's low-priced Plymouth. When sales declined, the company unveiled the first car with a V-8 engine, a major technological advance and one that added to sales. Later on Ford would work on a five-cylinder model, which was never released, and attempt to take a major portion of the middle-price market with the Lincoln Zephyr, a move that failed. The company continued to decline. Ford Motors produced 1,870,257 vehicles in 1929, not as much as the more than two million of Model T days, but enough to keep it even with General Motors. Then production fell, reaching 395,956 in 1932. Sales recovered between 1935 and 1937, but declined again in 1938, a year in which Ford sold only half as many cars as its major competitor.

There were many reasons for this erosion of a major American firm. In the first place, there was Ford himself, a brilliant engineer and a man of vision, but one to whom age, rather than bringing wisdom, had brought a sharpening of whatever flaws had existed earlier. Ford's anti-Semitism, known and even accepted earlier, lost friends as Nazi power grew in Germany, and sales declined when Ford began publishing diatribes in his Dearborn newspaper. Ford's paternalistic attitude toward labor, applauded in the 1920s, soured as his security chief and the power behind the throne, Harry Bennett,

1. Alfred E. Sloan, Jr., *My Years with General Motors* (New York, 1964), p. 199.

conducted severe reprisals against labor leaders. Ford's refusal to join in the NRA codes pitted him against Roosevelt in a battle he could not win insofar as public opinion was concerned. His high-handed attitude toward his dealers, accepted in the Model T years, haunted Ford as his distributorships eroded in the depression. He refused to give power to those around him who might have revived the firm—most notably his son Edsel and Charles Sorenson, who was probably the finest production man in the industry. Instead, Bennett's influence over the failing Ford grew, and earned him the hatred of consumers, who purchased Chevrolets and Plymouths instead of Model As and V-8s.

Finally, there are two other factors to consider. It is doubtful that, with the best of management, Ford could have maintained its short-lived sales edge over General Motors, a firm with greater resources, organization, and talent. If Henry Ford was a production wizard, Alfred Sloan was an organizing genius, and the 1930s called for organization as much as, if not more than, engineering. Tied to this was a second factor: despite the V-8, Ford lacked the technological skills needed in the new age.

> A further deficiency in Ford engineering lay in the relative dearth of college-trained men. The company method as fostered by Henry Ford was to take a promising high school graduate and complete his training in the shop. The candidate usually took correspondence school courses in addition. Many such men remained mechanics. In this respect they resembled Ford himself. "I did not consider Mr. Ford an engineer," remarked Roeder. "He was an excellent mechanic and he had a tremendous amount of ideas." Like him, many of his assistants in the engineering field lacked the intensive technical training that the universities were now giving.[2]

Chrysler Corporation lacked Ford's resources and tradition and could not match General Motors' organization and breadth

---

2. Allan Nevins and Frank Ernest Hill, *Ford: Decline and Rebirth, 1933–1962* (New York, 1963), pp. 58–59.

of market, but it possessed excellent management, a good research staff, and imaginative engineers, who were encouraged in their work. Finally, Walter Chrysler was able to develop a distribution network that though relatively small, was of a high quality.

Like the other major manufacturers, Chrysler continued to introduce technological improvements in the 1930s. Plymouth, headed by ex-Ford executive Fred Rockelman, introduced a four-cylinder free-wheeling model in 1931 which gained modest acceptance, and in the following year its six-cylinder engine, supported on rubber mountings with a new body, took sales away from Chevrolet and Ford. Plymouth was the third largest selling automobile in the industry by mid-decade, with Dodge and Chrysler sales increasing impressively. In 1934 the firm showed a profit of $13.7 million on sales of $372 million; in 1937 sales were $770 million and profits were $63 million. Chrysler retired in 1935, leaving a solvent company in the hands of K. T. Keller, who the founder had brought with him from General Motors.

The success of Sloan at General Motors and Chrysler and Keller at Chrysler, the decline at Ford, the difficulties at Hudson, Packard, and Studebaker, the major changes at REO, and the failure of many other firms, indicated that the industry had undergone a great transformation in the period from 1929 to 1937. The founders—most of them engineers—had been replaced by managers. The specialty firm had disappeared, while the broadly based, well-financed firm had prospered. Ford, which was the exception, suffered but did not fail due to the great strength with which it had entered the depression. Not until it emulated General Motors would Ford return to greatness.

The Big Three did demonstrate that the oligopolistic industries which had developed in the 1920s could survive under the depressed conditions of the 1930s. A firm in such an industry that had a management aware of possibilities and adequate finances could hold its own and even flourish during the depression. Such was the case in the tin can industry, where Continental and American expanded greatly, and in radio set manufacture, where RCA prospered and a small, well-financed and -led Zenith grew. It was even true in such fields as baseball, which became an industry in the 1920s, and in which the New York Yankees, with good leadership and finances, could expand and dominate in the 1930s.

This pattern was not to be found in industries marked by price competition in the late 1920s, and where natural oligopolies had not appeared on the eve of the depression. It was not present in industries where rapidly expanding markets, young technologies, and relatively low capital needs (or government subsidies) were required. It was not found in industries in which founder-engineers were more important than second-generation managers. The one industry that fit all of these conditions was aviation, which came into its own during the depression, and in which oligopolies did not appear until late in the decade.

The history of American commercial aviation properly began in 1909, when the Army purchased an airplane from the Wright brothers. Although the military was generally skeptical about air warfare until the late 1930s it was the largest single purchaser of airplanes then as now. Thus, the industry was always supported by government sales.

There were few manufacturers on the eve of World War I. At the time, most airplanes were used for experimentation or as sideshow attractions. The Wrights and Glenn Curtiss thought there were great commercial possibilities in air travel, but neither could gain enough customers or sales to make expansion worthwhile. Such investment bankers as Morgan, Lehman Brothers and Kuhn, Loeb refused to take an interest in the companies that asked for loans. World War I changed the situation. On the day America entered the war, there were less than a dozen qualified military pilots in the nation. By then the army, realizing that planes were valuable for reconnaissance and defense, asked for a large buildup in that area. Congress responded by voting $640 million for military aviation in 1917. By the end of the war, almost $1.25 billion had been spent on aviation.

The young aircraft industry in 1917 was in no condition to fill the needs of the armed forces. Up to that time, the industry had produced less than 200 aircraft; during the war, the nation turned out more than 1,500. In order to make this record, the industry had to turn to the resources of others, the most obvious candidate being the automobile industry. It was reasoned that since aircraft were motor-driven vehicles, as were automobiles, the technology of the latter could be easily applied to the former. Even before America entered the war, the Wrights had sold their patents and factory to a syndicate which also controlled the Simplex Automobile Company, and which later would purchase Glenn L. Martin Company, and merged it with other holdings to form Wright-Martin Aircraft. Glenn Curtiss' operations were also taken over, and reformed as the Curtiss Aeroplane & Motor Company, which was controlled by John Willys of Willys-Overland Company. Other automobile leaders backed Orville Wright in his new Dayton-Wright Airplane Company. General Motors sought aircraft contracts, as did Ford and other auto firms.

Howard Coffin, who was an executive of Hudson Motor Car Company and was affiliated with Dayton-Wright before he joined Baruch on the War Industries Board, encouraged the industry to enter aviation. Coffin was named head of the Aircraft Production Board, and was later succeeded by an old friend and associate, Edward A. Deeds, of Dayton Engineering Laboratories Company (Delco). Both men favored the automobile industry when awarding contracts. Dayton-Wright received advances of $2.5 million, Lincoln Motors $6.5 million, and smaller amounts went to other automobile and automobile-related firms. In general, the money was poorly spent. Coffin and Deeds disliked Glenn Martin, whose bomber was superior to anything then in production. Instead of rewarding Martin with a contract, they sought to use converted British and French planes. At the same time, they hoped to encourage American manufacturers, and pushed hard for the development of the Liberty engine, which was considered better than the British Rolls-Royce then in use. But the American engine could not be adapted to the foreign planes. The Liberty, produced by automobile engineers, had a drive shaft so placed as to make it admirable for cars, but unusable for aircraft. Some 2,500 Liberties were produced, but none saw action in the war. Indeed, by the time of the armistice, not a single American combat or pursuit plane was in France, and only a few heavy aricraft, most of them DeHavilland and DH-4s made from British designs by Dayton-Wright, reached Europe before the war had ended.

Despite the enthusiasm of Coffin and Deeds, and notwithstanding the personal interest of President Wilson, the transformation of a segment of the auto industry to airplanes posed many difficulties. Subcontracting was a failure, machine tools were invariably late or unusable, and money proved no substitute for technological skills. The President ordered an investigation of the muddle, headed by Justice Charles Evans Hughes. It showed that Coffin and Deeds had used their positions to gain contracts for their own firms, Dayton-Wright and Delco. For example, Deeds specified that all Liberty engines must use Delco ignition systems, and the DeHavilland contract was given to Dayton-Wright under rather shady circumstances. Hughes charged Coffin with a conflict of interest and recommended a court-martial for Deeds. Although Deeds was later cleared, one of his associates on the Aricraft Production Board was indicted on criminal charges.

Sales to the military declined during the 1920s, while hopes for expanded operations in the private sector were not realized. Air power supporters like General "Billy" Mitchell propagandized tirelessly and demonstrated to some that modern war would require fleets of military planes; they lost to advocates of conventional warfare, as symbolized by Mitchell's court-martial in 1925. In that year the *Shenandoah*, a Navy dirigible, was destroyed in a spectacular accident which took fourteen lives, and this seemed to spell the end of hopes for lighter-than-air ships. Although military aviation was glamourous, and exploited by Hollywood in such films as *Hell's Angels*, it was to languish for much of the interwar period. Army aviators would attempt to set distance and speed records, and in so doing encouraged technological progress, but firms hoping for military contracts were disappointed. Of the forty factories producing airplanes for the military in 1918, only three were still open a decade later.

As for the civilian market, in the early postwar years it was noted for "gypsy flyers," who would perform at circuses and county fairs, usually in converted warplanes. Most of the automobile companies, stung by the Hughes investigations and seeing better opportunities elsewhere, all but abandoned aircraft. Both Ford and General Motors returned to the field later, but for the time being, they concentrated on automobiles.

Despite these setbacks, there was progress in aviation during the 1920s. Most small firms closed in 1919, and the demand for new planes was dull so long as wartime surplus planes glutted the market and the need for commercial vehicles was minor. Such dramatic events as the Roosevelt Field to Paris flight of Charles Lindbergh, himself a gypsy pilot, set the nation wild in 1927, and for a while the air age was the talk of Wall Street. Stock in Wright Aeronautical, the firm that built *The Spirit of St. Louis*, rose from 25 to 245 in the nineteen months that followed the flight, as did the securities of other aircraft firms. Although there was no major rise in new orders in this period, the Lindbergh flight had important repercussions in the organization of holding companies and new firms.

More important than the Lindbergh flight and the glamour of aviation, however, were two other developments: the attempts to organize air transport services and the decision on the part of the federal government to subsidize airmail. Without these, the industry might have stagnated, if not declined. The dependence upon government contracts meant that the industry would develop its routes rapidly, and so set the groundwork for the carrier operations of the future. The fact that surplus warplanes could be purchased for little more than $300 aided those who wanted to enter the air transport field. The first development did not aid manufacturers, and the second actually discouraged many from entering or remaining in the business. Glenn Curtiss, for example, retired from aviation at this time, while Glenn Martin and William Boeing, after failing to convince Congress not to release surplus airplanes, considered air transport a more attractive field than production. Thus, in the late 1920s, the aircraft industry took on the appearance of radio and motion pictures. Like them, it divided at first into two broad areas—production and carrier-related business.

In 1911, stunt flyer Earle Ovington carried mail from Nassau Boulevard to Garden City on Long Island, and so became the first carrier of airmail in the nation. During the next few years Congress and the Post Office discussed the possibilities of airmail, but nothing came of it until 1918, when Congress voted $100,000 to the Post Office for further experiments in the field. The first flights were made by army planes, but within a few months the Post Office Department had its own DeHavilland DH-4s, together with civilian pilots, and took over the operation. The following year saw the first transcontinential airmail delivery, and throughout the 1920s the airmail network spread rapidly. This in turn encouraged the builders and operators of airfields, manufacturers, and parts supplies, and even some firms, which began to plan new planes for commercial flights. Airmail was feasible, although the price was high, and several pilots lost their lives in obsolete planes. In addition, the railroads, sensing a powerful competitor, demanded an end to government aid to private aviation.

Airmail had its advocates in Congress, including Congressman Clyde Kelly of Pennsylvania who, in 1925, introduced a bill to encourage airmail operators and commercial aviation by having the Post Office turn its operations over to the contract firms, which would receive up to four-fifths of the revenue from the mail transported. The bill passed, and the first contract signed under its provisions was with Colonial Airways, then headed by Juan Trippe. In time, Colonial formed part of the group that became Pan American Airways. National Air Transport, which received the Chicago-Dallas route, became Braniff Airlines. Varney Air Service and Gorst Pacific Air Transport received contracts, and in time helped form United Air Lines, while the precursors of Eastern Airlines and Capital Airlines also received Kelly Act contracts. The air transport business, then, had its true origins in the Kelly Act. Like the railroads, air transport would not have been possible without government aid.

The first airmail carriers used World War I planes, which were modified for commerical purposes. Such planes were inadequate for the needs, and manufacturers were encouraged to develop new designs. One of these, William Boeing, designed and constructed a fleet of biplanes to be used in mail service. The new B-40s were bigger than the World War I planes, and powered with a new engine, designed by Frederick Renschler, which was far superior to the old Liberty engine. Renschler of Pratt & Whitney together with Boeing, who headed his own firm, produced the first plane designed specifically for commercial purposes, and it sold well both to the airlines and the military. This close collaboration led to the merger of Renschler's firm with Boeing Aircraft and Boeing Air Transport; the new firm was called United Aircraft & Transport Corporation, of which Renschler became president and Boeing chairman of the board. To this was added Hamilton and Standard, the nation's leading producers of propellers, and Sikorsky Airplane Company, a major factor in flying boats and amphibians. Thus Renschler, backed by National City Bank, became the dominant figure in the industry.

The formation of United was made possible by the same forces that led to the attempted industry-wide domination by Paramount in motion pictures and RCA in radio: the belief that such rationalization was possible in a young industry, and the aid of investment bankers at a time when securities values were at an all-time high. The time was ripe in 1928, in the afterglow of the Lindbergh flight, when airplane and related issues were the glamour stocks on Wall Street.

Other firms soon followed the merger path. Clement M. Keys, with the aid of Bancamerica-Blair Corporation, the brokerage house of Hayden, Stone, and General Motors, formed North American Aviation Company in 1928. Capitalized at $25 million and with excellent sponsorship, North American quickly took over Eastern Air Transport, Sperry Gyroscope, and Ford Instrument, as well as more than a dozen other smaller firms in the field. Keys also brought together Curtiss Aeroplane & Motor Company and Wright Aeronautical Corporation to form Curtiss-Wright, the final arrangements for which were completed in 1929.

Still another giant firm spawned in the late 1920s was the Aviation Corporation, better known as AVCO. It was formed by Lehman Brothers, which placed W. Averell Harriman in the post of chairman of the board. AVCO was capitalized at $40 million, and shares were sold to the public at a time when the firm had practically no assets. With the money gained from the stock sales, AVCO started to purchase operating companies, including Juan Trippe's Colonial Airways and other carriers, several airplane factories, aviation schools, broadcasting stations, and even a busline. By the end of the decade

AVCO had some eighty subsidiaries and the largest transport mileage in the nation.

Throughout this period, Congress continued to pass legislation to aid the industry. The Kelly Act was amended several times and, in 1930, the McNary-Watres Act, which increased payments and set up a new base for subsidies, was signed into law. Old contracts were renegotiated under the new law by Postmaster General Walter Brown, who initiated the first complete study of the industry. Brown concluded that only the Big Three—North American, AVCO, and United—had the capital to compete on a national basis. The forty-odd other firms were undercapitalized and unable to accept contracts under the new law. Brown reasoned that if the smaller units could be consolidated, true competition could develop and the industry would be in a healthier condition. The major problem was in creating competition for United, which had integrated its lines far better than the other two major firms.

Under Brown's leadership, Transcontinental Air Transport merged with several other firms—including subsidiaries of AVCO and North American—to form Trans World Airlines. An AVCO subsidiary, American Airways, was merged with other firms and given contracts along southern routes. Thus, the airline system was created by the Post Office Department from components of the Big Three and a union of smaller independents. Still, the Big Three controlled air traffic through stock ownership and joint directorships. They were determined to continue in the lucrative passenger and freight fields, which in the late 1920s and early 1930s were coming into their own. While airmail remained the backbone of transport, it only doubled from 1928 to 1932, while passengers carried rose in the same period from 50,000 to 541,000; freight went from 217,000 pounds to 1 million pounds and miles flown from 10.6 million to 50.9 million.

The industry was hurt by the depression, but not as much

as most others. Still, the rapid growth of aviation, resulting in part from Wall Street influence, led to an investigation by Senator Hugo Black of Alabama. Black claimed that the aviation firms were guilty of violating the Sherman Anti-Trust Act, citing as evidence the fact that United, North American, and AVCO had received twenty-four of the twenty-seven airmail contracts outstanding. The firms replied that the industry had developed in the way that it did through the intercession of Postmaster General Brown. Black was unable to find sufficient evidence to recommend antitrust actions against the Big Three insofar as their manufacturing affiliates were concerned, and despite lengthy hearings he could not find Pan American Airways a conspiracy although it had a near-monopoly over international travel. But he did charge American Airways, United Airlines, Transcontinental & Western, and Eastern Air Transport of violating the Sherman Act. On February 9, 1934, President Roosevelt responded by cancelling all contracts for domestic airmail and turning the job over to the Army Air Corps. The change proved disastrous; the Air Corps had less experience in flying than the private lines, and the weather turned against it. Charles Lindbergh made several important speeches condemning the change. By May, after several fatal crashes, the commercial airlines were again carrying the mail.

Under the terms of the new Air Mail Act of 1934, the private system was accepted, but the legislation provided for the separation of the lines from their manufacturing parents. United was divided into several firms. Renschler headed the new United Aircraft Corporation, the largest component, which included Pratt & Whitney, Hamilton Standard, Sikorsky, and Chance Vought. Boeing took command of Boeing Aircraft, while United Air Lines was made independent of both manufacturing firms. North American sold Trans World Airlines to the Atlas Corporation, while AVCO divested itself of American Air Lines. The divestitures were completed in 1938, when North American sold Eastern Airlines to a group headed by

Eddie Rickenbacker. The new lines were placed under federal control in 1938, with the establishment of the Civil Aeronautics Authority.

The Black investigations marked a watershed in the development of the industry. Some firms turned to manufacturing for the government, which was expanding the army and navy air arms, while trying to compete in the commercial markets as well. Among these were North American, Boeing, and Lockheed, a small firm which went bankrupt during the depression but was revived after being reorganized. Smaller firms producing speciality planes for the military included Brewster, Grumman, and Martin, all of which had important interests in naval aircraft, and Consolidated Aircraft and Bell, which sought army contracts. The young private plane market included dozens of small firms, the most important of which were Piper, Beech, Bellanca, Taylorcraft, and Aeronautical Corporation of America. AVCO, United, and Curtiss-Wright produced motors, parts, complete planes, and military products, and were all that remained of the hopes of large, vertically integrated "General Motors of the air," which were considered possible in the late 1920's.

The market for commercial aircraft in the early depression years was poorer than it had been in the last years of prosperity, but the growth of military orders prevented mass bankruptcies. The industry produced 6,034 units, in 1929 of which the armed forces took 677. In 1933, the worst year of the depression, the nation produced 1,057 planes, of which the military took 466. Production reached 3,623, in 1938 with military orders accounting for half. Although these figures seem to indicate a sharp decline, it should be noted that the value of products, a more significant figure, which included parts and services, rose. In 1937 the value of products was $149.7 million for 3,230 airplanes, while the 1929 figures were $71.2 million for the 6,034 units. Sharp competition held down profits, however—there were some two hundred aircraft firms in 1935.

By mid-depression, some firms were well in the black and prepared technologically for the World War II expansion.

TABLE 2

Statistics for Selected Aviation Firms, 1937

Firm	Sales (000's)	Gross Profits (000's)	Net Income (000's)
Bell Aircraft	$ 1,708	$ 271	$ 66
Bellanca Aircraft	1,592	317	151
Bendix Aviation	40,595	12,415	2,950
Boeing Airplane	5,545	1,140	382
Curtiss-Wright	24,116	7,314	2,545
Douglas Aircraft	20,950	4,173	1,632
Lockheed Aircraft	5,210	1,198	212
Glenn Martin	7,839	2,179	1,451
North American	8,249	3,485	716
United Aircraft	28,755	10,141	4,630
Wright Aeronautical	16,654	6,925	2,608

SOURCE. U.S.,Temporary National Economic Committee, *Investigation of Concentration of Economic Power, Part 31-A: Supplemental Data Submitted to the Temporary National Economic Committee* (Washington, 1941), pp. 18213–18440.

Bendix, which appeared to have been the largest in the industry, actually was more allied to the automobile industry in this period. Curtiss-Wright and United remained strong, as was expected. For a while it appeared that Boeing would become the giant of the commercial airplane market. In 1933 United Airlines placed a $2.5 million order for 55 new Boeing transport planes. Douglas retaliated with a newer, better model, which it sold to Trans World Airlines, causing United to spend an additional $1.5 million on remodeling its Boeings. During the next two years, the two manufacturers competed for domination of the market.

The fastest growing company was Douglas Aircraft, and this was the result of the introduction in 1936 of a novel airplane, the DC-3, which was the major new product of the decade, and one which enabled the industry to partially break away from government domination. According to C. R. Smith, president of American Airlines, "The DC-3 freed the air lines from complete dependency on government mail pay. It was the first air plane that could make money just by hauling passengers. With the previous planes, if you multiplied the number of seats by the fares being charged, you couldn't break even, not with a 100 per cent load. Economically, the DC-3 let us expand and develop new routes where there was no mail pay."[3] The DC-3 enabled passenger traffic to grow rapidly in the late 1930's. By 1940, 3,185,000 passengers were being carried yearly by the airlines, as compared with the less than 494,000 in the first year of the New Deal.

On the eve of World War II, then, the industry had several major producers of airplanes, a developing technology, and a sound passenger structure. The oligopoly situation of the late 1920s had been changed to one of competition in production and franchised oligopolies in the case of the airlines. In choosing between markets, the manufacturers assured a degree of competition—more than was the case in automobiles, but less than that in chemicals. In 1939, the first year of the war, United Aircraft reported $52 million in sales, while five firms—Curtiss-Wright, Lockheed, Douglas, North American, and Martin—had sales of between $24 million and $49 million. Just as government airmail contracts enabled the industry to grow in the 1920s, so government contracts resulted in a developed industry in the 1940s. Continued military demands in the years that followed made most manufacturers government-oriented, and the first of the important monopsony firms of the post–World War II era. Government regulations, especially those of the Civil Aviation Board, placed the airlines in a situation

3. Lloyd Morris and Kendall Smith, *Ceiling Unlimited* (New York, 1953), p. 300.

similar to that of the railroads. Thus, the industry.was never to have a period in which it might have developed naturally.

The opportunities brought by the depression to strong firms in oligopoly industries, such as automobiles, and to new industries which had federal aid, such as aircraft, could be seen in other parts of the economy as well, thus substantiating the view that the New Deal, rather than restoring competition, actually completed the concentration begun in the 1920s. This was the case in many fields. In retailing, for example, the chain stores of the 1920s suffered declining sales and profit margins, but they were able to survive while smaller units closed shop. The response to the challenge was not one of retrenchment, although some thought in such terms initially, but rather one of innovation.

The large chain operations attempted to maintain their positions by stressing sales rather than profits, in the hope of surviving the depression. A & P, the leading food chain, was successful in this; during the 1930s its market share reached a high of 11.9 percent (1933), and never fell below 9.9 percent (1939). During this period, however, the firm's profits fell from $29.5 million to $20.4 million, as its rate of return on investment declined from 26.6 percent to 12.7 percent. A&P opened its first supermarket in 1936. In that year, twenty of the firm's 14,700 stores could be described as being of the newer type. Success in supermarket operations led to rapid expansion, and by 1939 the firm had 1,127 supermarkets out of a total of 9,100 stores. Not even the passage of the Robinson-Patman Federal Anti-Price Discrimination Act in 1936, under the terms of which independent retailers were protected from the price-cutting practices of large chains, could prevent the growth of supermarkets, the enrichment of the chains, and the disappearance of the small family grocery stores.

Bigness prevailed in cigarettes as well, although the circumstances were different. On the eve of the depression, the cigarette industry was dominated by American Tobacco, Lig-

gett & Myers, and R. J. Reynolds, with Lorillard, Brown and
Williamson, and other firms in a secondary role. The depression
offered an opportunity for renewed competition, as the smaller
firms and new companies rushed to the market with lower
priced brands. The Big Three retaliated by entering into agreements on tobacco purchases, engaging in price-fixing, using
cut-throat competion methods against the smaller firms, and
in other ways uniting to protect their positions. In 1946, in
American Tobacco Company v. *United States,* the government
succeeded in convicting the Big Three of unfair practices, but
by then their industry positions were again secure.

TABLE 3

Operating Revenue and Profits For Three Leading Copper Companies

COMPANY

YEAR	Kennecott Sales	Profit (000)	Anaconda Sales	Profit (000)	Phelps Dodge Sales	Profit (000)
1930	$ 77,559	$24,666	$179,333	$ 18,793	$83,970	$ 515
1931	48,501	10,007	96,388	(3,131)	50,320	(988)
1932	23,094	(616)	52,296	(16,893)	21,997	(3,752)
1933	39,818	9,294	72,481	(6,822)	24,709	(84)
1934	53,593	13,860	99,150	1,960	36,345	3,225
1935	66,674	22,534	127,679	11,314	53,957	6,392
1936	98,442	39,374	160,883	15,959	64,917	11,393
1937	138,864	67,507	233,917	31,732	83,129	12,741
1938	89,061	32,575	144,207	9,836	62,595	8,956
1939	127,009	50,035	183,675	20,482	75,516	12,279

SOURCE: U. S. Federal Trade Commission, *Federal Trade Commission Report
on the Copper Industry,* Part 1, *The Copper Industry of the United States
and International Copper Cartels* (Washington, 1947), pp. 125-166.

One would expect the copper producers to suffer severely
in a depression which affected every branch of heavy industry.

Indeed, on the eve of the depression many firms were faced with increasingly higher costs for exploration, a static price structure, and foreign competition. The situation worsened with the depression; in 1932 the price of copper fell to an unprecedented 4.8 cents a pound, forcing many mines to close. The firms were able to recover somewhat during the early New Deal, but the recession of 1937 led the industry to new depths of despair. Yet, the National Recovery Administration codes and an international copper cartel, which operated in the last part of the decade, assured not only survival for the leading firms, but a measure of profit. The Big Three copper producers ended the decade with larger profits than they had at its beginning. For them, the period from 1931 to 1933 marked the bottom, with low demand and prices, but afterwards there was sharp recovery. True, the price of copper securities remained depressed throughout the 1930s, as did those of other industry groups, but earnings increased substantially. In 1930, Kennecott earned $5.31 a share; in 1939, it earned $10.58. In the same years Phelps Dodge went from $0.40 a share to $7.19 a share, and Anaconda from $3.63 to $4.06.

Research was the key to the development of the chemical industry in the 1930s. There were hundreds of specialty firms and several giants in 1929, none of which dominated all aspects of the diverse industry. Du Pont, Allied Chemical, and Union Carbide were major factors in several products, while Dow, American Cyanamid, and Monsanto led in others. While leadership was shared, it should be noted that in any given product or process, the three or four top firms controlled more than half the business. Further, given the heavy capital costs, research expenditures, and marketing problems, entry into any part of the industry was difficult.

The chemical industry prospered during the 1930s, and more products emerged from its laboratories in this decade than during the 1920s. In part this was due to the foundations laid during the prosperity period, and the tradition of research. By 1937, the industry had 300 researchers for every 10,000 workers; iron and steel had only 20 per 10,000. That year, du Pont announced that some 40 percent of its products had been unknown eight years before. The new products included synthetic camphor, Duco paint, viscose rayon, and cellophane. The last item a product of du Pont's affiliation with Comptoir de Textiles Artificiels, the French firm that had developed rayon, was an instant success. And the most spectacular new du Pont product, nylon, was yet to come.

> The most important discovery ever made in du Pont's laboratories, of course, was the invention of nylon. The chemist responsible for this accomplishment was Dr. Wallace H. Carothers, a brilliant young man who was lured away from Harvard by du Pont after the company decided to support a program of fundamental research. In 1935, Carothers developed a polymide that he called "66" polymer, a fiber that was strong, tough, elastic, water-resistant, and capable of withstanding high temperatures. In 1938, du Pont completed the pilot plant and a year later large-scale production of nylon got under way. Nylon so nearly ruined the market for rayon that du Pont, once the only rayon manufacturer in the United States, has recently stopped making any of that fiber.[4]

The Carothers project cost du Pont $27 million, of which $21 million was spent on a pilot plant. Nylon was not marketed until 1940, at which time the needs of war prevailed over those of the civilian market.

Summary

It would be incorrect to reason from the foregoing material that the American economy was in sound shape during the 1930s. The misery of the period, the business failures, the

4. William H. A. Carr, *The du Ponts of Delaware* (New York, 1964), pp. 301–302.

general dislocation, and the psychological depression are well known. The statistics seem to corroborate those who would argue that this was the nadir of American business. From a gross national product of $104.4 billion and personal income of $84.8 billion in 1929, the nation fell to a GNP of $74.2 billion and a personal income of $47.2 billion in 1933. Not until 1939 did the GNP exceed that of 1929; not until the United States entered World War II did personal income recover. And even then, it was the war, not normal recovery, that enabled economic renewal to take place. In 1929, 3.2 percent of the civilian labor force was unemployed; in 1939, the figure was 17.2 percent.

But to argue that because the 1930s was a period of depression—the worst in the nation's history—it also was one of unalloyed gloom for American business, is also incorrect. This was not the case in petroleum, automobiles, aircraft, chemicals, and many other fields. In the industries marked by oligopolies, large-scale operations, self-financing, and increasing markets, many firms did surprisingly well considering the general economic climate. Furthermore, the leaders in practically every industry not only survived the period, but often emerged stronger than they had been in 1929. The falling away of competitors, the difficulty of access for new firms, government aid in many forms, and the response to the challenges were important reasons for their successes. Productivity, or output per man hour, increased 25 percent during the 1920s; during the depression, productivity increased 20 percent, a remarkable performance considering the high plateau from which the advance was made. American business, then, was far better prepared for the ordeal of war than the raw statistics would seem to indicate.

CHAPTER VII

Government-Business Relations in World War II

The World War I experiences of the War Industries Board formed a basis for many business practices in the 1920s and government-business relations during the depression. During the war, for the first time, American businessmen and statesmen had been forced to consider the problems of total economic mobilization, and a whole generation of bureaucrats had been trained in its techniques. At the end of the war, Baruch and several of his aides had suggested that their work be continued during peacetime, through the creation of an agency whose task it would be to prepare for future emergencies. This advice was not heeded, although a small planning branch was provided for in the National Defense Act of 1920, and the Army Industrial College was broadened somewhat. The generals remained interested in the concept, however, and during the 1920s planned allocations of material for what was called "M-Day" —mobilization day. Navy leaders did little in this direction, while air corps requirements went unconsidered for the most part.

The War Department made public a mobilization program in 1930, which was revised in 1933, 1936, and 1939. In general, the program contemplated the creation of a War Resources Administration, headed by a single individual, which would operate in a manner similar to that of the WIB. Should there be a future war, it was thought, the nation might have to be mobilized faster and to a greater extent than had been the situation during the period from 1914 to 1919.

These plans were either ignored or attacked for the most part. The prosperous America of the 1920s wanted no talk of future wars, and depression America was more concerned with domestic problems. The generals and businessmen who spoke of war preparations were considered special pleaders, profiteers, warmongers, or worse.

Those who opposed preparation were given ammunition by *Fortune* magazine which, in 1934, published an article entitled "Arms and the Men," which demonstrated that some large firms had made great profits during World War I. The public response to the article led to the establishment of a Senate committee to investigate the munitions industry. Although this group—the Nye Committee—failed to prove that businessmen and bankers had worked to involve the nation in the war, the publicity it received convinced many that the business community had gained fortunes from the misery of what was by then an unpopular war. The hearings served to reinforce the general antibusiness sentiment of the depression period, as liberal reformers, old antitrusters, pacifists, and small businessmen joined in antimilitarist groups.

Although the public was more concerned with economic problems in 1938, President Roosevelt was aware of the growing tensions in Europe. In that year he sent Bernard Baruch on a fact-finding mission to verify rumors of war preparations among the powers. Baruch reported that the major nations were already on a war footing. Germany had more than 3,300 bombers, Russia between 1,300 and 1,600, and France almost 1,000. In comparison, the United States owned 301. The differences in other military goods was equally unbalanced. Further, the Germans and others had already mobilized their economies for war, while the United States lacked even a plan. The President recognized the problem, and immediately began preparing the economy for possible war. Bypassing Secretary of War Harry Woodring, in whom he had little confidence, Roosevelt turned over war preparations to Assistant Secretary Louis

Johnson, who received open support from Baruch. Politically, this meant a new alliance between the administration and conservative Democrats, and an opening toward rapprochement with the business community. As the President would say later on, Dr. New Deal was being replaced by Dr. Win-the-War.

During the next year, Johnson supervised a program of stockpiling, established a priorities system to go into effect in case of national emergency, and mapped a plan of conversion for business. None of this was done with the fanfare that usually accompanied New Deal measures; Roosevelt, for political reasons, did not wish to antagonize the isolationist liberals whose aid he needed on domestic programs. The strategy worked, as most members of this group approved a $525 million defense budget in July 1939.

The next step was to organize a body to coordinate procurement under the new budget. Roosevelt was loath to give full authority to any one man, although several experienced individuals—such as Baruch—were willing to take the job. The President was noted for his habit of setting up rival forces in the same field, to check each other and at the same time gain wider support than could any single one. Examples abounded in the New Deal—Ickes and Hopkins clashed on relief, and Hull and Welles on foreign relations. Thus Roosevelt sought to avoid the formula which Wilson had finally arrived at in World War I: the creation of a "czar" to coordinate all aspects of the preparedness program. He established the War Resources Board, headed by Edward R. Stettinius, Jr., chairman of the board of U.S. Steel and a "progressive" businessman. Stettinius chose Walter Gifford of American Telephone and Telegraph, John Lee Pratt of General Motors, and Robert Wood of Sears, Roebuck, to serve with him on the board. Thus, the President hoped to complete the bridge to the business community, again thinking politically rather than planning efficiently. Significantly, none of these men had any experience in war mobilization; those who had were ignored insofar as appointments were concerned, although Roosevelt made a point of consulting with Baruch for show purposes.

The War Resources Board held a series of conferences and submitted a report in October 1939 which was not released until after the war. An important election was coming up, and the war in Europe had begun. Roosevelt announced that the United States was not going to war, and so was uninterested in plans for war. With this, the board was dismissed. Instead, Johnson was told to continue his mobilization-planning programs and to do so with the minimum of publicity.

The European war would not wait for the American election. As it became more evident that Hitler would conquer France, Roosevelt was forced to act openly. On May 25, 1940, he created the Office for Emergency Management, and three days later he formed a Council of National Defense and appointed an Advisory Commission as its executive. The National Defense Advisory Commission was made up of Ralph Budd of Chicago, Burlingham & Quincy Railroad, William Knudsen of General Motors, Stettinius, and representatives of government, the colleges, and labor unions. Roosevelt refused to name any of these as chairman, foredooming it to uselessness. Known as the "Headless Horsemen," the commission members were charged with effecting a concerted war mobilization program, a task made impossible by the lack of a directing force. Still, Sidney Hillman, president of the Amalgamated Clothing Workers and a member of the commission, was able to prevent several strikes in war plants. The NDAC also managed to facilitate the production of military aircraft.

Major problems usually landed in the offices of Donald Nelson, a former vice-president of Sears-Roebuck, who was named Coordinator of Defense Purchases by the commission. Nelson managed to coordinate the efforts of several executive procurement agencies, and he established methods by which the armed forces could grant contracts without competitive bidding, a procedure which facilitated procurement but at the same time tended to favor large firms over smaller ones. Later on, steps were taken to assure a role for small- and medium-size business, but from the first the pattern set by the NDAC held: the war effort would be led by the large firms which had consolidated their positions in the 1920s and dominated their industries in the 1930s.

Although Nelson later claimed that he admired Baruch, and supported the old WIB leader's suggestion that all power be concentrated in a single office, at the time he sided with those who favored divided authority. Personality played a major role in the early organization of the war effort. Roosevelt was unwilling to grant complete control to any single individual, and most members of the NDAC, unsure as to who might get the position if one were to be created, supported the President. Accordingly, there were few protests when, after the 1940 election, Roosevelt moved to reorganize the commission. The President established in its place the Office of Production Management, jointly directed by William Knudsen and Sidney Hillman. Knudsen, who was to be in charge of industrial production, organized a staff of prominent businessmen and placed each industry under the leadership of one of them. Hillman, who headed the labor effort, also brought businessmen to his staff, along with several labor leaders. Others with important positions were Stettinius, who headed the industrial materials sector, and Leon Henderson, who was charged with controlling inflation.

The confusion of the early war period was compounded when, on June 25, 1940, Congress authorized the Reconstruction Finance Corporation to undertake emergency defense financing. Chairman Jesse Jones acted quickly to implement the order, setting up the Rubber Reserve Company, the Metals Reserve Company, the Defense Supplies Corporation, and the Defense Plant Corporation. Others would follow, as the RFC became a major factor in the defense effort. Unfortunately, Jones' office also proved the great bottleneck of the period. It insisted that each program be studied from a cost position before authorization was given. As a result, several projects vital to the defense of the nation were delayed while Jones' accountants examined the books. Jones did relent after a while and eased conditions somewhat, but throughout 1940 and 1941, the RFC imposed fiscal controls on necessary defense programs.

In the period between the attack on Poland and Pearl Harbor, therefore, the politics of war preparation were mismanaged, confused, and marked by political expediency. In addition, the NDAC and RFC, together and singly, acted to aid big business at the expense of smaller producers. At the same time, the Temporary National Economic Committee, completing its massive study of the American economy, concluded that the economy was dominated by a few large firms, and recommended new antitrust actions. The TNEC charged not only that large contracts were given to the big firms, but that a few states seemed to dominate the defense picture. In its final report in 1941, the TNEC concluded:

> The business groups now engaged in the production of the materials which will make America the arsenal of democracy are as dependent upon Government aid for the money with which to build and operate necessary plants as the jobless men upon the W.P.A. R.F.C. loans and defense funds for the construction of factories and the development of power come out of the same deep and ever-deepening deficit from which reliefers get their meager pay checks.
>
> There is scarcely a person in Washington engaged in this great national effort of defense who does not realize that the problem of reconstruction cannot possibly be solved by production for war, and that preparation must be made for the day when this defense effort is no longer necessary.
>
> What will happen when production of bombs and weapons is no longer needed and the hour of industrial demobilization comes? What employment are we then to offer to the millions who cannot create their own jobs? . . .

The committee therefore recommends the vigorous and vigilant enforcement of the antitrust laws, confident that an awakening business conscience will realize the necessity of complete cooperation in the elimination of monopolistic practices. Enlightened self-interest upon the part of those who own and manage the commercial and industrial organizations of our time will prompt them to cooperate.[1]

Clearly, such an approach did not come to terms with the realities of 1940–1941, when an all-out industrial effort was needed to aid the Allies; for that matter, neither did the OPM, with its divided authority and lack of enforcement powers. On the other hand, Donald Nelson proved himself resourceful and capable in the procurement agency, where he worked with Sidney Weinberg, a partner in the investment banking house of Goldman, Sachs. Nelson and Weinberg established an Industry Advisory Council, which set up hundreds of small committees to work out individual procurement needs. Still, the machinery of the OPM almost broke down in 1941, as Roosevelt called upon industry to construct 50,000 airplanes and a two-ocean navy, while failing to delegate the power needed to facilitate production. Recognizing this, but still unwilling to give a clear mandate to a single individual, the President established the Supply, Priorities, and Allocations Board on August 28, 1941, placing it over the still-functioning OPM, and giving it the authority to allocate scarce materials to the armed forces. The SPAB was made up of members of the OPM, together with Harry Hopkins and Henry Wallace, both of whom were close to the President. Nelson was named executive director of SPAB, and retained his post as head of the procurement division of OPM as well. It appeared that he was emerging as the key man in the civilian effort, and Knudsen was losing ground. This suspicion was verified when,

1. United States, Temporary National Economic Committee. *Final Report and Recommendations of the Temporary National Economic Committee* (Washington, 1941), pp. 8–9.

a month after the Japanese attack at Pearl Harbor, Knudsen was dropped and Nelson named head of still another agency, the War Production Board, which replaced several large older ones and was granted enforcement powers.

Nelson was well prepared for his task by his procurement experience at Sears-Roebuck and his work at OPM and SPAB, and his staff was drawn in part from all three. At the time it appeared FDR had finally decided to emulate Wilson in selecting a single person and agency to coordinate the war effort at home. Such was not the case. Instead, Nelson found himself trapped by a web of confusion and deception, duplication and vagueness, at which the President was a master. Unable to grasp fully the outlines of his task, unsure as to the limits of his authority, Nelson faltered, and the WPB under his direction was a cautious, ineffectual agency. Later on it was learned that Roosevelt had not, in fact, granted Nelson the mandate many thought he had received. Apparently the President had toyed with the idea of selecting several others, including William O. Douglas, before accepting Nelson, and had never felt comfortable with the former industrialist.

The procurement problem was further complicated by political infighting, at which Nelson was a novice. At first the WPB chief had the enthusiastic support of Harry Hopkins, the closest of Roosevelt's inner circle, who had dissuaded the President from setting up a three-man committee consisting of Wendell Willkie, Nelson, and Douglas. Henry Wallace, then Vice-President, backed Nelson, in return for which he expected the WPB chief's aid in forwarding his political aspirations. The administration economists, led by Robert Nathan, also supported Nelson, hoping that he would succeed in putting their plans into motion.

As it developed, Nelson had no skill for politics and made many enemies. He soon demonstrated an amazing lack of knowledge, hidden by his acknowledged administrative skill. As a result, the WPB, more powerful than any of its predecessors, failed to coordinate the economy efficiently. To be sure, the task of World War II was far more complex than that faced by the WIB in World War I. But the efficiency of the latter organization cannot be explained solely by this fact; nor can the failures of the WPB be excused only on the grounds that Nelson had a more difficult task. Unfortunately, Nelson lacked the authority given Baruch, who gave the impression of being an assistant president. Had Roosevelt given Nelson the kind of support Wilson accorded Baruch, the WPB might have been more successful. But such was not the case.

Although the WPB retained most of its powers throughout the war, and was the principal agency in the mobilization effort, political pressures and Roosevelt's penchant for dividing authority led to disagreements and conflict. James Byrnes, whom Roosevelt had earlier named to the Supreme Court, resigned to become a troubleshooter in the procurement field. One of his first tasks was to end the feuds that had developed between and within the various agencies. His major problem was the split between Nelson and Charles E. Wilson, former president of General Electric who was serving as chairman of the Production Executive Committee of the WPB. Byrnes suggested that Roosevelt ask for the resignations of both men, and then appoint Baruch to the same job he had held during World War I. Roosevelt responded a few months later by creating the Office of War Mobilization, which supervised the entire war effort and controlled the WPB. Its director was Byrnes, who now became "assistant President." The transfer of power from Stettinius to Knudsen to Nelson to Byrnes was now completed. The political tensions were not over, however. Throughout the rest of the war Byrnes clashed with Hopkins, Wallace, and many others, as the struggle for succession to the presidency at times eclipsed the war effort. Nor was Byrnes able to still the internal conflicts in the various agencies. Eventually the Nelson–Wilson feud grew so heated that Nelson resigned to accept a mission to China, while Wilson returned to General Electric. Vice-Chairman Julius Krug succeeded Nelson as the head of the WPB and remained at the job until the end of the war. Other personality conflicts continued, and lines of power were still not clearly defined on V-J Day. The Roosevelt administration, then, did a poor job in coordinating the economic side of the war effort, and that was one of FDR's most serious failures.

President Wilson's organization of the economy during World War I was more efficient than was Roosevelt's in World War II, yet the economy performed better in the second war than in the first. The gross national product rose from $103 billion in 1938 to $184 billion in 1944. Roosevelt hoped for the production of 50,000 airplanes a year at the start of the war; in 1943, American industry delivered 84,400 and in the following year, 95,237. During the war American factories turned out more than 300,000 airplanes, 77,000 ships, 86,000 tanks, and 2,700,000 machine guns. Manufacturing output increased 128 percent from 1939 to 1944, as almost all industries shared in the war effort.

Clearly, the administration cannot be credited with such a spectacular performance. The origins of the success of mobilization can be found elsewhere, in four general reasons. In the first place, World War II did not erupt suddenly, as had World War I. American industry had begun to fill war orders before the attack on Poland. Then from 1939 to 1941 businesses received an ever-increasing volume of orders, at a time when the nation was not yet officially at war. In this period, large-scale conversions were made. Ford, for example, accepted important military orders in this period, while General Motors produced many items for all branches of the armed services. Yet, both firms continued to sell automobiles as well; indeed, production actually increased, rising from 2.5 million vehicles in 1938 to 4.8 million in 1941. No civilian vehicles were produced after January 1942, as the industry became wholly devoted to the war effort. But its conversion was more gradual than had been the case for most large firms in World War I.

A second factor was the entrance of many businessmen into the government in the war period. Baruch had used dozens of business leaders to head important WIB agencies; Roosevelt called upon industry to fill similar posts, and hundreds volunteered their services. The World War II "dollar-a-year men" had the experience of the New Deal to draw upon; they were used to working with government, and accepted the role of government in their industries more easily. These were men who had grown up in the age of corporate capitalism; unlike their World War I predecessors, they were not founders or ideology-bound rugged individualists, who might cause trouble on the lower echelons. Increasingly, big government and big business came to resemble each other, and the transition from a large corporation to a government agency was not too difficult.

The fact that American big business survived the depression, and in many cases emerged stronger than before, was the third factor in the success of the mobilization effort. Fortunately for the nation, the antitrust program of the late New Deal had not been implemented when the government realized the need for bigness in war. It is unlikely that the large contracts of the period could have been met by the nation's smaller concerns. As it was, one-third of all the government's war contracts were handled by ten corporations which, to be sure, subcontracted a good deal of the work. General Motors alone was granted $14 billion worth of contracts, and well over half the prime contracts went to the top three automobile makers. Chrysler became a major producer of tanks; Packard converted to the fabrication of marine engines; Willys became famous for its Jeep (although more of the small vehicles were made by Ford). After a difficult start the second-largest automobile manufacturer became the leading producer of heavy bombers, and Ford's other accomplishments showed how a major manufacturing firm could tool up for war.

The totals [at Ford] were impressive: 8,685 Liberator bombers, 57,851 aircraft engines, 277,896 jeeps, 93,217 military trucks, 26,954 tank engines, 4,291 gliders, 2,718 tanks and tank destroyers, 13,000 amphibians, 12,500 armored cars, 13,893 Universal Carriers, 2,400 jet bomb engines, 87,000 aircraft generators, 53,000 superchargers, 1,202 anti-aircraft directors, magnesium and aluminum castings and gun mounts. Though Ford made no ammunition, no guns, and relatively few motor vehicles, it led in the manufacture of high-power aircraft engines and large bombers. It was also the leading manufacturer of gliders, and supplied engines of its own design for the medium tanks made by Chrysler and General Motors. It contributed the final body design of the jeep, assisted in re-designing the medium tank, and designed an amphibian and a reconnaissance car.[2]

Although the large firms dominated the procurement effort, small companies also benefited, through special orders, subcontracting, and the production of those goods in which they held an industry position prior to the war. The heavy influx of orders caused the number of business failures to decline sharply. In 1939, there were 14,768 such failures, while in 1945 the number was 809. On the other hand, some half-million small- and medium-size firms disappeared through mergers and consolidations in the war period. Finally, new firms opened their doors during the war, and remained to grow in the postwar period.

With the coming of war, the bicycle industry converted to parts manufacture, and several medium and small firms merged to concentrate on bearing production. A. C. Gilbert Company, well known as a toy manufacturer, bought out several small firms in the same and related industries and concentrated its facilities on the production of precision parts. Majestic Metal Specialties, turned from making lipstick cases to incendiary

---

2. Allan Nevins and Frank Ernest Hill, *Ford: Decline and Rebirth, 1933–1962* (New York, 1963), pp. 226–227.

bombs. Talon Inc., a leading zipper manufacturer, continued its production of zippers for war use, but bought out some other firms to gain their facilities to produce bomb-tail fuses. Nemo Corset Company filled several large orders for WAC undergarments, and also delivered flare parachutes to the Air Corps. N. A. Woodworth Company, a small firm with twenty employees when the war came, became a vital subcontractor for Curtiss-Wright. H. Leslie Hoffman, a lighting equipment salesman, purchased several defunct plants, formed Hoffman Radio, and sold $4 million a year of radio equipment to the armed forces. Cases such as these were multiplied by the hundreds in all parts of the country. It can be seen, then, that the war provided excellent opportunities for entrepreneurs who were willing to cooperate with the government and bid for contracts, or ally themselves with the major producers. Still, few major new firms emerged from the war; the successful small firms became medium-sized, some firms grew large, and the large businesses became gigantic in comparison to their prewar size.

The fourth and final factor that enabled American business to respond so successfully during the war was the nature of government contracts. There were two important aspects to this factor: taxation and procurement. As part of its attempt to take the profits out of war, the government decided to levy an excess profits tax on industry. Such taxes had been tried with little success in World War I, and experience with the Vinson-Trammell Act of 1934, which imposed profit limitations upon war-related industries, was equally poor. Nonetheless, it was decided that all profits above normal would be taxed at a rate of between 85 and 90 percent. The firm was permitted to choose any year between 1936 and 1939 as being "normal" for tax purposes.

There were several problems with this law. In the first place, the base period was one of abnormally low profits, and so penalized all firms that returned to what would ordinarily be considered normal production and discouraged competition for new contracts. Second, some firms—especially in chemicals —had spent large sums on research in the late 1930s, and so showed little profits. As a result, they were taxed in wartime for products developed in peace. Finally, it encouraged business to waste money, since such waste could be charged to costs, and so not be reflected in profits.

> In curbing inflation and preventing waste, the two other specific objectives which Congress sought, the wartime Excess Profits Tax was powerless. When the law took eighty-five cents of every profit dollar many businessmen thought it better to have the fun of spending the whole dollar as a "business expense" than to give most of it to the government; and so luxuries such as "office cars," "executive airplanes," "travelling secretaries," and "entertainment" became, by the scratch of an auditor's pen, "Legitimate business expenses." Lawrence Ottinger, president of the United States Plywood Company, summed up the businessman's point of view on this wasteful procedure when he said, "In effect the Government promised to throw six dollar down any rat hole where we threw a dollar." The rat holes of war were well filled. As a check on inflation in commodity prices excess profits taxes were unavailing, because the more the government paid for war goods, the less was turned over to it in excess levies. No ceiling was placed on the price of materials going into war goods because the same result was achieved by contract renegotiation.[3]

The procurement program was a buckshot operation; if enough shot is fired, it will hit the mark, although most will be scattered. The administration and business engaged in many wasteful operations, and horror stories of such waste abound. On the other hand, so much was spent that there was more than enough for necessary programs.

From the first, President Roosevelt succeeded in aiding the Allies in their struggle with Hitler. Even before the blitzkreig in the West, American supplies were destined for Great Britain

3. Francis Walton, *Miracle of World War II* (New York, 1946), pp. 264–265.

and France. On June 6, 1940, the Navy Department delivered the first of one hundred scout bombers to the Curtiss-Wright factory; under a World War I law, they were being turned in as "overage." Actually, they were the latest operational models, destined to be sent from Curtiss-Wright to Europe. In the same fashion, another 100 airplanes, 600,000 British Enfield rifles, and 800 French 75-millimeter World War I guns were shipped to the Allies, along with large quantities of munitions and small arms. Then, on March 11, 1941, the President signed the Lend-Lease Act, which authorized the "lending" of American arms to the Allies. Congress appropriated $7 billion for the program, and the funds were quickly used to put the economy on a wartime basis. By December 7, almost $6 billion of the money was spent.

> Besides the indirect effect of Lend-Lease orders upon the expansion of America's war production capacity, hundreds of millions in Lend-Lease funds were directly invested before Pearl Harbor in new factories, shipyards, processing plants, storage depots, and other facilities in this country which, taken together, made an important addition to our industrial plant. These investments, now totalling nearly $900,000,000, have been made in 34 out of the 48 states in the union. They range in size from more than $142,000,000 for war plants in Michigan to $14,000 for a dry skim milk plant in North Dakota.... Lend-Lease also financed the construction of ammunition docks, heavy-lift piers and floating cranes in American ports which since have loaded munitions for American troops as well as for our allies. It has helped to build a whole system of storage depots from coast to coast and many halfway stations that have contributed to a more orderly flow from factory to shipside of war materials for our own and other United Nations forces.[4]

Government largesse made it possible for Lend-Lease to contribute substantially to the defense of Britain. But even Stettinius was obliged to state that the program involved a

4. Edward R. Stettinius, Jr., *Lend Lease: Weapon for Victory* (New York, 1944), pp. 100–101.

good deal of waste and duplication. Although it was to have been administered by a Cabinet committee, consisting of the Secretaries of State, Treasury, War, and Navy, which would have been difficult enough, in practice Lend-Lease was controlled by several groups. First, the program was administered by an Emergency Management Office. Then it was—in theory—turned over to the Lend-Lease Administration. In fact, Lend-Lease was divided among several existing agencies and a few new ones, most of which were controlled by Hopkins. Each office had its own pet projects, and often they operated at cross-purposes. For example, as a result of duplication, the United States sent so much fuel oil to neutral Spain in 1941 that that nation's per capita supplies were greater than those of the United States. Shipments of canned food to Russia went uneaten for a while, as the Soviet people did not like American cooking. Machines sent to Britain arrived with too few parts, too many, or poor instructions. It was inevitable that such problems would appear in a program as large as Lend-Lease. Many could have been avoided, however, had it been conducted by a single authority instead of several. Still, the huge volume of spending—almost $282 billion for war between 1941 and 1945—enabled the nation and the Allied cause to overcome whatever wastes did exist. The power of the economy, then, more than compensated for the lack of efficiency in government.

Not all industries were able to respond satisfactorily to war demands. Steel, for example, was still recovering from the labor strife of the 1930s, financial problems, and poor plant location. In 1938, the nation produced 32 million tons of steel, a sharp decline from the 63 million tons of 1929. The mills were then operating at 20 percent of capacity, and only the larger firms were able to survive the recessions of 1929 and 1937. As a result, few were able to modernize their facilities, or for that matter saw any reason to do so. The larger firms concentrated on producing strip-sheet steel, which was used in great quantities by the automobile industry. Bethlehem still led in structural shapes, Republic in light steels, National in flat rolled steel, and U.S. Steel in most other shapes. Few firms, with the exception of National, attempted to move to new markets. Steel capacity, which had stood at 55.6 million tons in 1920, had risen to 64.8 million tons by 1929. In contrast, capacity was still below 70 million tons in 1937, an indication of the industry's lethargy during the depression.

In 1938 and thereafter the industry was called upon to expand rapidly and meet the need for new shapes and products. Most firms could not carry the heavy burden of new construction, or had the wish to do so; they expected the recession to return after the war, and had no desire to be burdened with new, unusable capacity. As a result, the government had to construct facilities for the industy, and then turn them over to the private firms to operate. The industry spent less than $100 million for plant improvement and expansion in 1937. In 1940, the figure rose to $180 million, the limit of what private industry was then prepared to spend. Expenditures reached more than $700 million in 1943, well over half of which represented government investment in new plants. Twenty-nine modern integrated plants were constructed wholly with government funds, and twenty more were joint ventures with private firms. In some cases, such as that of Republic, the government built upon existing skills and facilities. Writing of the period in 1943, Republic's president said:

Of course, Republic's operations were crucial, too. Republic already was almost entirely on a war production schedule. Since 1939 we had raised our ingot capacity 30 percent and our pig iron capacity had more than doubled. We were rolling ship plate at a rate five times our prewar peak. Even this gives no real conception of Republic's unique value to the United States as it went to war. When we were putting the company together I hadn't been in the least interested in the business of making rails or heavy structural shapes. What had excited me was the great chance

I saw to exploit the vast potentialities of light steels, almost literally new metals. Our electric furnace capacity, concentrated at Canton, was incomparably the greatest in the United States when the war started in Europe, yet we have since expanded twelvefold; this, of course, included an enormous goverment-owned plant at Chicago, which we designed, built and are operating for the government. As long as a year after France fell there was not an airplane made in this country that did not have somewhere in it vital pieces of Republic's electric furnace steel. Indeed, in the year of Pearl Harbor one-half of *all* the steel in American-made airplanes had been poured from our furnaces. Knowing as I do who was getting that steel and into what crucial places it was going both here and abroad, I do not see how Hitler could have been checked without the special metals made by Republic. Surely in what has happened there must be glimmerings of light to show people that their hard-pressed government could not get this steel from *plants*. That steel came from *management*. Since the emergency began $150,000,000 has been spent erecting government facilities designed and built by Republic on Republic property. Why? So Republic's management could get steel out of those facilities.[5]

Several important facilities were located on the West Coast. Prior to 1941, there had been only one steel plant in the Pacific area, a small Colorado Fuel and Iron operation. Now a huge integrated plant, operated by Henry Kaiser, was located at Fontana, California. Ore was brought in from almost 200 miles away. Few thought the plant would be competitive, but through a combination of modern techniques and excellent management the Fontana Plant produced 675,000 tons of ingot steel a year. A second western plant, costing $202 million and operated by U.S. Steel, was located at Geneva, Utah. An Armco-operated facility was located at Houston, Texas, to serve the Gulf region. Similar plants were located elsewhere in West and South, most against business advice, but necessary to serve war factories. As a result, the industry of 1945 looked quite dif-

5. Tom Girdler, in collaboration with Boyden Sparkes, *Boot Straps* (New York, 1943), pp. 417–418.

ferent from the industry of a decade earlier. The giant firms still dominated the field, but their operations were spread all over the nation. World War II resulted in the creation of a truly national steel industry, destroying the near-monopoly held by the upper Midwest and Birmingham.

The American petroleum industry was in healthy shape when the war erupted, and prepared for the burden it was to undertake. Domestic reserves were high, refining capacity strong and modern, and research productive. Exports were less than 10 percent at the time, however, and it was feared that once overseas military demands were made, they would cut deeply into reserves and production. Rationing was instituted, but even then, at no time did the military take more than 34 percent of output. Indeed, civilian consumption of refined petroleum products rose from 1.11 million barrels in 1939 to 1.18 million in 1945. Gasoline rationing lasted until after V-J Day more to preserve rubber tires, still in short supply, than because of a shortage of fuel, although this was not known until later.

The aircraft industry was a major market for steel, and the fastest growing consumer of petroleum products. Although in better shape than the petroleum industry in 1939, it was to experience growth pains unknown to the oil men.

The aircraft industry had been dominated by the automobile firms during World War I. The same companies, or their successors, played a major role in producing World War II aircraft. This was necessary due to the relative weakness of most firms in the industry in 1939. On the first day of the war, only two American firms—Pratt & Whitney (United Aircraft) and Curtiss-Wright—were prepared to produce modern engines, and the engines were inadequate for military needs. Many new World War II engines and some planes were designed and produced by automobile companies. Even then, the usual bureaucratic problems held back industrial development. It is significant to note that even the B-29, the most advanced of American bombers, had been conceived during the peace period, while its predecessor, the B-17, was a product of early 1930s design.

Added to the difficulties were interservice rivalries as to whether the army or navy would control air power. And within the services, there were many powerful voices raised which doubted the necessity of a strong air arm. One defender of air power, Alexander De Seversky, writing in 1942, said,

> The common denominator of all the objections to an independent Air Force is that the United States has built air forces of a sort under the aegis of the two other services and can therefore improve them without limit under the same monitorship. It would only complicate further an already complex picture, the argument runs, to set up a "third" aviation when we already have Army and Navy aviation.
>
> The answer is that *at present we have no air power at all.* We have a miscellany of airplanes, good, bad, and indifferent, and no air power in the sense that we have defined the idea in these pages. If the production program of 185,000 planes announced by the President in his great address of January 6 is carried out in full, we shall be no nearer genuine air power—since these planes will not reflect a unified aerial strategy to be used by a unified air command.[6]

De Seversky did not succeed in gaining his objective of a separate air force at the time, but large-scale expansion did take place in 1942. Knudsen, then in charge of procurement, supervised the operation, as several large facilities, most of them completely financed by the government, were constructed. In order to take advantage of large pools of skilled labor, plants were constructed for Curtiss-Wright in St. Louis, Pratt & Whitney in Kansas City, and Boeing in Wichita. Favorable weather conditions, plus the location of new steel plants, led to the establishment of a second center on the West Coast, including the Lockheed and North American Aviation com-

6. Alexander P. De Seversky, *Victory Through Air Power* (New York, 1942), p. 279.

plexes in California and the old, but expanded, Boeing plants in Seattle. A large supply of technological skills led to the growth of a third complex in the New York area, which included Sperry, Republic, Grumman, Fairchild, and Brewster.

At first, the government attempted to spread its contracts in such a way as to prevent the formation of oligopolies in military aircraft. Still, by the end of the war, such firms as Boeing, Douglas, North American, and Lockheed had emerged as industry giants, while Bell, Chance-Vought, Republic, and Grumman were strong secondary firms. This development was both natural and desirable; the smaller firms lacked either the technological skills or the management to compete for war orders. An example of this was the failure of Brewster to deliver most of its planes on schedule. The firm passed through the hands of several managements, each hoping to solve its difficulties. None were successful, and in the last months of the war, the navy withdrew its final contract from Brewster, thus spelling the end of the company.

It soon became clear that the established firms would dominate the market for war planes. They performed their tasks with skill, a striking contrast to the procurement situation in that industry in World War I.

The contribution of the aircraft industry to the war effort cannot be measured solely in terms of deliveries to the AAF. As the following table clearly reveals, the Air Force received just over half the total number of aircraft turned out in the United States between July 1940 and August 1945:

Recipient	Number of Aircraft
U.S. AAF	158,880
U.S. Navy	73,711
U.S. other	3,714
British Commonwealth	38,811
USSR	14,717
China	1,225
Other foreign	4,901
Total	295,959

Of this grand total, 230,287 aircraft were actually procured under AAF cognizance regardless of the ultimate recipient. . . . On the

basis of the production figures... the top fifteen manufacturers
under AAF cognizance were:

	Aircraft Accepted	
Manufacturer	AAF	Navy
North American	41,839	0
Consolidated	27,634	3,296
Douglas	25,569	5,411
Curtiss	19,703	6,934
Boeing	17,231	291
Lockheed	17,148	1,929
Republic	15,663	0
Bell	12,941	1
Martin	7,711	1,272
Beech	7,430	0
Ford	6,792	0
Fairchild	6,080	300
Cessna	5,359	0
Piper	5,611	300
Taylor	1,940	0

When the aircraft under Navy cognizance are added in, the
order is changed substantially, especially when the four firms,
Grumman, Eastern, Chance-Vought, and Goodyear, which produced nothing for the AAF, are added into the sequence with
17,448, 13,449, 7,898, and 3,940 aircraft, respectively.[7]

The growth of air power, a good part of which was devoted
to bombing raids, and the need for navigational devices, range-
finding equipment, and other electrical products, gave great
impetus to research. Several new products came out of the
war, including radar, which had been the subject of experiments
in Great Britain since the 1920s. Such developments as radar,
sonar, the Norden bomb sight, and even prosaic collating
machines were needed by the armed forces, and provided contracts for the prewar electrical industries. Naturally, the bulk
of the contracts were given to the large firms, such as General
Electric, Westinghouse, and RCA, but other companies were

7. Irving Briton Holley, Jr., *United States Army in World War II, Special
Studies, Buying Aircraft: Material Procurement for the Army Air Forces*
(Washington, 1964), pp. 560–562.

able to gain awards for specialized equipment. Sperry Gyroscope, United Aircraft, International Telephone and Telegraph, Zenith Radio, and others in the electrical, radio, and aircraft industries entered military electric production and gained useful knowledge. In addition, hundreds of small firms, many of which did not exist in 1938, were able to capture contracts for parts or assembly. As a result, the nation had a strong electrical technology by the end of the war, one which would provide the background for the electronics industry of the 1950s.

Far more than had been the case in World War I, science and technology played key roles in the mobilization effort. In 1941, the Office of Scientific Research and Development was established under Vannevar Bush and James Conant. The OSRD recruited scientists and technicians for special projects, and also underwrote basic research in most scientific areas. This program underscored a development in business techniques that had its origins in the chemical industries of the 1930s: the rise of scientists to important managerial positions. The more complex technologies of the 1940s could not be handled by conventional businessmen, so scientists were placed in command of business and government programs related to the war effort, working under the direction of the military and in conjunction with businessmen. Government agencies oversaw the effort but contributed little in the end, and at the start of the war probably did more harm than good. One writer summarized the programs this way:

> The lessons to be gleaned from our economic mobilization effort are many. One which is seldom high-lighted is that it is possible to initiate defensive measures of far-reaching importance in time of peace. We did learn to plan, and in many ways to plan well, even though it took us until 1942 to put plans in workable form. Another lesson which should have been learned is that the capacity of American industry to produce should not be underestimated. Our production limits had not been reached in World War II when

cutbacks and reconversion began; this is a fact for engineers, politicians and potential enemies to ponder on. What seems to be the most valuable lesson of all is the final proof, if proof were needed, of the effectiveness of a team composed of the scientists, the industrialists and the military, supported by the determined workers of America. This is the team which won the War, regardless of what happened in Washington: it was a team of men and women who understood the partnership which must exist in wartime between the laboratory, the production line and the fighting front.[8]

Even while the nation was in the midst of war, the Administration planned for the eventual conversion to peace. In 1943, the Office of War Mobilization asked Baruch to head an advisory unit on this matter. The Baruch report, issued in 1944, recommended such things as the G.I. Bill of Rights, and several programs for settling war contracts, and selling war surplus. In addition, there was the major problem of disposing of some $15 billion worth of government-owned facilities, most of which were on lease to private concerns during the war.

The war with Japan ended on August 15, 1945, three months after the German surrender. Contracts were cancelled, as expected, and by mid-1946, 10 million military personnel had been discharged into the labor market. All went surprisingly well, and the feared depression did not materialize. Wartime controls continued well into the peace period, as the problems of reconversion were not solved in some areas until the 1950s. One major concern of business, the disposal of the government facilities, was undertaken by the Surplus Properties Board, headed first by Guy Gillette and later by Stuart Symington. Under the direction of these men, most facilities were sold either to their wartime operators or high bidders outside the field. In some cases the program changed the nature of major industries. In aluminum, for example, the purchases of government facilities made Reynolds Metals and Kaiser Aluminum

8. Courtney Robert Hall, *History of American Industrial Science* (New York, 1954), p. 399.

and Chemical competitors, though at the time not serious threats, to the giant Aluminum Corporation of America. Kaiser also purchased the Fontana Steel works, which became the nucleus for Kaiser Steel, as well as several war surplus plants, including Ford's Willow Run operation, which was to house the short-lived Kaiser-Frazer Motor Company. But this was the exception; the program of the Surplus Properties Board did not cause many changes in the structure of control of the early postwar years. Other factors were at work, however, and were acting to transform the economy and the organization of business.

Summary

The mobilization program before and during World War II was not as efficient as it had been in World War I. In attempting to divide authority and retain true power for himself, Roosevelt hindered efficient economic integration such as that which marked the Wilson-Baruch era. Not until well into the second year of war did the President delegate major responsibilities to James Byrnes, and even then, the conflicts of the previous years remained.

American war production did not appear to suffer unduly from this lack of efficiency, and by the end of the war American business was outproducing all other belligerents combined in most areas. This was due to several factors. In the first place, big business was far stronger in 1938–1939 than most contemporaries had realized. Small- and medium-size firms suffered greatly during the depression, but the large concerns emerged without undue difficulty, and often stronger than they had been in 1929. Next, hundreds of "dollar-a-year men" went from business to Washington, and were able to expedite the shift from peace to war production. Finally, managerial combinations of scientists, businessmen, and military leaders were usually able to overfulfill production goals, helped at all times by plentiful government grants.

CHAPTER VIII

Monopsony and Conglomerates in Postwar America

Few economists expected the survival of the American variety of capitalism during the recession of 1937 and in the months that followed. Socialism, permanent pump-priming, nationalization, a form of fascism—all were predicted at one time or another by the most respected economists of the period. Only then, they said, could the prosperity of the late 1920s be duplicated. Never before or since had the nation seen its economic future in such dark terms. These predictions were inaccurate, of course, as the United States prospered during the war, and did even better in the generation that followed.

The statistics told only part of the story, but they did indicate the extent of the prosperity. The Gross National Product in 1939 was $90.5 billion. The exigencies of war led to an increase to $212 billion by 1945. With the Japanese surrender, many businessmen expected the same type of economic decline that followed the end of World War I. Indeed, the GNP did dip slightly in 1946, and the nation was crippled by the worst wave of strikes in its history, followed by a sharp inflationary spiral as wartime controls were ended. But pent-up consumer demands were not easily satisfied, and the GNP rose to $231.3 billion in 1947, and to $257.6 billion the following year. There was a minor recession in 1949, and the figure went down to $256.5 billion. Since that year, the course of the economy has been upward, although at varying rates. In 1950, the figure stood at $284.8 billion, in 1960 at $503.8 billion. Economic growth had become the rule; depressions such as those of

1873, 1893, and 1929 were seen as relics of the past, never to be repeated in the future.

This remarkable record was made possible by a combination of factors, the most important of which was the impact of government spending on the economy. While none could deny that government had become the most important single factor in the economy, it should be stressed that this change came about through evolutionary and pragmatic development and practice; at no time did political and economic philosophers gain control of the decision-making process. The problems of a mature economy on the one hand and the needs of the defense and space establishments on the other dictated a rise in government spending; the inability of the private sector to undertake needed programs, coupled with an unwillingness to invest in low-profit areas, spurred government spending onward. By the mid-1960s, one out of every eight American workers was employed by local, state, or federal government, and government purchases accounted for some 21 percent of the GNP. Government agencies spent $170.5 billion in 1963, and employed almost 10 million workers. By 1966, governments were spending over $1,000 for each man, woman, and child in the nation.

On the other hand, it should be noted that most of this money was used to purchase goods and services from private corporations. The postwar company presidents all were dedicated to the American variety of free enterprise, and did not establish government-owned and -operated corporations, which had been considered by some before World War II. Although the Atomic Energy Commission still controlled much of atomic power, major research was carried on by such firms as Westinghouse, General Electric, and North American, while privately owned utilities accounted for most of the commercial uses of atomic energy. Space exploration was initiated and carried on by the government, but through large contracts given to such private firms as McDonnell Corporation, North American, Litton Industries, Grumman, and many others. The use of satellites for communication, first explored by government agencies, was carried out by a government-created but private firm, Communications Satellite Corporation. All of these were largely dependent on government contracts for their work.

In the field of weaponry, the government accounted for most purchases, which took some 10 percent of the GNP, but almost all contracts were filled by private firms. Defense had become the biggest business in the nation, bigger than automobiles. Even here, there were other factors to consider. Whereas during World War II, military spending accounted for 38 percent of the GNP, its comparative role had declined due to the rapid growth of the economy as a whole. Similarly, although government spending on the federal level had risen sharply, GNP rose even more rapidly. In 1946 the federal debt was $269 billion; by 1961 it had passed the $288 billion mark. In this same period, the per capita federal debt fell from $1,905 to $1,573, while the percent of federal spending for debt interest remained around the 10 percent mark. In other words, although the activity of government in the private sector rose dramatically, other areas increased even more rapidly and the economy as a whole stayed in the hands of private corporations, albeit many were dependent upon government orders for their existence.

> The extent to which large weapons firms are the large firms in the economy generally can be determined by comparing the membership lists of the 100 largest defense contractors with the membership of a list of the 100 largest industrial firms in the economy as measured by their sales. The appearance of the same names on the two lists indicates either that their extensive weapons business alone makes some firms large enough so that they are counted among the largest industrial corporations, or that corporations, large from their commercial business, have entered into weapons making. In either case, the implicit assumption in such an analysis is that it makes a difference whether the weapons business is carried on by the very largest of the corporations in the economy; that the very large corporation is a distinct and unique institution.

...The marked change in the extent of overlapping membership occurred in World War II as a consequence of the expansion of the aviation industry. In 1939 not a single aircraft company was on the list of the 100 largest industrials. Between 1939 and 1945, 24 of the top 100 defense contractors joined the ranks of the 100 top industrial companies, and indeed companies on the list of the 100 defense contractors account for 24 of the 28 newcomers. Fifteen of these newcomers were aircraft companies. And it is not simply that these companies barely made the list, since four—Curtiss-Wright, Consolidated Vultee, Douglas, and Bendix Aviation—were among the top 25 companies in 1945.[1]

It appeared such spending was a vital factor in saving the nation from depressions, that the United States had been lifted from the slump of the 1930s by military procurement and remained prosperous in the postwar world due to a continuation of such spending. Some economists thought that should "peace break out" the nation would fall into a serious slump, not unlike that of 1937. Others thought the rapidly growing civilian market could take up whatever slack developed, while a third group, often Marxist in ideology,[2] believed the federal government would continue to dominate the economy, no matter what the demands upon it might be.

Even should this last analysis be accepted, it could still be argued that the government's effect upon business was as much psychological as economic. The Full Employment Act of the early Truman administration committed the government to intervene in the economy should depression threaten. It may well be that the expectation of government support gave businessmen confidence and emboldened them during recessionary periods.

1. Merton J. Peck and Frederic M. Scherer, *The Weapons Acquisition Process: An Economic Analysis* (Boston, 1962), pp. 118–121.
2. See Victor Perlo, *Militarism and Industry: Arms Profiteering in the Missile Age* (New York, 1963), for a work of this genre.

The emergence of government as the largest single factor in the economy caused some entire industries to become monopsonistic. In other industries, usually considered competitive, monopsonistic firms were the result. This was most evident in the aerospace complex. Prior to World War II, this industry was relatively small. The need for planes led to rapid expansion, and the cold war continued this growth, most of it based on military procurement programs. Some firms, such as North American Aviation, chose to abandon most of their civilian business, concentrating instead upon airplane, missile, and space efforts paid for by the government. General Dynamics, much of whose business was government-related, attempted to enter the civilian airplane field, with near-disastrous results; by the 1960s, it too was tied to the government. On the other hand, Boeing and Douglas maintained a balance between government and civilian sales. To these, and many other aerospace firms, complete reliance upon the government implied a certain lack of freedom. To be sure, the government was in a position to place large orders which the civilian market could not match, and would support research projects such as space exploration, an area which private companies would otherwise not enter, but there also were drawbacks to government work. Budgetary considerations could result in widespread "stretch-outs," such as occurred in the early Eisenhower years. Further, margins were small, and profits could be renegotiated long after payment was made. Finally, changes in defense stances could result in the destruction of a company. There was also the question as to whether the government was a single purchaser or many. In fact, the different branches of the armed forces and government agencies often bid against each other for the services of the defense suppliers, and weapons systems had to be promoted by these firms in a manner not too dissimilar to the pattern set in private industry.

Success could bring large rewards; North American's capture of the Apollo project resulted in multibillion dollar contracts and security for several years. General Dynamics' fortunes were rescued by its being awarded the TFX airplane contract. A small firm such as McDonnell Corporation could enter the billion dollar ranks when it learned to "play the game" correctly. McDonnell grew large on contracts for its Phantom jet, and then still larger with the award of the Gemini project. Likewise, failure could be near disastrous. Martin, by misunderstanding the drift in procurement politics, and Republic, by concentrating on a single weapons system, suffered heavy losses, and Republic was eventually forced to merge with Fairchild-Hiller to remain solvent. Paul Hardiman, Inc. which grew rapidly as a builder of government installations, went bankrupt when attempts to gain new contracts failed. After failing to win a prime contract, North American merged with machinery-maker Rockwell Manufacturing, to form North American Rockwell, with almost half its business in non-defense areas. Several disastrous contract miscalculations almost destroyed Lockheed, and the firm had to be bailed out by government guarantees of loans in 1971. Unable to compete with Boeing in civilian planes and lacking the financial abilities to compete for giant defense contracts, Douglas merged with McDonnell to form McDonnell Douglas, a new giant in the industry.

Large defense suppliers resorted to several policies. In the first place, their government-liaison forces were enlarged, and defense companies became lobbyists, often working in conjunction with regional interests. Thus, Kansas and Washington supported Boeing, whose major plants were at Wichita and Seattle, while California and Texas supported General Dynamics, and New York lobbied for Grumman. This development proved crucial in the awarding of the TFX airplane contract. General Dynamics and Grumman concentrated on filling the requirements as set down by Secretary of Defense Robert McNamara, while Boeing tried to please the admirals and generals who that firm believed would overrule the Secretary. In addition, congressmen and senators applied whatever pressures they could for their companies. In the end, McNamara prevailed over the military and the naval leaders and Texas and New York won over Kansas and Washington; General Dynamics and Grumman won the contract. At the time it appeared not only a defensible method of contract awards, but one that would save billions of dollars in a period when defense costs were mounting. Such was not the case. The TFX proved the most costly procurement blunder of the post-war era. The plane, while demonstrating the feasibility of new designs, was plagued by disasters, design changes, and cost problems. A congressional investigating committee looked into the matter, and in 1970 reported the plane should never have been built. McNamara was charged with playing politics, while others who had been in the Defense Department when the contract was awarded were accused of conflict of interest. At the same time it was learned other defense companies had been bypassed, although they had superior products and lower costs than their competitors, due to lack of political support.

Another policy aimed at lessening the impact of monopsony was one aimed at seeking new customers. Although it failed to capture airline business, General Dynamics did produce civilian electronic items and industrial gasses, and merged with Material Service Corp., a large producer of building supplies. Martin followed the same path, joining with American Marietta, a conglomerate that produced cement, chemicals, and household items. Grumman entered the private airplane and boat industries; other defense firms found similar niches.

Foreign armies and air forces were also dependent upon American suppliers for their hardware. The United States became the military producer for the Western world in the postwar era and sent large shipments to uncommitted nations as well. The market grew rapidly in the 1960s. By 1969 aerospace firms had sales in excess of $28 billion, and exports of $3.1 billion made them a major source of foreign earnings. From 1962 to 1966, General Dynamics, a leader in the field, sent $1.1 billion of war materials overseas, most of it the ill-fated

TFX (now called the F-III) and Tartar missiles. Lockheed's total was $960 million in aircraft alone, while a Lockheed-General Dynamics joint venture in Polaris missiles did well, netting the firms $427 million. The automobile companies also profited from overseas defense business: Chrysler's M-60 tank grossed $154 million and General Motors' 155-millimeter howitzer brought $57 million.

As might be expected, there was criticism of such sales. Some charged that by selling war goods, American companies were helping foment wars. The response was that the arms were sold to allies, and if we didn't provide them, the Soviet bloc would. Far more serious, however, was the growing belief that the nation was in some ways coming under the domination of a "military-industrial complex." It could be argued that the military-industrial complex first appeared during World War I, with Baruch and the War Industries Board its progenitors. During the 1930s, when antiwar sentiment was strong, the defense companies and their political appendages were known as "merchants of death." Then, when World War II erupted in Europe and the need for arms became apparent, the companies came under the umbrella of what was then known as the "arsenal of democracy."

In his farewell address to the nation on January 17, 1960, President Eisenhower warned against the rise of a powerful, permanent, nexus of the leaders of the armed forces and the war production-oriented corporations.

> Until the latest of our world conflicts, the United States had no armament industry. American makers of plowshares could, with time and as required, made swords as well. But we can no longer risk emergency improvisation of national defense; we have been compelled to create a permanent armaments industry of vast proportions. Added to this, 3½ million men and women are directly engaged in the Defense Establishment. We annually spend on military security more than the net income of all United States corporations.
>
> This conjunction of an immense Military Establishment and a large arms industry is new to the American experience. The total

influence—economic, political, even spiritual—is felt in every city, every statehouse, every office of the Federal Government. We recognize the imperative need for this development. Yet we must not fail to comprehend its grave implications. Our toil, resources, and livelihood are all involved; so is the very structure of our society.

In the councils of government we must guard against the acquisition of unwarranted influence, whether sought or unsought, by the military-industrial complex. The potential for the disastrous rise of misplaced power exists and will persist.[3]

Although the speech was widely reported and viewed on television as the last official statement of a popular President, little was made of his warning at the time. In 1962 President Kennedy recognized the existence of close connections between war production-oriented corporations and the Pentagon but indicated that he saw no important danger from that source.

The situation changed sharply in 1963 and the years that followed, the catalyst being the Vietnam war. Increasingly the military-industrial complex came to be blamed for American participation in the conflict, in tones not unlike those of the Nye Committee investigations of the 1930s. Although the nation's leading military men had warned against involvement in a land war in Asia ever since the end of World War II, the search for scapegoats led to their door. In addition, critics of the war charged that the major American corporations were profiting from the conflict, in effect reaping rewards while the nation was in moral agony.

It became almost impossible to separate the issue of Vietnam involvement from the question of the military-industrial complex in the second half of the 1960s. "Doves" noted, with Senator William Fulbright of Arkansas, that the nation had spent in the period from 1946 to 1967 $904 billion for military power while in the same period only $96 billion had been spent

3. *New York Times,* January 18, 1960.

for education, health, and labor programs funded by the federal government. "Hawks," such as Senator Richard Russell of Georgia, responded that such was the price of defending the nation. The hawks likened defense spending to an insurance policy; you don't want to use it, but it is vital when emergency situations develop. The doves had difficulty answering this argument, and were unable to show specifically how the military-industrial complex had influenced the Eisenhower, Kennedy, or Johnson administrations to enter the Southeast Asia area, open the war, or escalate it.

On the other hand, antiwar scholars were able to show convincingly that the nexus of military leaders and defense contractors did exist. For example, some 90 percent of all weapons procurement was being done without competitive bidding. Defense contractors had the use of more than $13 billion of government-owned installations. In 1968 more than 2,000 retired officers with the rank of navy captain or army colonel or above were on the payrolls of defense-oriented corporations; Litton Industries alone had forty-nine such individuals in management posts. Congressional investigations uncovered waste, inefficiency, and duplication in many key programs. Furthermore, the kind of politicking that had taken place during the TFX contract award seemed more widespread than had been suspected earlier in the decade. Many universities were involved in defense planning through individual grants to researchers or the establishment of special institutes on campuses. Finally, labor unions were involved, as, through lobbyists, they attempted to win contracts for firms and higher wages for themselves. In this way, the military-industrial complex of Eisenhower's speech was transformed into the military-industrial-political-educational-labor complex of the late 1960s, an entity so large and nebulous that its convolutions were impossible to trace completely.

Businessmen who defended their roles and those of their firms in supplying war materials usually made three points in rebuttal. First of all, the military-industrial complex had to be defined with more precision than was the case in the late 1960s. The firm with little but war and war-related business was a rarity. For example, the defense portion of the twenty-five leading prime contractors in 1969 accounted for less than one-seventh of their total business. Next, they defied their critics to show how they had attempted to influence foreign policy decisions, especially in the area of the Vietnam war. Finally, they claimed, war and war-related business was far less profitable than had been claimed.

> The critics are suspicious of any activity, including research and development, because of what they contend are the "fat profits" in aerospace participation.
> What is the profit picture?
> The most penetrating and exhaustive analysis of corporate profits was a study of the Logistics Management Institute nonprofit organization, which compared the profits of 40 companies substantially engaged in defense production with 3,500 companies not engaged in defense.
> The results of the broad-based analysis showed that profit on sales for the commercial and industrial companies was almost double that for defense-related works, and profit for investment in nondefense efforts since 1963 was 40 per cent to 74 per cent greater.[4]

Such defense also noted that several major prime contractors—General Dynamics, Lockheed, and North American among them—were in poor financial shape as a result of accepting government bidding under current contract rules. Rather than profiting from the Vietnam war and increased business, they were in worse shape in 1970 than they had been in 1960. They aggressively sought high profit margin work in non-defense areas, a shift made increasingly more urgent as defense spending began to decline in 1969.

4. Robert Anderson in *New York Times,* November 15, 1970.

The desire to diversify had other motives, however, some of them directly related to government attitudes toward business in postwar America. For example, the federal government encouraged subcontracting to small businesses and set up several agencies to aid entry into government work. Despite efforts to grant subcontracts to the smaller firms, the program generally failed. Such businesses often lacked the technical ability and financial resources to undertake more significant work, a fact cited by prime contractors when it was noted that the smaller firms' role in electronics, aircraft, and missile work declined steadily throughout the 1950s and 1960s.

Another reason for the decline in small business participation could be found in the practice of granting subcontracts to large firms, in this way "spreading the risk" among monopsonistic competitors. Thus, two corporations bidding on the same contract would each be engaged in webs of subcontracting arrangements, which meant that neither would be unduly harmed if the contract was lost. Republic, Grumman, Rohr, Martin-Marietta, and many other prime contractors also engaged in the subcontract business.

The government's economic and psychological domination over the economy as a whole and the businessman individually could be found in nondefense areas as well. The antitrust program of Arnold and others had been suspended during the wartime emergency, along with the suggestions of the Temporary National Economic Committee. After the war the government indicated a willingness to resume the antitrust program. At that time, there came into vogue a new interpretation of the Sherman Act, which was reflected in *American Tobacco Company v. United States*.

This condemnation of *"the power to abuse* rather than the *abuse of power"* simplified the task of proving an antitrust violation. No specific intent to monopolize had to be shown. More than this, no proof of an explicit agreement among the Big Three (cigarette manufacturers) was required. Statistics which showed that the companies bought and sold at identical prices and purchased fixed shares of the supply were accepted as sufficient proof of an illegal agreement. "The essential combination or conspiracy in violation of the Sherman Act," said the Court, "may be found in a course of dealings or other circumstances as well as in any exchange of words." Under this doctrine, conscious parallelism of action in an oligopolistic market may be held to be an illegal conspiracy.[5]

United States v. *Aluminum Company of America,* was decided in 1945, with Circuit Judge Learned Hand writing the decision. Hand concluded that Alcoa was innocent of specific charges of conspiracy, but nonetheless asserted that a monopoly situation did exist.

We disregard any question of "intent." ... By far the greatest part of the fabulous record piled up in the case at bar, was concerned with proving such an intent. The plaintiff was seeking to show that many transactions, neutral on their face, were not in fact necessary to the development of "Alcoa's" business, and had no motive except to exclude others and perpetuate its hold upon the ingot market. Upon that effort success depended in case the plaintiff failed to satisfy the court that it was unnecessary under Section 2 to convict "Alcoa" of practices unlawful of themselves. The plaintiff has so satisfied us, and the issue of intent ceases to have any importance.[6]

Thus, Judge Hand stated that intent to monopolize was not necessary for the court to find the existence of monopoly, and to enforce the provisions of the Sherman Act.

The decision and its implications were thought to have opened a new era in antitrust prosecutions. This did not occur;

5. Merle Fainsod, Lincoln Gordon, Joseph C. Palamountain, Jr., *Government and the American Economy* (New York, 1959), p. 583.
6. Irwin M. Stelzer, ed., *Selected Antitrust Cases* (Homewood, Ill., 1955), p. 19.

if anything, the court decided fewer major cases in the postwar period than it had in any similar period since the passage of the act. This was due to the great care taken by businessmen not to violate the act, the willingness of the Justice Department to attempt settlements out of court, and the nature of new business combinations, many of which fell outside the purview of the acts. In fact, the rise of a new merger movement after the war made antitrust legislation appear antiquated and inadequate, if not irrelevant.

Paradoxically, the merger movement of wartime and postwar America up to 1950 often served to increase competition rather than limit it. Nowhere was this more evident than in the steel industry. Prior to the war, the industry was dominated by such large corporations as U. S. Steel, Bethlehem, Republic, and Jones & Laughlin, while specialty firms had significant segments of local and unique markets. With the exception of Jones & Laughlin, which acquired the Otis Steel Company in 1942, none of the big firms consummated an important merger after World War II began. On the other hand, through several minor acquisitions, Inland Steel was able to gain a major market in the Midwest during and after the war, while Colorado Fuel & Iron, a small factor in 1945, rose to medium rank through the acquisition of Wickwire Spencer Steel in that year. Steel could be considered more competitive as a result of these mergers than it would have been without them.

Elsewhere, the merger movement acted to rationalize production and distribution, usually resulting in lower costs and economies of scale. In chemicals, Air Reduction Company, a large producer of industrial gasses, acquired Commercial Gas Company in 1941, along with Solid Carbonic Corporation. Four years later the firm merged with Home Oxygen Company. National Cylinder Gas Company took over seven competitors in the same period. At the same time, the gas divisions of Union Carbide, General Dynamics, and Allied Chemical continued to expand, and new companies, such as Air Products, entered the field. By 1950, there were fewer firms producing and selling industrial gasses, but the prices were lower, and competition was not destroyed. Similarly, the merger of Lockheed and Vega and that of Consolidated Aircraft and Vultee did not lessen competition in aircraft. Similar situations could be found in the textiles, dairy, and other industries. Mergers resulted in fewer companies, but the evidence that they led to consumer exploitation or that large firms exercised their powers in an irresponsible fashion was—with several notable exceptions—scanty.

Despite this, leading members of both houses of Congress called for a revamping of the antitrust laws, especially the Clayton Act. To these men, the heart of the Clayton Act was Section 7, which, in essence, forbade combinations or mergers which might create a monopoly or restrain commerce. Even when the act was passed in 1914, many progressive senators and representatives felt that it was too weak, and repeated attempts were made to amend the act so as to give Section 7 "more teeth." The leaders of the congressional group, including Senators Joseph O'Mahoney and William Langer and Congressmen Emanuel Celler and Estes Kefauver, introduced several amendments in the postwar period, but until 1950 all failed of passage. Kefauver, who soon became a senator, was the leader of the group, and he enlisted the aid of members of the Federal Trade Commission in his fight. In a 1948 report, the FTC stated:

> In practice, competition has proved to be a somewhat crudely working but, on the whole, highly effective theory and system. Yet it would be blindness not to recognize the obvious fact that the effectiveness of competition, as the protector of the public interest, has been seriously weakened during the last several decades. In industry after industry, prices, production, employment and, in fact, all forms of economic activity have come under

the domination of the Big Four, the Big Six, or in some cases, the leader.[7]

The work of the legislators bore fruit in the Celler-Kefauver Amendment of 1950, which discounted intent insofar as finding antitrust violations were concerned. If a firm had a large share of the market as a result of mergers, the courts could dissolve it even if no restraints of trade could be discovered. Size, together with market share, would be sufficient cause for such action.

The renewed interest in antitrust led major corporations to consider the penalties as well as the benefits of growth. Some analysts believed that General Motors set its prices so as to enable Ford and Chrysler—not to mention the smaller firms—to compete successfully. It was thought that General Motors tried to gain a 20 percent return on equity, a higher rate than was the practice at Ford or Chrysler. Should it lower prices, the argument went, the other firms would be forced into dissolution or mergers, in which case the Justice Department would try to dismember General Motors. Thus, the large auto maker set a price umbrella over car prices, in much the same way that U.S. Steel used a similar device in steel during the early twentieth century. A comparable situation was said to have obtained in computers: International Business Machines did not undercut competitors and dared not enter into mergers for fear of antitrust actions. While there was no direct proof of these practices, the activities of the large firms showed more restraint than many thought normal.

On the other hand, the courts were not as inflexible in blocking competition as they could have been. Nor was the Federal

7. U. S. Federal Trade Commission, *Report of the Federal Trade Commission on the Merger Movement: A Summary Report* (Washington, 1948), pp. 68–69.

Trade Commission unwilling to allow the growth of already large companies. Flour milling, for example, was dominated by Pillsbury, General Mills, Quaker Oats, and other large firms. Competition was intense, profit margins low, and the industry mature. It was natural for small firms to seek mergers, and for large ones to expand their markets by taking on additional brands. As a result of the industry situation, Pillsbury acquired the assets of two competitors, Ballard and Ballard Company, and the Duff's Baking Division of American Home Products Corporation. The government claimed that Pillsbury substantially lessened competition in flour milling by these actions. The case was brought before the Federal Trade Commission in 1953, which decided that the mergers should be allowed. The commission gave the Celler-Kefauver Amendment an interpretation different from the one the framers themselves thought necessary.

> If... respondent should continue to acquire competitors at the rate it has since 1940, and other large companies should do the same, the urban markets in the southeast may come to be dominated by a few large milling companies. This, of course, has been the trend in other industries. In some of them, under the policy of the Sherman Act, competition between the big companies continues to protect the consumer interest. But, as we understand it, it was this sort of trend that Congress condemned and desired to halt when it adopted the new Clayton Act anti-merger provision.[8]

The ambiguity of such decisions, many of which came down during the mid-1950s, satisfied neither Kefauver nor big business. The former continued to argue against bigness as the curse of business and the exploiter of consumers. Businessmen countered by stating that the very foundation of antitrust thinking was antiquated. It was reasonable to put restraints on a

8. United States of America before the Federal Trade Commission in the Matter of Pillsbury Mills, Inc., in Stelzer, ed., *Selected Antitrust Cases*, pp. 70–76.

railroad, for example, when it was the only means of transportation between New York and Chicago. But what was wrong with a single line between the two cities in the 1950s? If the line operated in an arbitrary fashion the consumer could have recourse to busses, airlines, or private automobiles. In the post–World War II world, steel competed with aluminum, scotch whiskey with rye and bourbon, beer with soft drinks, and duplicating machines with copiers, to give a few examples.

Business's response to the antitrust policies came in the growth of the merger-oriented corporation, one which was most often described as "conglomerate." In this type of company, the companies acquired were usually in a business having no *direct* relation to that of any other corporate division of the parent company. There were three basic reasons for such mergers and the rise of conglomerate corporations. First, the FTC could not complain of loss of competition if a manufacturer of textiles acquired the assets of a chain saw firm. Thus, the conglomerates, which spread investments over several industries, could not easily be accused of antitrust violations. Next, the conglomerates were often formed by firms whose original business was tied to defense procurement programs. These firms, operating in a monopsonistic environment, feared that if "peace broke out" they would suffer severely. Such had been the case when defense companies had been hit by cancellations after World War II. If the firms had been diversified, the impact of the cancellations would have been less.

Finally, conglomerates were formed by a new breed of businessmen, men who were interested in creating economic empires through the purchase of companies which would then be reinvigorated through efficient management. In analyzing conglomerates, the FTC seemed to fail to understand them fully, or perhaps did not feel it wise to admit that its own programs had led to their popularity. In one report, the FTC stated:

Conglomerate acquisitions, sometimes referred to as circular acquisitions, are those in which there is little or no discernable relation between the business of the purchasing and the acquired firm. Of all the types of mergers, the reasons for this particular form of acquisition are the most difficult to ascertain. Intent to remove a troublesome competitor or to become the leading producer of a particular product, so often present in horizontal acquisitions, generally does not exist in conglomerate acquisitions. Desire to acquire sources of supplies or end-product fabricating facilities, which characterizes vertical acquisitions, is not a factor in conglomerate mergers. Instead, the motives underlying conglomerate acquistions appear to include such diverse incentives as desires to spread risks, to invest large sums of idle liquid capital, to add products which can be handled with existing sales and distribution personnel, to increase the number of products which can be grouped together in the company's advertisements, etc.

But in addition to these factors, there is present in most conglomerate acquisitions a simple drive to obtain greater economic power. With the economic power which it secures through its operations in many diverse fields, the giant conglomerate corporation may attain an almost impregnable economic position. Threatened with competition in any one of its various activities, it may sell below cost in that field, offsetting its losses through profits made in its other lines—a practice which is frequently explained as one of meeting competition. The conglomerate corporation is thus in a position to strike out with great force against smaller business in a variety of different industries. As the Commission has previously pointed out, there are few greater dangers to small business than the continued growth of the conglomerate corporation.[9]

This report, issued in 1948, could find few conglomerates to offer as examples. It observed that most were found in the drug and drug-related fields. The prime example was American Home Products, a corporation which, since its incorporation in 1926, had acquired sixty firms, thirty-two of these from 1940 to 1948. This large conglomerate produced both ethical and proprietary drugs, floor wax, coffee, Italian foods, lubricat-

9. Federal Trade Commission, *Report of the Federal Trade Commission on the Merger Movement*, p. 59.

ing oil, cheese products, paints, insecticides, and beauty preparations.

If the report was incorrect in its conclusions regarding the reasons for conglomerate mergers, it was accurate in predicting the growth of such corporations. The most spectacular companies of the 1950s were the results of conglomerate philosophies of management. Since the FTC and the courts were bound to a concept of the firm that went back to the turn of the century, they could not regard the conglomerates as violators of the antitrust laws. Thus, National Tea Company, with a minute part of the total industry share, could be prosecuted, while Litton Industries, one of the giant firms of the 1960s and the prime example of the conglomerate philosophy, was never seriously threatened by antitrust activity, although it was larger and grew faster than National Tea. Charles "Tex" Thornton, the founder and head of Litton, offered an answer to the lack of government prosecution when responding to a question regarding the firm. When asked about the activities of his large enterprise, he replied, "We are in the business of opportunity," meaning that Litton would move into any area which showed promise, and had no fixed conception of limits. The antitrust implications were clear: U.S. Steel was primarily a steel producer; General Motors was in the automobile business. Both could and did fear government charges that they dominated their industries. But Litton made certain that it had small shares of many fields, and further took care not to be identified with any single area. How, then, could the Sherman Act of the Harrison administration and the Clayton Act of the Wilson administration be brought to bear upon this large firm with this new theory of what constituted an industry?

Litton began in 1953, when a small electronics company, Electro-Dynamics Corporation, acquired the assets of a similar firm, Litton Industries, and took its name. In 1954 Litton acquired West Coast Electronics, and in 1955 Ahrendt Instruments, USECO, and Automatic Sereograph were added. Other small firms were acquired in 1956 and 1957. Litton made its biggest move in 1958 by merging with Monroe Calculator, a company which at the time was larger than the acquiring firm. The mergers continued, and it seemed that Litton would grow more in that fashion than through internal expansion. This was not the case; during many years, Litton's internal expansion was larger than volume gained through acquisitions. In any case, the growth was phenomenal. In its first year of operation, Litton did $3 million worth of business; in 1958, the year of the Monroe merger, the figure was $83.2 million. Litton crossed the billion dollar mark in 1966.

The company's success was based on excellent management. Thornton, the key man, was a graduate of the Harvard Business School, a spawning ground for many of the new executives of the 1950s. From there he went into the Army Air Corps, where he made a reputation for efficiency and charm. After the war, he was one of the "whiz kids," who went to Ford to revive that moribund firm. Then he went to Hughes Aircraft, which he left to form Litton. Throughout his career Thornton was known as a promoter, a man who was best able to exploit the ideas of others. While this was true, and Thornton himself did not deny it, he was also a man of vision who realized that the concept of the corporation used by the FTC and by businessmen themselves was outmoded due to the new technologies of postwar America. Indeed, times were changing so rapidly that any concept of the firm was bound to become outdated in a relatively short period of time. Therefore, Thornton insisted that Litton make no hard and fast rules; the product rejected today might be accepted tomorrow. In this way, the organization would be receptive to any new opportunity that might come its way. Thus, at one point Litton refused to enter the highly competitive fields of computers and transistors, at the same time retaining the option to enter if and when conditions seemed favorable.

Along with imaginative management, Litton relied heavily

upon investment bankers, in this case Lehman Brothers. Most of the firm's acquisitions were made through transfers of stock. This preserved capital and took advantage of the fact that Litton's common stock sold for thirty or forty times its book value. By placing a high price on such securities, the investment community helped pay the bill for external expansion.

Many factors have helped bring about the conglomerate merger explosion, but one key explanation has been a rising stock market which has permitted mergers to be made on highly advantageous terms. Since most acquisitions take the form of an exchange of stock (usually tax free), companies whose securities trade in the market at high price-earnings ratios have found it particularly easy to purchase lower price-earnings companies at relatively small cost. If, for instance, two companies, X and Y, have earnings of $1.00 per share but the X shares sell for $20 and the Y shares for only $10, a merger can easily be arranged that is mutually attractive. Y shareholders might, as one possibility, exchange each of their shares for X shares having a market value of, say, $11 (this gain in value is usually free of tax). With Y's earnings added to their previous profits, X shareholders could also reasonably expect their own holdings to rise in price in view of the market's tendency to capitalize their corporation's earnings at a higher rate. Exactly this kind of swap is involved in Consolidated Food's proposed purchase of United Artists, the nation's most successful film distributor. Under comparable conditions Litton, ITT, and other firms have made many acquisitions on highly advantageous terms in the last few years.[10]

To some, Litton's mergers seemed haphazard, especially when, in the late 1950s and early 1960s, they took place at the rate of one every three or four months. Actually, each new firm acquired was accepted because it had a place in the "big picture" at corporation headquarters. For example, the acquisition of Monroe enabled Litton to expand into a nonmilitary area and have an outlet for the technological developments

10. Richard J. Barber, "The New Partnership: Big Government and Big Business," *The New Republic,* August 13, 1966, p. 18.

made at other divisions. The purchases of Royal McBee, several office furniture firms, and a Swedish cash register company complemented the technology and intensified the use of the sales force at Monroe. With this constellation of firms, it was natural for Litton to enter the field of small military computers. The purchase of Ingalls Shipbuilding, which on the surface did not appear to fit any pattern, did make sense to Thornton. Modern ships—especially submarines—use huge quantities of electronic equipment. Thus, Ingalls was a prime customer for other products made by Litton member firms. Hewett-Robbins, a materials handling company, was acquired and teamed with other branches of the complex to work on new, electronically controlled methods of handling bulk items. In almost each case, the acquired firm either became a customer of another Litton division, or an important supplier to other parts of the complex. The mergers continued, with some fifty firms a year being considered for the Litton complex.

During the drive for $3 million sales in 1954 to the billion dollar figure of 1966, Litton was not engaged in a single major antitrust action, because it made a point of being a challenger, not a dominant factor, in almost every field it entered. On several occasions the FTC asked for information, but at no point did it try to stop a major merger or initiate action against Litton for violation of Section 7.

Litton realized that the dynamics of modern society were such as to offer great rewards to those who understood them, and penalties to those who could not adjust to new conditions. Modern technology and business methods joined in postwar America. Litton, a prime example, was controlled by a new type of entrepreneurs from the business schools and by scientists; each was interested in and concerned with the areas usually considered the private preserve of the other. The Litton approach came to be accepted by others in the new technology-oriented firms of postwar America, as was seen in a 1966 interview with Litton president, Roy Ash, and senior vice-president, Harry Gray.

We've been roaming over a pretty wide range. Is there any large and obvious point about Litton that we've forgotten to mention?

ASH: There's one point that may be taken too much for granted. It's about our people. This is a "people business," and talking just about products and markets and research overlooks that point. Every business is a people business in some sense, of course, but we think we've brought together some particular kinds of people and provided them a very special environment. Our kind of man is the kind you usually think of as an enterpreneur—he thinks and acts as though he's in business for himself. Most of our executives would be if they weren't at Litton. They're highly motivated people.

When you talk about entrepreneurs, how many people are you referring to?

ASH: Well, first, the division managers—there are more than forty executives right there. But if you mean all the people who approach their responsibilities, like entrepreneurs, the number would probably be closer to a thousand.

Actually, some people have left Litton to go into business for themselves, and they've done remarkably well. Teledyne was started by your people and Walter Kidde was pretty transformed by some other Litton people. Tell us a bit more about your environment.

ASH: We have a level of enthusiasm in the company we don't want to lose. In some organizations, where a man's ideas are knocked down once or twice, he's not apt to come up with a third one. We try to sustain an atmosphere in which every idea is a good idea—unless proven otherwise. We want people to keep throwing in all the ideas they have.

Still, I'd imagine that the Litton environment must look kind of scary to some people on the outside—people whose companies you want to acquire, say.

ASH: Well, we can understand that not everybody wants to get into this kind of environment. I know we have scared some who may feel the pace of Litton is different from what they're used to.

I gather from the remarks about all your entrepreneurs that you view Litton as a collection of related small companies rather than as one large one.

ASH: That's right, and it gets back to your original question—about how we keep on growing when we don't have some big lock on a new technology or market. If, in fact, you look at Litton, not as a $1-billion company, but as a number of $10-million to $100-million companies, then you might see that we have a large number of individually strong positions. We're not totally dependent on any one field, but we have a lot of different capabilities.[11]

Another conglomerate, with a different history and philosophy of management, but with equally striking results, was Textron. Here again an enterprising entrepreneur was responsible for the creation of a giant enterprise. Royal Little, the man behind Textron, began the firm as Special Yarns in 1923, and remained in the textile business for the next three decades. During World War II, the company expanded rapidly, as did most in the field, and Little thought seriously of making it into a giant among textile companies. But the industry was slow-moving, marked by strong competition from specialty firms, and subject to swings in the business cycle. Accordingly, Little thought in terms of acquiring nontextile business. In 1952 the charter was changed to enable him to do this, and Textron (its name was changed in 1944) began its search. At first Little was unsuccessful, but he did acquire Dalmo Victor Company, a small manufacturer of airborne antenna, in 1954. Then others followed, some in textiles, others in electronics and related fields. In the process, Little discovered that he and his associates were well fitted to take control of medium-sized firms and then reinvigorate them. Thus, Textron went from a large textile producer to a company specializing in managerial talents. In 1956, the first truly big year for Textron mergers, Little acquired General Cement; Benada Aluminum; Myrtle Paint; Carolina Bagging; Campbell, Wyant, and Cannon Foundry; Bandon Veneer and Plywood; Hall-Mark; Federal Leather; and Fanner Manufacturing, all small firms. He also purchased the S.S. *LaGuardia,* a converted transport, which

11. "How Litton Keeps It Up—The View from the Inside," *Fortune,* 74 (September 1966), p. 182.

he renamed the S.S. *Leilani* and placed on the holiday route to Hawaii. Enough of the mergers worked out so that Little was able to sell off Textron's remaining textile affiliates to Deering-Milliken in 1963. Purchases of Bell Aircraft's defense business, Speidel, chemical companies, parts manufacturers, and others gave Textron a diffuse image. In 1965, the company estimated that aerospace and defense products accounted for 35 percent of its sales, industrial products 20 percent, consumer items 16 percent, metal products 17 percent, and agrochemicals 12 percent.

Although Textron and Litton were both conglomerates, there were several key differences between them. Litton acquired firms that fit into an open-ended pattern and could become an integral part of an already-existing enterprise. Textron often would purchase firms having no relationship with any other business the main firm was in; indeed, Little once observed that there was no central point for Textron's business. Thornton and Ash purchased firms with stock, and refused to accept companies that lacked good executive talent or were running in the red. Little wanted firms that were clearly stagnating, paid for them with cash whenever possible, and then brought in new management teams to transform the firm into a profitable enterprise.

The conglomerate movement affected older firms as well. In an effort to remain in the automobile field, Studebaker acquired several firms engaged in such varied pursuits as the production of petroleum additives, stoves, small power generation equipment, and parts. For a while profits from the new divisions compensated for losses in the automotive field. Then Studebaker sold off its Mercedes distributorships and left automobiles entirely. The company had been one of the buggy manufacturers that had gone into automobiles when it was clear that they were here to stay. In the 1960s, it left automobiles when it realized that small firms lacked the capabilities to compete. Then it merged with Worthington Corporation, a heavy equipment manufacturer. One might say that Studebaker learned that its business was not automobiles, but rather the acquisition and management of conglomerate enterprises, while Textron's was the invigoration of moribund firms, and Litton's was the management of an interrelated maze of companies.

The conglomerate idea appealed to many in postwar America, and some went so far as to leave profitable specialities to take on new lines of endeavor. W. R. Grace, known for steamships, airline operations, and banking, entered the chemical industry to gain a new growth area. By the mid 1960s, Grace was a major chemical firm, while its old businesses had become secondary or were sold off. National Distillers entered metals and agrochemicals, and diversified to an even greater extent. Philadelphia & Reading and Glenn Alden, both coal producers, realized that anthracite lacked growth. The former moved into clothing, boots, and became a major factor in the toy industry; its coal business was liquidated. Glen Alden remained in coal, but its greatest growth came in such diverse areas as motion picture theatres, leather, and clothing.

Some highly successful firms, finding themselves with excess cash, purchased growth companies or attempted to find bargains among depressed situations. Thus, Gillette acquired Paper Mate Pens and some small cosmetics companies, which accounted for a steadily increasing sales volume by the mid-1960s. Kern County Land, which leased large tracts to oil and cattle companies, purchased controlling interest in J. I. Case, a depressed farm equipment company which it helped return to prosperity; it, in turn, was taken over by Tenneco. Transamerica Corporation, which dealt mainly in financial firms, acquired United Artists, a film company which owned no studios but financed independent producers. Both gained by the merger; Transamerica had a new outlet for funds, while United Artists had fewer fears about money for its projects.

As has been indicated, stock transfers were important in the creation of conglomerates, especially those that followed the Litton example. The securities markets were also useful in making possible the growth of two interesting firms: Kaiser Industries and Ling-Temco-Vought.

Henry J. Kaiser, a capable and inventive wartime producer of several products, formed Kaiser-Frazer Corporation in 1945, purchased several war surplus plants, and entered the automobile business. This was made possible through the sale of Kaiser-Frazer stock, which brought in more than $53 million.

At first, all seemed well; the postwar shortage of cars enabled K-F to sell all its products. When supply caught up with demand, however, the company was stuck with large inventories and was forced to leave the automobile industry. But Kaiser quickly recouped some of his losses. In 1956 he formed Kaiser Industries, which retained stock control of Kaiser Aluminum and Chemical and Kaiser Steel and Permanent Cement, while the public purchased additional shares in the operating units. In addition, KI owned all the stock of Willys Motors (the producer of Jeeps) and Kaiser Engineers, a construction firm. Later on, Kaiser organized Kaiser Hawaii Kai, a land-development and hotel complex. There was little interaction between these units. Kaiser Aluminum and Kaiser Steel competed with each other for metal contracts, and Kaiser Engineers bid against other large construction firms for work at Kaiser installations. In a sense, the conglomerate was organizable due to the fact that stock ownership in the major parts of the corporation was shared by the parent organization and the public. Without such financing, the debt-ridden Kaiser-Frazer could not have been successfully converted into Kaiser Industries.

Ling-Temco-Vought presented a variation on this theme. It was the creation of James Ling, who brought together a variety of nonrelated companies to form a billion dollar conglomerate in less than a decade. The company began as Ling Electric in 1946, a small contracting company started by a returning GI after World War II. The firm was successful, and by 1955, when Ling sold stock for the first time, his gross was over $1.5 million a year. Within months he was able to purchase LM Electronics, and changed the name of his company to Ling Electronics. This was done by assuming $66,000 in back debts and $19,000 in cash. Since electronics was a key word at the time, the stock in his company rose rapidly, more than making up the acquisition costs. In this way, Ling learned that the stock market could be used to turn paper into assets, and he began a career of financial juggling that amazed the business world. He formed Ling Industries, floated a $750,000 convertible debenture issue for Ling Electronics, and merged the two companies. In 1959 he absorbed Altec Corporation, a manufacturer of sound equipment, paying for it by issuing shares in the new firm. The new Ling-Altec Electronics then began a career of picking up smaller companies for stocks and bonds in the parent. By 1959 sales passed the $48 million mark. Then Ling acquired Temco Electronics & Missiles, also for stock, and again changed the name of his firm, this time to Ling-Temco Electronics. By using money borrowed from Dallas banker Troy Post's American Life Insurance Company, he was able to engulf Chance Vought, this time changing his firm's name to Ling-Temco-Vought.

Throughout this period Ling sold off portions of the companies he no longer wanted or needed. Since companies were generally acquired for stocks and bonds and sold off for cash, he usually wound up with more money than he had started with. Furthermore, he learned that the parts are often worth more than the sum. Thus, he recouped a good deal of the purchase price for Chance Vought by selling a subsidiary, Vought Industries, to Divco Wayne for cash. Through careful manipulations and complex financing, together with a keen business sense, Ling's empire recorded $325 million in sales in 1962.

In 1964 Ling announced "Project Redeployment." It was the ultimate in this type of securities manipulation. First, he reorganized the company into three operating divisions—LTV Aerospace, LTV Electrosystems, and LTV Ling Altec—all controlled by Ling-Temco-Vought. Then he offered his stockholders the chance to trade each share they owned in the parent company for a package of one-half share each of the new subsidiaries plus $9 in cash. Ling realized that the operating companies would probably sell at a higher price-earnings multiple than had the parent company, and since the latter would retain sizable stock ownership in the three divisions, it would benefit through their higher securities prices. Furthermore, each of the new companies would be able to borrow money on its own, acquire new companies, and so expand the Ling empire. The plan was a success. By 1966, LTV Aerospace, with sales of $230 million, had emerged as a major firm in its own right and the parent company still had 75 percent of its stock. Ling-Temco-Vought also owned 75.8 percent of LTV Electrosystems ($120 million in sales), 89.4 percent of LTV Ling Altec ($25 million in sales), and 82.4 percent of Okonite ($85 million in sales), a wire and cable manufacturer acquired in 1965. Two years later Ling purchased Wilson & Company, the moribund meat-packing giant, for a package of securities. He then divided the firm into three subsidiaries (Wilson & Co., Wilson Sporting Goods, and Wilson Pharmeceuticals & Chemicals), exchanged them for LTV stock, and so recouped his purchase price.

Ling's largest acquisition was Greatamerica Corporation, a giant financial-transportation conglomerate in its own right controlled by his friend, Troy Post. The cost, some half-billion dollars, was paid through the issuance of a huge bond issue. Then Ling set about dismantling the company. First Western Bank and Trust was sold to World Airways for $63 million, and other life insurance subsidiaries were sold for an additional $60 million. Then Ling offered his stock and bondholders the opportunity to exchange their securities for a package of other parts of the old Greatamerica stocks, including National Car

Rental and Braniff Airways. And while engaged in carving up the old Post holdings, he purchased 62 percent of Jones & Laughlin Steel and attempted to do the same for that company.

The conglomerate movement's crest was reached in 1968, but even earlier, as acquisitions continued and the prices of securities rose, there were signs of trouble. Increased talk of antitrust action worried would-be merger candidates, and when the Johnson administration began a series of indictments against conglomerates early in 1969 the movement came to a halt. More important, however, was the inability of management to translate mergers into higher profits. At Litton, for example, the large office machine division suffered losses, while shipbuilding and other defense-related operations did not perform according to expectations. A-T-O Corporation and Susquehanna Corporation showed major dips in earnings, as did other "budding giants." Several major financial magazines, *Forbes, Fortune,* and *Barron's* in particular, ran articles exposing the tricky bookkeeping methods used by several major conglomerates to maximize earnings and so raise the price of their securities. The economic slowdown, which began in 1969, provided a major test of the conglomerators' management abilities and most failed. As interests rates rose and money sources dried up, the lifeline of mergers—credit—disappeared. James Ling, hailed as a genius in 1966, was the greatest victim of these adverse conditions. The Jones & Laughlin merger ran into legal difficulties compounded by the firm's unusually bad year in a declining economy. Unable to service his debt as easily as once had been the case, Ling was obliged to seek money wherever he could find it, paying high interest rates in an attempt to keep his firm intact and his control of it assured. In the end he failed, and in 1970 he was ousted from control of his foundering empire.

To some it seemed that Ling and others of his type were tracing the path of such pyramiders as Samuel Insull. Just as Insull had been a hero of the 1920s as well as a symbol of the "New Era," only to become the villain of the 1930s, so it appeared that Ling would go down as a fallen Prometheus. This was an exaggeration. All the major conglomerates survived the recession, but emerged as "multi-market firms" rather than the Cinderellas of a few years earlier. But the merger movement and "innovative" Ling-like practices were not completely dead. Studebaker-Worthington spun off STP Corporation, Turbodyne Corporation, Wagner Electric Corporation, and other subsidiaries while retaining a large amount of their stock. Syntex, itself a spin-off from Ogden, now entered the field, divesting itself of parts of two newly formed firms, Alza Corporation and Zoecon Corporation. Finally, Ling returned to the business world as president of a new company, Omega-Alpha Corporation.

Summary

The American economy grew steadily in the post–World War II period, rising from a GNP of $212 billion in 1945 to $1 trillion a quarter of a century later. Increased consumer desires were important in this growth, as was the necessity of many industries to catch up with demand after the war. Most important, however, was the growth of government needs, especially in the field of military procurement. As a result, a huge monopsonistic complex of enterprises developed, serving the government in the hopes of gaining large, long-term contracts.

At the same time, the growth of antitrust activity led firms to seek new forms of organization. The most important of these was the conglomerate corporation, a company consisting of a group of unrelated operating units. Such firms usually reflected the union of sophisticated graduates of leading business schools and scientists, both of whom considered "the business of opportunity" more important than the particular item they happened to be producing at any given moment.

CHAPTER IX

Big Business in an Age of Innovation

In almost every year of the postwar period, the share of sales and profits of the top 500 firms in the nation expanded, while that of small business declined. The message was clear: become large, merge, or go out of business. This was true even in such previously small business areas as restaurants, automobile parts, or textiles. The first group witnessed the rise of franchise operations, and the decline of independent units. Conglomerates entered the automobile parts industry and several, led by Gulf & Western Industries, began to dominate it. As for textiles, after decades of competition, a few firms, most notably Burlington Industries and J. P. Stevens, gained leadership positions. Despite the American dream of the independent businessman, and after seventy years of antitrust action, big business dominated the economy.

In 1966, *Fortune* published a list of the twenty leading companies in sales growth from 1955 to 1965. The first two were Ling-Temco-Vought and Litton; both were conglomerate firms with strong defense commitments, and both were led by strong individuals. In third place, was Jim Walter Corporation, a construction firm led by Jim Walter, who began as a builder of low-price houses and then expanded through mergers. Gulf & Western, a conglomerate in automobile supplies, motion pictures, and zinc mining was in fourth position, followed by Consolidated Electronics Industries, a holding company. The rest of the list followed the same pattern. Some were conglomerates led by strong businessmen of the new breed (Lear Siegler,

Air Products & Chemicals); while others were special firms in growth industries, protected by strong patent positions (Ampex, Xerox, Texas Instruments, Ethyl). It appeared that the firms that prospered were new companies headed by far-sighted businessmen in growth industries. The response to this was an obvious one: wasn't this always the case in American industry? The answer was, of course, affirmative, and this indicated that, despite the rapid growth of the postwar period and the great increase in innovation, the success pattern remained essentially the same as it had been for more than a century.

In some industries even the best management could not increase growth. McLouth was the only steel firm to show sustained growth in this period, and this small firm was able to do so because much of its product was used by General Motors, which treated the firm as though it were a semicaptive plant. Steel had several major difficulties. The industry was burdened with obsolete plants in poor locations; it was tied to the automobile industry, which in the 1950s was highly cyclical, and foreign steel, supported by price concessions made by overseas producers, cut into the American market. Finally, the wage-price squeeze hurt the industry, leading to price increases which further encouraged consumers to seek substitutes in aluminum, plastic, and the like.

The industry did, however, recover, primarily because of the seeming end, in the mid-1960s, of the sharp cyclical nature of the automobile industry, the introduction of new technologies and products, a rise in the price of foreign steel, an advantageous government procurement program, and a program of aggressive marketing.

In steel, as in many American industries, the automobile continued to be of major importance. During the late 1940s, the industry boomed, as postwar demand led to prosperity at the major and minor automobile firms, and allowed new-comer Kaiser-Frazer to hope for a permanent share of the market. Even during the 1950s, when good years alternated with bad, the growth pattern continued, as consumers spent approximately 5 percent of their disposable income on automobiles and automobile-related products.

Although the industry had all the attributes of maturity, there was constant change and innovation in automobiles. Ford was revamped in the forties and early fifties, and Chrysler in the early sixties, to meet the challenge of General Motors while Willys, Studebaker, Kaiser-Frazer, and Crosley disappeared from the scene, but these changes were not brought about by the pressures of competition. Instead, the automobile industry was obliged to meet the shifting demands of consumers, who had more disposable income than ever before, and whose whims were catered to by Detroit and Dearborn.

The innovations were not primarily of a technical nature, however; the last major innovation, automatic transmission, came before World War II, and refinements, such as fuel injection, self-sealing tires, and power boosts for steering and braking did not bring major changes to the industry. Instead, the remaining manufacturers concentrated on style changes and advertising in the postwar period. Newspaper advertisements by automobile firms cost $114 million by 1960; four years later the figure was $124 million. The new medium of television was also used—in 1964 some $39 million was expended by the agencies. These advertisements stressed style, beauty, and accessibility. Price competition, which had disappeared in the 1930s, did not return. Instead, the manufacturers stressed style changes. One year all would concentrate on color schemes, the next on such devices as tail fins or portholes. Critics noted that automobiles had no need for such styling, but the public seemed to prefer them, and sales rose irregularly during the 1950s.

This period also saw the complete reversal of the Ford philosophy of the 1920s; customers demanded more variety than ever before, and by the 1960s, a purchaser might, through the choice of options, ride out in a Chevrolet different from any of the millions on the road. In an affluent society, the purchaser, not the engineer, decided questions of design. In an effort to cater to the new market, General Motors produced new models. The Chevrolet II and Chevelle provided a lower-cost and upper-cost model in that line, and the Corvair a rear engine sports model, while the Corvette was a successful sports car. Ford tried to duplicate the lines, adding the Falcon (low-price compact) and the Mustang (medium-price sports model), as well as the successful Thunderbird (higher-price sports car). After several years of fighting the trend Chrysler joined in, dropping the medium-price DeSoto and adding the Valiant and Barracuda to compete with the low-priced and sports models.

Style competition offered rewards, but also posed problems. In the mid-1950s, Ford noted a gap in its line. Whereas Chevrolet customers "moved up" to Pontiacs, and Plymouth owners to Dodges, the Ford purchaser did not view the medium-price Mercury as a proper choice. Thus, the firm introduced the Edsel. The car did not catch the imagination of the public, however, and was dropped after several years at a loss of approximately $250 million. Still, Ford was able to survive and prosper; by the 1960s, the cycle in car sales flattened out and production rose steadily. Some 6.7 million units were produced in 1950; fifteen years later the figure stood at 9.3 million.

With the failure or disappearance of all firms but the Big Three plus American Motors, it appeared the industry would settle down to a period of oligopolistic competition. Such was the case, but there was one element of competition: that of foreign cars. At first, sports models dominated the imports. Then, in the early 1950s, Volkswagen of Germany began to sell increased numbers of its plain automobile in the United States. Hailed as the "Model T of the 1950s," it found wide acceptance among urban purchasers who applauded its maneuverability and appreciated its low price. In addition, in an era of high discretionary spending, the Volkswagen appealed to those who wanted "something different." Other small cars appeared—Fiat, Renault, Datsun, Hillman—but none had the popularity of the Volkswagen. American Motors President George Romney, realizing that his firm might be salvaged by going along with this trend, concentrated production on the Rambler, which was smaller than the Chevrolet or Ford, but slightly larger than the imports; for a while his company prospered. Then the Big Three counterattacked, introducing the Corvair, Falcon, and Valiant, and American Motors' sales declined as did those of the imports. Although Volkswagen sales remained high, the total number of imports dropped from 668,000 units in 1959 to 540,000 in 1965.

By the mid-1960s, the Big Three were in almost complete command once again. The industry was worried about charges that automobiles were unsafe and threats of antitrust action, but these seemed minor in the face of continued prosperity and hopes of more two-, three-, and four-car families. The manufacturers continued to stress style, and bowed to public pressures by adding several safety features.

In the late 1960s the industry was hit by four blows, each following close upon the heels of the other. First came the attack from an increasingly safety-conscious public, led by consumer champion Ralph Nader whose book *Unsafe At Any Speed* was a major attack on the way American automobiles were being designed, produced, and sold. Then came a revived assault by foreign manufacturers, led by Volkswagen but sparked by Toyota and Datsun, two energetic Japanese firms. By 1970 the imports had captured over 11 percent of the American market, and the rate showed no sign of slowing. The 1969–1970 recession hurt American manufacturers, as potential buyers either delayed purchases or turned to inexpensive models, often foreign-made. Finally, the automobile industry was charged with being the major contributor to pollution at a time when interest in ecology and the environment was at an all-time high.

At first the companies tried to ignore these threats, but by late 1968 they turned to meet the challenge and criticisms. All four American firms speeded up programs to produce a pollution-free engine and in other ways worked to lessen the problem. Increased automation enabled them to raise prices at a slower rate than wages were increasing. Most importantly, however, the American firms decided to meet the foreign challenge by producing competitive small cars. Ford's Maverick and American Motors' Gremlin and Hornet appeared in 1969, while the Ford Pinto and the General Motors Vega, the major American challengers to Volkswagen and Toyota, came out late in 1970. Chrysler concentrated its attention on its Duster which, though larger than the rest, was still smaller than the standard American sedan, and at the same time began to import Japanese cars (the Colt) for its distributors to sell. The new models were widely advertised, and by early 1971 gave indications of halting the increased American preference for foreign cars.

The auto industry set the pattern for other mature sectors of the economy. The tobacco manufacturers, like the Big Three auto makers, spent more on advertising than ever before, fought adverse publicity (regarding the possible cancer-producing qualities of cigarettes), expanded into nontobacco areas, and followed consumer preference in the affluent economy.

At the end of World War II, many industry forecasters believed that such old, established brands as Lucky Strike, Camel, Old Gold, and Chesterfield, would continue to dominate the market. But, as happened in the case of automobiles, the consumers demanded change and variety. Thus, the manufacturers introduced king-size brands, and by the mid-1950s, Pall Mall had replaced the older brands as the largest-selling cigarette in the nation. Then, as reports of cancer-producing properties of cigarettes were made public, the industry switched to filter brands, and Kent and Marlboro sales rose sharply, so that by the 1960s, they outsold nonfilters by a wide margin. The filters were followed by a vogue of menthol-flavored brands, such as Kools and Belair. Experiments with nontobacco cigarettes failed, but the public approved of such products as charcoal-filters, water filters (Waterford), and super-kings. Each firm competed with the others in the introduction of new brands. The president of American Tobacco earned the nickname of "brand-a-month," while Lorillard and Reynolds were not far behind.

Despite this, the industry was unable to meet the arguments of those who claimed cigarettes to be the major source of lung cancer, and sales leveled off as the antismoking campaign took hold. In 1969 the television networks gave time to antismoking groups after being ordered to do so under the equal-time provisions of the broadcasting code. Then, in 1970 the government banned all tobacco commercials from television, the order to go into effect in 1971. Statistics indicated that cigarette smoking had not declined as yet, but without the benefit of advertising on television, the major source of information for American consumers, the future of the industry was in doubt.

Industry leaders, well aware of their problem as early as the mid-1960s, had embarked on a program of diversification so as to lessen the impact of declining tobacco revenues. R. J. Reynolds, American Tobacco, Philip Morris, and Lorillard became conglomerates, expanding particularly in the areas of food, pet preparations, packaging, and shipping. In order to change its image, American Tobacco changed its name to American Brands, while Reynolds Tobacco became Reynolds Industries. Lorillard merged with Loew's, a large conglomerate, while Philip Morris continued to seek new acquisitions. Thus, the tobacco companies were able to survive and even grow, while their major product began to enter what many industry forecasters considered its decline.

Similar situations developed in clothing, specialty foods, supermarkets, home building, and many other mature industries. The oligopolistic pattern was either reinforced or reformed, as the firms in such industries tried to keep one step ahead of their competitors for what seemed a finite number of consumers and purchasers.

The case was somewhat different in the "growth areas" of the postwar period, such as electronics, television and office machines. In these industries, competition was keen, opportunities great, entry often comparably less difficult, and rewards greater.

Of the growth industries, electronics was the largest and most difficult to define. At the end of the war, less than one billion dollars of goods classified as electronics were being produced yearly. By 1950, the figure had risen to $2.6 billion, and in 1967 it passed the $15 billion mark. In 1967 scientists, the government, and businessmen were still not clear as to what constituted an electronic product. To most, it was distinguishable from the electric industry in that it dealt with the creation of power in one of several forms by the use of small amounts of electricity. In 1883, Thomas A. Edison observed that "something jumped" through a vacuum in a light bulb, causing deposits on the side of the bulb. Fourteen years later J. J. Thomson of England discovered the electron, and used this concept to explain the "Edison Effect." Within a few years, this theoretical discovery was translated by Marconi, de Forest, and others into commercial products, such as wireless and home radios. Most students of the field agree that this was and is part of the electronics industry, but it is not what was meant by the growing sector of the industry after World War II.

The electronics industry is remarkably difficult to quantify and classify. In the first place the speed with which it grows and changes from year to year renders the statistics seriously out of date before they can be scraped together and printed. Until World War II, electronics was almost synonymous with radio; today radio is only one portion. Even the electron tube is already being replaced in many products by the smaller transistor, in which patterns of communication are imposed upon electrons not as they leap through a vacuum but as they traverse a tiny lump of germanium or silicon. But even if the statistics were up to the minute, the industry would still be elusive because its products are not officially classified in a neat "electronics" bundle; they fall into many different industries and are not easily separated from the nonelectronic products.

"The first thing to be grasped about electronics as a business, A.D. 1957, is that this is an industry running on three different clocks," wrote William B. Harris in the April 1957 number of *Fortune*. "One part of the industry is already 'old' enough to have seen severe competition, strong forces toward concentration, and a number of business casualties; this is the world of the TV and radio manufacturers—a mature, dangerous jungle. Other parts of the industry are so 'young' that serious worries about competitors' costs are years away; this is the area of electronics where small businesses can still shoot up overnight.... Finally, there is that area of electronics—about half the industry—whose affairs are regulated by the clock of history itself; so long as relations between the U.S.S.R. and the U.S. are bad, military electronics will be a good business."[1]

To complicate matters further, these three parts of the industry were by no means distinct; most firms in the industry served at least two, and possibly all three, areas. General Instruments, for example, manufactured television tuners and other radio supplies, could be classified as a small business faced with severe competition, and also sold "electronics hardware" to the military.

It would be impossible to draw detailed generalizations about the electronics industry, since its consolidation period is still to come and many of its managers accept varieties of the conglomerate philosophy as enunciated by Thornton and Little. Still, some observations might be put forth, with the understanding that they are continually being revised.

---

1. Max Hall, ed., *Made in New York: Case Studies in Metropolitan Manufacturing* (Cambridge, 1959), pp. 245-246.

First, the electronics industry, unlike such older industries as steel, automobiles, merchandising, and food processing, grew, developed, and matured at a rapid rate. This was due both to the accelerated pace of change in postwar America, the large consumer market, the needs of the cold war, and the fact that electronic techniques and products were quickly adapted to already existing products. In 1940, Admiral Corporation did $4.7 million worth of business in electronics; ten years later the figure was $230.4 million. In this same period, the electronics sales of Motorola went from $9.9 million to $177.1 million; Sylvania rose from $14.3 million to $162.5 million, Zenith from $52.3 million to $335.3 million, and RCA from $127.8 million to $586.4 million. General Electric, the leader in the field in 1940 with $532.7 million, sold $1.96 billion worth of electronic products in 1950.

The rapid rise in an industry noted for shifting and complex technology required a new type of manager. Whatever remained of the myth of the young boy who rose from clerk to company president was shattered; the key to leadership in electronics was a Ph.D. degree in one of the sciences, or an M.A. or Ph.D. from one of the better graduate schools of business, where the student took several courses in science and knew how to understand what the scientist was saying. In some firms, the old-line businessman, the financial vice-president, the son of the founder, etc., remained in power. Even then, his key men would often fit the scientific mold. This was particularly true in the case of new firms. Ramo-Wooldridge, which later merged with Thompson Products, was formed and guided by Dean E. Wooldridge, a physicist, and Simon Ramo, a Ph.D. in electrical engineering who was a research associate at California Institute of Technology. Arnold Beckman, founder and president of Beckman Instruments, a leading producer of medical electronics equipment, was a former chemistry professor at the same school. W. R. G. Baker, who guided General Electric's electronics program, had a Ph.D. in engineering. Elmer Engstrom, who became president of RCA and Frederick Kappel, who held the same post at American Telephone and Telegraph, were also engineers. Russell Varian, co-inventor of the klystron tube, also organized Varian Associates, which produced the product. A Harvard physicist and two of his students formed EGG, a rapidly growing electronics firm.

A second generalization would be that the new firms were highly competitive, so price wars and technological innovation were the rule. The transistor that cost $3.50 in 1958 sold for $1.70 in 1960, and the later model was a more sophisticated device. Philco's high-performance switching transistor, introduced at $100 in 1956, was changed, modified, and improved, but in 1960 it sold for $6.75. With such competition, firms that could not afford large research and development costs or could not adapt at a moment's notice to new technologies and markets, often failed. Many were merged into larger firms. The mergers were facilitated by the electronics stocks' high price-earnings ratios. Thus, a share with a book value of $5 might sell for $200 on the open market. The firms took advantage of this to acquire other firms for stock rather than cash. In this way the stock exchange "worked" for the merger movement in electronics, as it did for conglomerates. The acquired firm usually was taken over not for its markets, patents and products—these could be made obsolete in a matter of weeks—but for the men working for it. Often, a poor firm with a good research staff or a special expertise—or even a single exceptional person—would be considered for a takeover.

Finally, the demands of the electronics industry had a part in changing plant location determination, the nature of American education, and marketing methods. During the 1920s, firms located their facilities in areas close to raw materials or to markets, while such factors as labor supply and land costs were considered to be of secondary importance. Electronics, which required smaller factories, light but expensive raw materials and finished products, and a highly trained, often irreplaceable skilled and professional labor force, had different requirements. In the first place, the manufacturer did not worry as much about transportation facilities as had previously been the case; if he produced sophisticated components, for example, most of his supplies could be brought in and shipped out by truck and airplane. Insofar as plant location was concerned, the manager would often look for one near, but not in, a large, centrally located city. New York, once a center for the production of radio parts, was able to capture little of the television market. The Midwest was preferred for the production of components, and the assembly of the final product in some cases, since air freight costs were lower when products were sold to a national market. The only bulk item in television, the cabinet, was usually constructed close to sources of hardwood. Then, depending upon relative economics, the electronics products would be shipped to the cabinet factory for assembly, or vice-versa. Television manufacturers saw few benefits, and many drawbacks, in location in large urban areas.

At a time of prosperity, such as the 1940s, early 1950s, and 1960s, manufacturers had to take rising labor costs into consideration, and so tended to move away from high-cost urban areas to low-cost rural or suburban ones. On the other hand, since electronics firms depended to a large extent upon key men, their needs and demands had to be taken into consideration. Such people required recreational facilities, the benefits of urban life without its disadvantages, and the intellectual stimulation of large, excellent centers of learning and culture. Towns were quick to learn this; in the 1940s and early 1950s, they stressed tax benefits in their search for new businesses; in the late 1950s, they concentrated on appeals to those who desired higher education for themselves and superior public schools for their children. Education itself became a resource. This meant that large research laboratories would develop in the suburbs of large cities near excellent schools. Thus, the outskirts of New

York became more appealing than the city proper. Boston underwent a renaissance, and its famed Route 128 became a leading electronics research area, due to its complex of colleges and universities. Los Angeles was also chosen because of its technology-oriented graduate schools. Where there were no such institutions, the states hastened to create them. Florida Atlantic University was founded and located near the missile complex at Cape Kennedy. The New York State University at Stony Brook was situated in Suffolk County, near New York, in the expectation that it would draw business there. As the electronics industry expanded, these complexes and others like them grew and proliferated, while at the same time the central cities lost more businesses and found it impossible to attract firms engaged in the "new technology." Some fabricating and manufacturing plants remained in old locations, but the research branches were invariably elsewhere.

While the largest single consumer of electronics supplies was the government, the civilian sector also expanded rapidly, led by television and computers. Of the firms with over $100 million in electronics sales per year in 1951, five were basically defense oriented, while seven were to a large extent engaged in television production. In addition, some giants—General Electric, General Motors, International Business Machines, Honeywell, Western Electric, and Westinghouse—were defense suppliers, but did not consider the government to be their major market for electronics products.

One key to both the civilian and military markets was the new technology revolving around the transistor and integrated circuits. Most of the major electronics firms either engaged in transistor manufacture in the early period, or considered entry at one time or another. The transistor—a small device which was used to replace tubes and was sometimes called a semiconductor—was invented in the Bell Laboratories in 1948. It had advantages of size, reliability, and speed, and its uses multiplied rapidly. By 1966, more than $820 million worth of the small items were produced yearly.

Were it not for antitrust practices, Bell Laboratories, a division of American Telephone and Telegraph, might well have become the leader in semiconductor technology and production. As it was, the firm used the devices primarily to develop its complex communications systems, and left most of the production to others. The major reason for this was fear of charges of monopoly. In 1949, the Justice Department attempted to separate Bell Laboratories and Western Electric from the parent firm. To counter this move, American Telephone offered to leave the transistor business by agreeing to license all producers for an advance royalty of only $25,000. Even this nominal sum was not paid by most, for American Telephone had a cross-licensing arrangement with RCA, and that firm, also for antitrust considerations, offered patents for nothing. By the early 1950s, the scramble for market position among producers had begun in earnest.

Several older firms with an interest in electronics quickly entered the field. Sylvania, General Electric, Westinghouse, and RCA all began pilot programs in transistors and other similar devices, and many old-line firms are still major factors in the industry. On the other hand, the bulk of sales went to those newer firms whose origins went back to the marriage of professional managers and scientific leaders.

The leader in semiconductors was Texas Instruments, the predecessor of which was chartered in 1930 as a company engaged in geological research. Its founders, Clarence Karcher and Eugene McDermott, were both scientists who hoped to obtain business from Texas-based petroleum companies. The firm was reorganized in 1941, and during the war was a minor supplier for the defense industries in the Dallas area. By that time leadership had passed to John Jonsson, a self-made man with a background in engineering, who had previously been at Alcoa. During the war, Jonsson worked with Patrick Haggerty, also an engineer, who at the time was with the Navy Department. Haggerty joined the company after the war, and for a few years he and Jonsson attempted to make it a leader in electronics, as well as to expand its original line of business. By 1950, the firm was selling $7.5 million worth of products and services a year. Realizing that its future lay in technology and unwilling to commit itself to any single product, the firm took a new name, Texas Instruments. Haggerty later claimed that the name was chosen because of its noncommittal nature. As an indication of this, Texas Instruments merged with Intercontinental Rubber in 1953, and considered entering the relatively new field of synthetic rubber. Other mergers followed, most of them with electronics firms in the Texas area.

Jonsson and Haggerty had determined that TI would become a new technology-based company when Bell Laboratories announced the licensing of transistor patents. They paid the fee, and began studying the technologies involved. When they realized the potential in transistors, they decided that it would not be necessary to merge and become a conglomerate to achieve large size; the transistor market was so large that internal expansion alone could match the growth rate later achieved by the great conglomerates like Litton and Textron.

Having decided to concentrate on transistors, Jonsson and Haggerty began to search for qualified personnel to handle management and research. Gordon Teal of Bell Laboratories was one of these and Willis Adcock another; both were scientists with business interests. Under their leadership, Texas Instruments became the leader in transistor technology, and later the prime innovator for micro-circuits and integrated circuits. Indeed, so highly qualified was the firm that such giants as IBM were content to purchase their transistors and other items from Texas Instruments, rather than enter the field themselves. By the end of the 1950s, TI was the leading firm in a rapidly developing industry. Its success illustrated most of the points made earlier. The firm was led by businessmen and scientists; it was located in Houston, a city which had all the advantages of location, education, and labor force. Texas

Instruments was adaptable, and sought opportunities, as did Litton—in 1965 it won the contract to produce a fused metal to be used in new quarters and dimes. Finally, the firm showed that entry was much easier in fields concerned with new technology than those involved in the old.

By the early 1960s, dozens of small firms that had entered the transistor field a decade earlier had either been absorbed by larger concerns or had left the field entirely. Texas Instruments had some 20 percent of the market, and was content with this share, since the market for products was increasing at a rate of more than 15 percent per annum. Fairchild Camera and Instrument was a distant second, retaining its position as a result of researches into silicon transistors and several other devices, for many of which it had a research edge on Texas Instruments. Another new firm, Transitron, a product of two brothers, David and Leo Bakalar, was also a major factor and bid for industry leadership. It, too, had teams of research scientists, a good location (Boston), and new managers. But Transitron fell behind in research and development, which in the early 1960s meant that it was several months behind TI and Fairchild. As a result, the firm's sales fell drastically, and it almost went bankrupt. General Electric, RCA, Motorola, Raytheon, Philco, and Sylvania were all producing transistors, but none was able to match Texas Instruments product specialties.

Fairchild and Motorola competed for second place in transistors. Early in the decade, Fairchild's position was seemingly secure, while Motorola was not even in the top ten. Motorola's rapid rise was not unexpected, however. An old-line producer of home radios and later the leading manufacturer of two-way radios and other communications devices, Motorola was a large manufacturer of television sets as well by 1967. As such, the firm was vitally interested in electronics, especially solid-state devices, which afforded compactness and reliability. Motorola entered the transistor field, in the belief that one day transistors would replace tubes in television sets. After a small beginning in the 1950s, the firm became a major supplier of transistors and other electronics devices. The rapid rise of Motorola was still tied to the rise of television, however. This was one of the most dynamic growth areas in the 1950s and 1960s.

Although the use of transistors in television sets did not take place until the mid-1960s, the industry proved a boon to the electronics producers. The average set had a minimum of twenty electronic tubes, against six for most radios, and many more connectors, condensers, switches, etc. In 1947, television contributed little to industry volume; by 1950, sales had crossed the $1.3 billion mark. Fifteen years later more than $2 billion was being spent on sets alone, and the total market for consumer electronics products was well over $3.7 billion. Clearly the television market was a major factor in the plans of the electronics industry.

There was a rush for entry into television and the competition was intense. In 1947 there were fourteen manufacturers of sets; by 1950, the number had passed eighty. In 1966, the field was dominated by a few "majors"—RCA, Zenith, Motorola, Admiral, Magnavox, General Electric, Sylvania, Philco, and Westinghouse, with a handful of minor firms, many of them operating on a regional basis. In this, the television industry of the post World War II period resembled radio after World War I. Intense competition, hopes of high profits, and large-scale spending led many to enter, but also allowed few to survive. The major difference, of course, was that television was dominated from the first by the radio firms, whereas early radio had to start from scratch.

Television resembled radio in other ways. Just as the firms manufacturing radios had hoped to control both set production and stations, so several large television set producers tried to gain control of stations in the early days. RCA accomplished the feat, becoming the second largest set producer (after Zenith) and the owner of NBC. CBS, the second largest network, attempted to enter set production, but abandoned this effort in the late 1950s. ABC, the third network, did not attempt to enter set production, but in 1967 was merged with International Telephone and Telegraph, which controlled European set manufacturers.

The television industry affected not only set manufacturers, stations, and networks, however; if it had, it would deserve to be treated as a logical extension of radio, since no major new firms entered the field after 1947. Instead, the industry adapted the conglomerate philosophy to its own needs and, in effect, redefined the industry. By the mid-1950s, television embraced small firms engaged in making commercials (MPO Videotronics) advertising agencies, studios engaged in producing series (Desilu) electronics firms producing recorders and other devices (Ampex), independent producers (Plautus Productions), and motion picture firms selling their film libraries to networks. In a sense, the television industry did not really exist, nor for that matter did motion pictures, advertising, or talent representation. Instead, by the mid-1950's, there was a single complex known as the entertainment industry.

Some firms recognized this earlier than others. Music Corporation of America, the leading talent representation firm in the nation, purchased Universal Pictures, interests in phonograph record firms (Decca), and organized a subsidiary to produce television series. When the Justice Department demanded that the firm relinquish either its talent affiliate or its other interests, MCA left the former field, its original business. By the early 1960s, MCA dominated the television series market and produced films for television release as well as for the theaters. Walt Disney also recognized the power of the new medium; he continued to produce highly successful movies and also appeared on the Disney program on NBC, which not only brought in profits but also provided built-in advertising for his other interests, which included Disneyland in California.

The motion picture firms were slow in grasping the significance of the change. For a while they attempted to combat television, stating that "movies are better than ever." But as audiences dwindled, they were forced to use their facilities for television. By the early 1960s, they discovered that more was to be gained by linking forces with the new medium than by fighting it. Television consumed talent in huge amounts and needed the backlog of old feature pictures owned by the film industry. By 1966, motion picture firms had accepted television completely, and joined the new entertainment industry. Paramount, which became part of Gulf & Western Industries, Warner Brothers, which came under the control of Seven Arts (a television-oriented firm), and others were intertwined with the new industry.

Television was electronics, but also entertainment. Engaged in both fields, RCA attempted to straddle them. It was led in this attempt by David Sarnoff, one of the few businessmen of the 1920s and 1930s who was able to adapt to the new dispensation, and become one of its leaders.

> To pioneer and to profit—these two motivating forces have run like impulses of alternating current through the history of the Radio Corporation of America. Indeed, General David Sarnoff believes that the secret of corporate success lies in the ability to push forward the frontier, at the same time never forgetting the importance of making substantial deposits back at the bank. But this philosophy, which has given R.C.A. and Sarnoff himself a clear place in business history, faced a stern test during the last decade, when R.C.A. arrayed itself on the frontier of color television. Before the time came when color's account could be written in black on the company's books, R.C.A. had to sustain a long and costly effort, laying out $130 million over a thirteen-year period. Meanwhile, electronic data processing, the company's other principal recent effort, which began on a major scale in 1958, entailed an expenditure that has reached $100 million; even by R.C.A.'s own estimates data processing will not turn profitable before 1964.[2]

2. Walter Guzzardi, Jr., "R.C.A.: The General Never Got Butterflies," *Fortune* (October 1962), 102.

On the surface, it would appear that Sarnoff was frivolous, to say the least, in attempting two such large-scale projects at the same time. If RCA were indeed to become the leading firm in the new entertainment industry, why expend so much time and effort on computers? The answer was simple. In Sarnoff's mind, even the entertainment industry, as large as it might be, was not autonomous, but rather had links to other industries, some old and some new. One of the new ones, electronics, seemed fruitful to the general, so he entered this great growth field in the late 1950s. Sarnoff seemed intent on showing that RCA could outdo Litton at its own game; it would become a conglomerate, entering new fields related to older ones and merging with already-existing firms whenever possible. By the mid-1960s, RCA went one step further, and began to resemble Textron; it entered publishing, education, and apparently any other field in which its technology and skill could prove profitable. But RCA's major drive outside of entertainment remained in computers. As Guzzardi stated, RCA did not become profitable in this area until the mid-1960s. At that, it was one of the few firms, outside of IBM, able to show profits in this highly competitive field, although it left the field in 1971.

The computer was born during World War II out of a shortage of scientists and mathematicians. The first computer, designed by John Mauchly and J. P. Eckert, Jr. and known as ENIAC (Electronic Numerical Integrator and Computer), was in effect a giant adding machine for complex figures. It was constructed by a group of IBM and Harvard scientists, including John von Newmann, and was completed just before the end of the war.

> To be sure, the machine was not all it might have been. Built under the pressure of wartime schedules, it was hardly an example of engineering finesse. For one thing, it was rather bulky. It occupied 1,500 square feet of floor space and weighed more than 30 tons. It included miles of wires, half a million soldered connections, and about twenty thousand vacuum tubes. A television set

with only twelve to fifteen tubes may become fairly hot, so you can imagine how much heat ENIAC generated. It was a potential furnace as well as a computer. An air-conditioning system helped keep the operating level down to about 100 degrees Farenheit, and the machine was designed to shut itself off automatically when the air conditioning failed. Otherwise, temperatures would have soared, and it would have melted its own connections.[3]

The IBM-Harvard group was not the only one interested in computers. Others, recognizing the need for high speed "arithmetic machines" were also at work. Several firms, led by Sperry-Rand, constructed similar models. Eckert and Mauchly, realizing that they lacked the capital to enter the business on their own, approached Thomas Watson of IBM and offered to sell their fledgling operation to that giant company; Watson refused, believing that his firm's future lay in other directions.

Eckert and Mauchly eventually wound up at Remington Rand, producer of the UNIVAC. The UNIVAC division produced several fine machines, but Remington Rand, (which eventually merged with Sperry & became Sperry-Rand) lacked the ability to market them effectively. Thus, when IBM decided to enter the field in 1953, it was still largely unexploited. Concentrating on sales and service, as well as production and research, IBM was able to take the lead in all areas by 1956, and was never to relinquish it. By the mid-1960s, it produced well over 70 percent of all computers in the world.

By the early 1960s, there were dozens of firms producing computers. Generally speaking, they could be divided into three groups. The first of these were the old-line producers of business machines, who looked upon computers as a logical extension of their lines. Into this group fell such firms as IBM, Burroughs, National Cash Register, Clary, and the UNIVAC division of Sperry-Rand. A second group was comprised of

3. John Pfeiffer, *The Thinking Machine* (New York, 1962), p. 27.

firms that had expertise in electronics and sought to sell computers produced by their engineers. RCA, Control Data, Minneapolis Honeywell, General Precision, Scientific Data Systems, and a host of small firms were in this category. Finally, there were those firms who needed computers for their internal operations, produced them for special needs, and then attempted to sell them to others. General Electric was the major firm here. American Telephone & Telegraph, the largest user of computers in the early days, would have been a logical entry into the race, but once again, antitrust problems led the firm to withdraw from computers, although remaining a producer for its own needs.

The computer industry could be entered successfully only by firms with large amounts of capital, effective scientific and sales forces, and a management that was willing to gamble and could afford large losses and massive accounts receivable. A rule of thumb employed in the early 1960s was that it would take one dollar of capital for each projected dollar of sales in the first few years, and in the case of many firms this proved an underestimate. As might have been expected, dozens of companies fell by the wayside, despite the fact that their machines were good, and in some cases better, than those of their more successful rivals.

IBM dominated the industry. The giant firm produced a wide range of machines, had excellent sales and services, and was well financed. The company's finance arm was strong and well managed, and since most IBM computers were leased, the firm resembled a finance company as much as one engaged in production. IBM was also a leader in public relations, labor relations, and showed sophistication and diplomatic understanding in its overseas dealings. In the 1960s the company came to epitomize the best in American technology, management, and planning.

The other firms usually tried to make markets in areas where IBM had small problems, or where the firm encouraged competition by ignoring it or erecting price umbrellas. Honeywell, for example, copied the sales approach pioneered by IBM, and made certain its new machines were compatible with IBM's. In 1970 Honeywell merged with General Electric's computer division, thus making it a more formidable competitor. The merger also signaled the end of General Electric's attempt to win a substantial share of the market on its own. Control Data Corporation, another major firm, specialized in giant computers, many of which were sold to the government and universities. The UNIVAC Division of Sperry-Rand, once the leader in the field, suffered setbacks in the late 1950s and early 1960s, but made a spirited comeback under new management in the late 1960s, and continued to challenge IBM across the full line of products. The others—National Cash Register, Burroughs, and smaller firms—accounted for most of the rest of the market. They either considered computers only a small part of their overall operations or lacked funds, depth, reputation, or technological background to challenge IBM head-on. Such challenges could prove dangerous and costly. Xerox, the leader in office copiers whose management and service departments rivaled those of IBM, merged with Scientific Data Corporation, a well-managed firm whose computers sold well in the lower end of the cost spectrum. When Xerox announced a challenge to IBM, the giant returned the complement by releasing a new line of office copiers.

IBM produced few machines in the low-cost area, thus permitting firms concentrating on such products to flourish. Digital Equipment, Hewlett-Packard, Varian Associates, and Data Machines were able to show good profits here, since most of their products were purchased outright rather than leased, and required less in the way of research and development than the IBM and CDC giants. Furthermore, IBM showed little interest in non-digital machines. The analog computer, which compared sets of data, was not produced by IBM and most of its competitors. Electronics Associates, Beckman Instruments, Veeder-Root, and Westinghouse, all produced analog instruments which, since they usually were purchased outright, were able to show profits more readily. In addition, several small firms specializing in the application of computer techniques and the development of programming, rather than the production of hardware, were able to survive and, in some cases, prosper. Computer Usage Company, Corporation for Economic & Industrial Research (CEIR), Computer Applications, Computer Sciences, and others were able to compete for a while with the service departments of the giants. Finally, many firms prospered by supplying parts to the large manufacturers; as we have seen, Texas Instruments sold millions of transistors to IBM and the others. Potter Instruments was able to sell its memory systems successfully; Addressograph-Multigraph initially concentrated on readout devices; and hundreds of large and small firms either adapted or organized to serve the rapidly growing industry.

A shakeout—or to be more precise a series of them—was in the making. All of the above companies, with the exception of Texas Instruments, would be acquired or leave the business during the 1970s. Potter Instruments would go into bankruptcy when several of its customers developed their own devices and stopped ordering; Addressograph-Multigraph would fail in an ambitious expansion program, causing it to collapse. But other firms entered the industry, and several enjoyed spectacular success.

Toward the end of the 1970s it had become evident that the computer industry—itself spawned from the office machinery industry—had evolved into the data-processing industry and from there into the information-processing and -distribution industry, with the end still not in sight.

Summary

The advent of television, electronics, and computers in the post-World War II period was one of the more dramatic developments in American business. In those years, the GNP increased from $21.34 billion in 1945 to one trillion dollars a quarter of a century later. The increment in GNP *alone* was more than the total Soviet GNP in 1970. The achievement, indeed, was remarkable, especially when one considers the fears of the mid-1940s and the general belief that mature capitalistic nations would lose their ability to innovate and grow.

The generation that commanded the American economy in the immediate postwar period was, in its way, the most dynamic in American business history. In terms of growth, innovation, and ability to adapt to new circumstances, the American businessman had performed remarkably well. Not a single field was the same in the late 1960s as it had been a decade earlier. Food packing, housing, clothing manufacture, chemicals, shiping—all witnessed the impact of technological innovation and a rethinking of basic assumptions. Nor was the large corporation content to exploit the domestic market alone; in the 1950s and 1960s, American firms exporte huge amounts of capital. In 1950, American overseas investment was $11.8 billion; by 1965, it had risen to $49.2 billion. During this period, their investment in Europe rose from $1.7 billion to $13.9 billion. The figures for Latin America rose more slowly, going from $4.4 billion to $9.3 billion, but American firms in Asia and Africa raised their investment from $2.1 billion to $10.8 billion.

To be sure, most of this money was invested in those nations with solid economies, stable politics, and records of friendship with the United States. Still, it was clear that the Americanization of the world would be accomplished as much by force of business and investment as by any other medium. In 1970, IBM not only dominated the American computer market but was the largest factor in every country in which it was represented. Heinz and Campbells were major world food companies; Procter & Gamble's soap products were sold in all continents; Levitt Homes constructed large projects in France and elsewhere; Coca-Cola had become ubiquitous—the growth of American business overseas was sometimes called the "Coca-Colonization of the world."

American students in leading graduate schools of business, such as Harvard, Columbia, Chicago, and Stanford, found themselves being crowded out by foreigners, who were eager to learn the key to corporate success and, then, to transplant the seeds in their own countries. During the mid-1960s, in retrospect the high noon of America's power and reputation, the nation's giant corporations and their newer companions seemed vigorous, self-confident, and capable of continuing on in this fashion for the indefinite future.

CHAPTER X

Decline, Revival/
and Renewal

Within a decade the power, self-confidence, and reputation of American big business that had prevailed in the mid-1960s was replaced with uncertainty and deep soul-searching. By then, all talk of an "American Century" had been turned aside, and scores of writers were examining what to them promised to be the coming age of Japan, a time during which that nation's major businesses would encircle the globe, capturing markets for both mature and advanced products previously controlled by American firms, and transforming the United States into what two scholars called "the first great post-industrial agrarian society."[1]

The reasons for this change in status and perception were dissected in scholarly works, the popular press, and television specials. Among the more obvious factors were the economic and social malaise caused by the dual traumas of the Vietnam War and Watergate, followed by the "oil shocks" of 1973 and 1979, from which the Europeans and Japanese recovered more rapidly and in better style than the United States. The dollar glut of the late 1960s, resulting from aggressive American investment abroad and a chronic balance-of-payments deficit, fore-shadowed the decay of the postwar Bretton Woods accords and its ultimate abandonment by the United States in 1971. That abandonment cut the dollar from gold and harmed its position

1. Edward Feigenbaum and Pamela McCorduck, *The Fifth Generation: Artificial Intelligence and Japan's Computer Challenge to the World* (New York, 1983).

as the world's central currency, a psychological as well as financial blow and one of no small importance.

The decade of the 1970s was marked by "stagflation," the simultaneous ailments of recession and inflation, a phenomenon most economists had previously thought couldn't happen. Not only did stagflation savage the economy, but it left policy-makers bewildered and confused. Add to this a low level of leadership from the White House—a disgraced Richard Nixon, a well-meaning and liked Gerald Ford who was nonetheless perceived as being inadequate, and an ineffectual Jimmy Carter—and you have a recipe for stagnation and a paralysis of will.

Yet there surely was more to it than that. It might be argued, for example, that American business had achieved its pre-eminent position due to the terrible destruction of Europe and Japan during World War II. Both nations recovered smartly in the 1950s, the result in part of American aid, but also of the innate talents of their peoples. After all, Japan had been a rapidly growing economic power during the interwar period, and Germany, the United Kingdom, France, and other European nations possessed entrepreneurial and managerial talents every bit as good as those produced in the United States. Then, too, businessmen from both areas had traveled to America to learn the reasons for its successes, studying them at graduate schools of business administration and the corporations themselves, while even more businessmen received their indoctrinations at overseas branches of American companies. Thus, the relative decline of several American industries during the 1970s was largely due to the groundwork laid in the preceding two decades and the application of lessons learned from the likes of IBM, MMM, General Electric, General Motors, and dozens of other finely managed American corporations.

Viewed in this light, it might appear that the great American economic surge of the quarter century following World War II had resulted as much from the postwar maladies of Europe and

Japan as anything else, and that it was bound to be altered once a more normal situation existed. Yet the American economy remained quite powerful and innovative, especially in new technologies. The perception was otherwise, however. Americans were often pictured as being quite retrograde, especially when compared with the Japanese, who in this period came to symbolize efficiency.

Key American corporations took the lead in several of the more exciting and rapidly developing industries, information processing and transmission and electronics in particular. Industry insiders knew that many of the Japanese successes in such areas as consumer electronics and automobiles were due to technology transfers from the United States; Japan's industries could turn out better and more inexpensive products than the Americans, but often only after American companies blazed the path. Such was the case for a wide variety of products from cameras to hand-held calculators to watches, television sets, and tape recorders.

Sentiments of inferiority extended even to those industries where the Americans held a lead. Critics who in 1983 noted that the Japanese companies *sold* more 64K RAM microchips probably didn't realize that IBM *manufactured* more of them than all the Japanese firms combined, with American Telephone & Telegraph a close second. Even then both companies purchased additional supplies from vendors for use in their computers and related devices. Many of the same individuals who warned that the Japanese were ahead of the United States in the manufacture of several products assumed that this could continue indefinitely, that the American firms were incapable of meeting the challenges, and that the Japanese advantage in some fields could be duplicated in all. None of this was true. Of the top three manufacturers/marketers of semiconducters, two—Motorola and Texas Instruments—were American. (Nippon Electric was in the number 2 position.) In the mid-1980s the American firms still enjoyed a wide advantage over their Japanese counterparts in technology transfers.

Thus the situation was much more complex than is usually imagined, and, taken as a whole, it presents a picture of combined growth, stagnations, and decline, which has ever been the case in American industry.

These forces could be found at work in several key industries, the more striking and important of which were steel, automobiles, and information processing. The first is an industry undergoing crucial alterations due to the development of new technologies and the appearance of foreign and domestic rivals. Such also is the case with the automobile industy, where the challenges have been met with more positive and potentially successful reactions. As for information processing, the American companies hold a strong lead, and foreign competition— trumpeted for more than a decade—has yet to materialize in a significant way.

Along with virtually all other aspects of American business, the automobile complex was badly shaken by the "oil shock" of 1973, when, due to price boosts by the Organization of Petroleum Exporting Countries and the Arab oil boycott, fuel costs rose sharply and shortages developed. The average price for a gallon of gasoline rose from $0.36 a gallon in 1972 to $0.53 in 1974, going to $0.62 by early 1977 before leveling off. A second boycott two years later, resulting from the Iranian Revolution and further OPEC action, caused new shortages, at the end of which a gallon of gasoline fetched $1.23. On both occasions, prices and shortfalls resulted in a greater demand for small, efficient cars, which, given the nature of the market, meant a turning away from Detroit's "gas guzzlers" and an increased demand for imports, especially those from Japan.

Were this all there was to the matter, Detroit might have thrown back the foreigners in much the same way it had during the previous decade. Indeed, when the mania for small cars subsided in 1974-1975, the automakers became convinced such would be the case. Only in retrospect did they realize the ailments were deeper than that.

One of the problems was a growing perception that

foreigners—especially the Japanese—not only turned out more economical cars, but also designed and manufactured them with greater care and ability. The American products were plagued by recalls; stories of defects became standard fare in popular magazines and television specials; friends regaled one another with difficulties encountered with domestic cars and the superiority of the imports.

An outstanding example is provided by the case of the Volare/Aspen, introduced by Chrysler in 1976 as a successor to and replacement for the popular Reliant/Dart. Due to errors in carburetor design, the cars stalled when accelerating from a slow turn—usually in traffic. This led to a recall. The brakes faded badly: another recall. Due to improper galvanizing, the fenders rusted badly: a third recall. There were reports of hoods flying up at high speeds: the fourth recall in little more than a year. All of these corrections cost the corporation $200 million, along with much of its good will and reputation, and played a role in causing Chrysler's near demise.[2]

The malaise wasn't limited to Chrysler. Ford skimped on safety measures in its compact Pinto, resulting in fires when the cars were struck in the rear; costly lawsuits and bad publicity followed. General Motor's vaunted X-Cars, introduced in 1979 as an "import stopper," had more than a dozen recalls, the government fining the corporation for one recall involving defective brakes.

Added to constant recalls was the matter of "sticker shock," or the escalating price of cars after 1973, the result of inflation combined with the need to conform to governmental safety standards. For example, the Pinto, which listed for $1,999 in 1969, sold for $2,225 in early 1973 and had gone to $2,695 a year later. The 1971 Chevy Nova, considered a compact, sold for $2,870; the 1978 Chevelle Malibu, advertised as an "economy compact," cost $4,295.

2. Michael Moritz and Barry Seamon, *Going for Broke: The Chrysler Story* (New York, 1981), pp. 15-16 ff.

The instinctive reaction on the part of customers was to hold on to their old cars awhile longer, to settle for used cars, or to downgrade the type of car purchased. All three approaches were tried. By 1980 the average age of the American car was more than seven years, higher than at any time since the immediate post-World War II period, and the prices of used cars soared. At the same time, Americans considered the relative value of domestic and imported models, and increasingly they came down on the side of the foreign sedans—especially those manufactured in Japan, the continuation and acceleration of a trend that began in the mid-1960s. In 1965, imports accounted for 563,000 sales, which was less than 6 percent of the total. As recently as 1969, 1.8 million foreign-made vehicles were sold, this being 19 percent of all purchases.

By 1980, the imports were taking more than one out of every three sales, 3.1 million in all. Of this amount, close to 2 million were Japanese, twice the number imported four years earlier.[3] That year, the four domestic companies reported total losses of $4.2 billion, and the industry was in its worst condition since the Great Depression. The Japanese companies manufactured 7 million cars that year; the American figure (exclusive of captive Canadian factories) came to 6.4 million. When trucks and buses were included, the combined American-Canadian total came to 9.4 million, the Japanese to 11 million. Clearly American manufacturers could not claim to be the world's leading automobile makers.

Even before then, however, Detroit had developed programs to recoup lost ground. Starting in 1979, the four domestic companies put into operation a five-year $80 billion program to upgrade facilities, alter operations, and in other ways turn out cars that might match the imports in terms of value, quality, and performance. Each firm had its own approach. General Motors decided to downsize its entire line. Ford kept some of its larger

3. United States, International Trade Commission, *Automotive Trade Statistics, 1964-80* (Washington, 1981), pp. 2, 4.

cars while attempting to develop a group of popular subcompacts and compacts. Chrysler, which skirted close to bankruptcy in 1979 before being saved by a federal loan program, pinned its hopes on the K-Car, the Reliant/Aries subcompacts that replaced the Volare/Aspen. American Motors sought a corporate savior and found one in the French national company, Renault, which purchased control of the company and then announced that one of its models would be manufactured in American Motors' factories as the Alliance.

As Detroit struggled to revamp operations in order to match the Japanese in areas of value and quality, it often borrowed from ideas tried in Japan. General Motors led the way in creating "Quality of Work Life" programs, in which assembly line workers cooperated with management in improving the situation on the factory floor. Labor contracts were renegotiated. At Ford, for example, the workers accepted a 30-month wage freeze and deferred cost-of-living increases and acceded to reductions in paid time off. In return for these concessions, the company guaranteed a base income for "tenured" workers until they retired, a program similar to the Japanese lifetime employment principle, and a profit-sharing plan not unlike the bonus and profit-sharing plans often found in Japanese industry. "The wave of the future is greater participation by our work force in the business process," said a Ford vice-president. The corporation's chief negotiator, Peter Pestillo, said that "We aren't willing to treat our hourly people as the most variable cost we have."[4]

And it worked. The break-even point at General Motors declined from 5.6 million units in 1978 to 4.3 million in 1983, and that at Ford went from 4.2 million to 2.6 million. The most drastic improvement was at Chrysler, where in 1978 the break-even point had been 2.4 million. Management and labor slashed that figure to 1.1 million in 1983. By the mid-1980s, it had

4. John Simmons and William Mares, *Working Together* (New York, 1983), p. 51; [Frank Gibney, *Miracle by Design: The Real Reasons behind Japan's*] *Economic Success* (New York, 1982), p. 218.

become evident that the American automobile industry was on the rebound, prepared to contest the Japanese for market share.

In this period, the automobile was altered drastically. Alfred Sloan once remarked that the car of 1960 wasn't that different from the one turned out thirty years earlier. In contrast, the automobile of 1984 was a quantum jump ahead of those of a decade earlier. Low-carbon steel had been replaced by lighter, stronger materials such as aluminum and plastics; the 1984 cars contained around 200 pounds of aluminum, twice that used four years earlier, and approximately 300 pounds of plastic, three times that used in 1981. Aluminum radiators were replacing brass ones. Cooling systems could disappear completely once the new radical ceramic engine is perfected. This power plant, fabricated wholly or partly of high-temperature, tough ceramics developed in part in the space program, will last for more than 100,000 miles, and its supporters claim it will get better than 80 miles per gallon when wedded to the aerodynamic chassis designs which had already made their appearances. Research in these areas is being conducted in Europe and Japan as well as in the United States, with all major companies participating in the process. The changes could be seen at the new factories. The Buick installation in Flint, Chrysler's new mini-van complex in Canada, and Ford's revamped engine plant near Dearborn are among the most modern in the world.

By the mid-1980s, it had also become evident that a world auto industry was in the making. Chrysler had a partnership of sorts with Mitsubishi, Ford with Toyo Kogyo, and GM with Isuzu; at the same time GM agreed to enter into an arrangement with Toyota to manufacture small cars in one of its West Coast plants. American Motors came increasingly under the control of Renault. Throughout the world American, Japanese, German, French, British, Swedish, and Italian automakers were cooperating and comanufacturing cars and trucks. The four American car companies will all survive and probably grow, but their essential shapes will be strikingly different from what they were in the past.

The American steel industry suffered from malaises similar to those that crippled the auto industry, but the resolution there wasn't as happy. Instead, by the late 1970s and early 1980s, it seemed certain that the United States would continue to import many basic shapes from overseas, and that the major companies would survive only through a combination of strong demand and government intervention. Moreover, there was a decided move out of the industry by some of its leaders, and new entities entered the field and, by utilizing modern methods, threatened to further damage the old, ailing giants.

At one time during the late nineteenth century, the steel business was highly competitive. While it was true the major firms often came together to form pools, these always broke apart. Thus the Bessemer Steel Association, which was organized in 1875 by Andrew Carnegie and others and included Pennsylvania Steel, Bethlehem, Jones & Laughlin, Cambria, and Scranton as well as Carnegie itself, dissolved when the founder decided to cut prices and eliminate competition. Other, similar breakups would follow, with Carnegie usually the first to abandon the pool. "I can make steel cheaper than any of you and undersell you," he was purported to have argued. "The market is mine whenever I want to take it. I see no reason why I should present you will all my profits."

This practice often led to chaos and business failures, but it also spurred price competition and technological progress. There were several cycles of boom and bust during the late nineteenth century, but in general the steel companies improved the quality of their products, productivity increased, and prices fell.[5]

It was to bring an end to this competition and provide stability for the industry that J.P. Morgan purchased the Carnegie properties in 1901, added his own Federal Steel and related holdings along with dozens of other companies, and created

5. Peter Temin, *Iron and Steel in Nineteenth Century America: An Economic Inquiry* (Cambridge, 1964), pp. 109. ff.

United States Steel. Capitalized at $1.4 billion, it was the largest industrial corporation in the world. Just as the Pennsylvania Railroad symbolized the railroad age, so U.S. Steel was to stand for America's power in the era of the gray metal. It was the centerpiece of an industry that at the time was strong, innovative, aggressive, and rapidly expanding, when Pittsburgh was known as the Steel Caldron, and the United States was on its way to becoming the world's leading exporter of the metal.

As expected, Morgan substituted cooperation for competition. Judge Elbert Gary, placed in charge of U.S. Steel, actively sought to work in harmony with the smaller companies. In 1907, he institutionalized this policy with the famous "Gary dinners," annual meetings at which, as he put it, "Steel people [came] together occasionally . . . to tell one to the others exactly what his business was."[6]

While the dinners lasted only four years, their spirit remained. During the next half century, it was common knowledge that in most matters U.S. Steel would set the pattern, which all of the others would follow. In effect, Big Steel erected a price umbrella (a level under which all could survive), while the industry as a whole lobbied in Washington for protective tariffs and other beneficial arrangements. Technological progress slowed down; companies were loath to abandon outmoded facilities and practices; and management became imbred and unimaginative.[7]

The retrograde nature of the American steel industry was masked by the combined forces of war, secular changes in the economy, and the business cycle. Demand shot up during wars; the railroads still used a great deal of steel; automobiles would require even more; and during flush times, construction ate up the metal at a solid clip. Steel suffered through depressions, but not much more than other industries.

6. N.S.B. Gras and Henrietta Larson, *Casebook in American Business History* (New York, 1939), p. 607.
7. Robert Crandall, *The U.S. Steel Industry in Recurrent Crisis* (Washington, 1981), pp. 12 ff.; John Ingham, *The Iron Barons: A Social Analysis of an American Urban Elite* (Westport, 1978).

The country turned out 14.9 million short tons of all varieties of steel in 1901, having tripled production in ten years. Shipments for 1917 came to 50 million tons, this due to the requirements of war. A peak of 61.7 million tons was reached in 1929, followed by a decline due to the Great Depression. During World War II, the mills turned out more than 80 million tons a year, and after the war, when the United States helped rebuild Europe and Japan, demand soared, with 117 million tons sold in 1955, a new high. Big Steel appeared strong and self-confident. But the strength was an illusion and the confidence misplaced.

It was then that foreign competition increased, and other metals and plastics replaced steel in several applications. Nonetheless, the American industry, led by eight major firms, the largest of which was U.S. Steel, poured 131 million tons of steel in 1965. After this new high, sales fell off.

The European, Japanese, and even Latin American steel industries were rebuilding and modernizing in this period, often with government help. Not bound by the kinds of pricing regulations enforced in the United States, they were free to offer steel abroad at prices geared more to obtaining market share than any other consideration. In 1960, 3.4 million short tons of steel were imported into the United States, and the figure increased irregularly during the next two decades. By 1980, more than 15.5 million tons were coming into the American market, this being more than 16 percent of total domestic usage. Three years later, in a dramatic display of just how serious was the decline of the American steel industry, U.S. Steel entered into an agreement with British Steel to import semifinished steel slabs from that company. Soon after, Wheeling-Pittsburgh announced it would import slabs from Brazil's leading company, Siderbras.

Critics and union leaders argued that the foreigners were selling their product in the United States at a loss, this being a violation of American law. But the domestic companies conceded that even with transportation costs added, the foreigners could undersell them in their own backyards.

The reasons for this dramatic decline weren't difficult to uncover and could be located in such familiar areas as labor and raw materials costs, managerial errors, federal policies that had negative impacts upon the industry, the disappearance of raw materials price advantages, and the failure of the American companies to come to terms with new technologies.

Low-priced raw materials had been one of the major reasons the United States took the world lead in steel. Ore from the famed Mesabi range and other nearby pits had given American companies a price advantage the Europeans and Japanese couldn't match. These pits were running out by the early 1960s, however. Although new sources were found elsewhere, these were more costly, and the companies had to construct fleets of ore vessels and incur transportation charges, which wiped out the price advantage.

Shipping costs declined in this period, which benefited the European and Japanese importers, but shipping costs represented a new cost for the Americans. In 1956, for example, iron ore cost $9.63 a ton in the United States against $16.69 in Japan; by 1962, the price of ore for the Americans had risen to $11.78, while the Japanese were importing it at $12.97. Five years later, American ore became more costly than that used by the Japanese, and the differential expanded thereafter. By the mid-1970s, the American price was $27.62, and the Japanese, $15.81. There was a similar pattern in coke prices. In 1956, coke used by American steelmakers cost $9.85 a ton, while the Japanese were paying $22.14; the figures twenty years later were $56.04 and $53.60, respectively.[8]

While the American companies had more than their share of technological triumphs, they were slow to incorporate them in exisiting facilities or to erect new ones. The Americans licensed technology to the Europeans and Japanese, who led the way in

8. United States, Federal Trade Commission, *The United States Steel Industry and Its International Rivals: Trends and Factors Determining International Competitiveness* (Washington, 1978), p. 117.

such improvements as continuous casting, the utilization of computer controls in the mills, and the erection of new and more efficient electric furnaces, which use scrap rather than the more familiar mix of ore, coke, and limestone. Thus, while Japanese wages rose by 244 percent in the 1960s, unit labor costs actually declined by more than 30 percent due to greater productivity. In contrast, American wages rose by 39 percent, but as a result of the American firms' utilizing outmoded equipment, unit labor costs actually rose a trifle.[9]

Most industrialized nations have developed and enforce measures defining and limiting the amount of pollution companies are permitted to create. Those set down and patrolled by the Environmental Protection Agency are among the strictest in the world, and this too has contributed to the increase in the price of steel. In 1976-78, the companies spent some $600 million a year on environmental controls. To this should be added another $100 million a year for occupational safety and health measures. These programs increased the price of domestically manufactured steel by approximately 11 percent. The steel companies complained that these costs were too much to bear at a time when foreign-market pressures were increasing; environmentalists and foes of industry wrote and then administered the laws, which were never completely agreed to by the producers.

The fact remains, however, that the adversarial atmosphere between government and industry was far greater in the United States than elsewhere. In Europe, Japan, and Latin America, government generally worked with business to create standards that were then accepted and implemented. In the United States, environmentalists and foes of industry wrote and then administered the laws, which were never completely agreed to by the producers.

9. *Ibid*, pp. 113, 117.
10. William Hogan, *The 1970s: Critical Years for Steel* (Lexington, 1972), pp. 11-36.

Unable to compete economically with the foreigners, the steel companies, charging unfair competition and pointing to the possible loss of tens of thousands of jobs, were able to convince Washington to come to their aid. Beginning in 1969, the government entered into agreements with the Europeans and Japanese to limit their exports to the United States to 14 million tons a year. Then, in 1978, Washington developed and put into place the concept of "trigger prices." In effect, this concept conceded the Japanese advantages in steel, but at the same time provided a means of limiting imports. The costs of production in Japan would be calculated, and the calculations would serve as benchmarks upon which to base policy regarding imports. Should the foreign companies' prices decline below costs, action to keep their products from the American market would be taken. In the nature of things, however, trigger prices resulted in more squabbles and further pointed up the malaise within the American industry.[11]

The actions taken by the individual companies must be seen against this background of failure, economic ailments, erosion of market position, and growing awareness that the United States might no longer be competitive in steel. Out of this came three basic strategies: abandonment and amalgamation, diversification, and attempts, on the part of some old and new companies, to adapt to new technological and market conditions.

"You can have this steel facility for nothing," said a Republic Steel executive to a group of visiting scholars in the late 1960s. "But you'll have to take the labor force was well." The message was obvious if exaggerated for effect: both the plant and its workers were obsolete. Even so, foundry closings outran expansion efforts by the mid- and late 1970s. In 1977, for example, Bethlehem closed down two facilities, which between them were capable of turning out 2.6 million tons of steel; Youngstown shuttered a major facility rated at 1.7 million tons;

11. Crandall, *The U.S. Steel Industry in Recurrent Crisis,* pp. 40-45.

and ailing Alan Wood, a minor factor, razed its 1.1 million ton complex, effectively putting itself out of the business. U.S. Steel "retired" two plants rated at 2 million tons that year, another rated at a million in 1978, and another rated at 1.2 million in 1979. The others followed suit; in 1978-1979 alone, the companies retired facilities rated at 8.5 million tons, which was more than 5 percent of its capacity. While estimates varied, it was believed that an additional 20 percent of the nation's plants were uneconomical, with U.S. Steel in the worst shape of all.[12]

As indicated, the major integrated companies responded to the situation by acquiring other, usually relatively minor factors in the business in order to achieve economies of scale, and in addition, diversified into other fields. Bethlehem Steel, the second largest entity, went after but failed to acquire Cerro, a major factor in copper mining. It then purchased Kusan, a manufacturer of plastic parts, and took a majority interest in Multicon, a housing firm. National, then the third largest company, purchased an interest in an aluminum company, South Wire, and followed this with the purchase of a participation in American Magnesium. National acquired Granite City Steel in 1971 and nine years later United Financial Services, an important savings and loan holding company, for a quarter of a billion dollars in cash, signaling its new status by taking a new name, National Intergroup.

So it went throughout the industry. Armco entered finance leasing, insurance, nonmetallic composites, and plastics, while Inland made a major commitment to housing. Of the large integrated companies, only Republic failed to enter new fields in an important fashion, and significantly this company had one of the group's worst records.

Meanwhile takeovers and mergers abounded. In 1968 alone, five out of the top twenty steel companies were sought by conglomerates.[13] Youngstown Steel approached Lykes, a New

12. *Ibid*, pp. 140-41.
13. Hogan, *The 1970s: Critical Years for Steel*, p. 17.

Orleans-based steamship company, that year, and LTV, a major conglomerate headed by James Ling, began its courtship of Jones & Laughlin, at the time the nation's seventh largest steel company. Both takeovers succeeded, and later in the decade, LTV took over Lykes-Youngstown to become the third largest factor in the industry (behind U.S. Steel and Bethlehem but ahead of National and Republic). Other conglomerate takeovers included that of Crucible Steel by Colt Industries, Sharon Steel by NVF, and Lone Star Steel by Northwest Industries. Athlone acquired Jessop Steel; Teledyne took Columbia; and Penn-Dixie Cement purchased Continental Steel.

The most striking change came at the industry's leader, however. The U.S. Steel of 1981 was decaying and, unless the rot could be rooted out, inevitably would have crumbled. It might have been saved by adopting one of two new strategies: cutting back drastically on many operations and revamping as a smaller but more profitable entity or diversifying away from steel into some new and more promising fields.

The U.S. Steel of 1980 had revenues of $12 billion, which enabled it to place in the nineteenth slot on the *Fortune 500* roster, ahead of Western Electric and Eastman Kodak but behind the likes of Tenneco and General Electric. At year's end, the corporation had a cash-and-equivalents balance of slightly more than $900 million with the borrowing potential of at least as much. U.S. Steel's long-term debt was close to a quarter of a billion dollars, not particularly large as such things went. Chairman David Roderick might have used his resources to erect two modern, competitive facilities or to diversify into some new business.

Initially Roderick opted for the latter course and accepted an invitation to merge with Marathon Oil, which in 1980 was being pursued by Seagram and Mobil. *Fortune's* number 39 corporation with sales of $8.2 billion, Marathon had long been deemed by the investment community a likely takeover candidate.

The contest for Marathon was dramatic and even thrilling. Lost in the contest were the problems of U.S. Steel, the question of why this once-powerful company had decided to decrease its commitment to metals and go into petroleum. The reason was obvious: large integrated steel companies had little reason for optimism given the situation in the early 1980s. Unlike automobile companies, they had little chance of recovery and renewal. Today, U.S. Steel is as much an energy company as it is a steel operation, and it is likely to continue along this path during this decade and the one to follow.

This wasn't the end of it, however. In September 1983, LTV and Republic agreed to merge. Five months later, Roderick stunned the industry by announcing a plan under which U.S. Steel would purchase National Intergroup's National Steel for cash and stock that came to more than $1 billion. The combined firm not only would enjoy new economies of scale but in addition, would be able to close down duplicate facilities. While the Justice Department challenged the LTV-Republic merger, causing the parties to abandon their plans, it appeared the U.S. Steel-National combination would be permitted to proceed.

While the major integrated companies faced a bleak future, smaller and more aggressive domestic firms have done quite well, and in their experience may be found an indication of where the steel industry is headed.

Starting in the early 1970s, several old and new companies entered the steel industry on a specialized and regional basis, and today there are some fifty of them stretched across the country. While producing a wide variety of products they share several common attributes. They are located in low-wage, often rural areas and employ work forces that have rejected unionization. To this, they marry the most modern technologies. All produce steel by means of electric furnaces, which today account for close to a quarter of total production, almost five times the share of a quarter of a century ago. Proximity to markets replaced proximity to ore sources as a matter of prime consideration.

Scrap availability and prices weigh more heavily in mangerial decisions than almost any other production factor.

The names of these "mini-mills" aren't familiar to those outside of the industry. Some of the more important new companies are Nucor, Northwestern Steel & Wire, Florida, Georgetown, Connors, and North Star. Others are specialty steel companies, which have embraced the new technology and market approach, and these include Laclede, Lukens, and Atlantic.[14]

Perhaps the best known of the new companies is Nucor Corp., which began life as Reo Motors (a motor vehicle manufacturer) and became Nuclear Corporation of America in 1955. After a foray into high technology, it purchased a small steel company in 1962. Other purchases, followed, with Nucor generally scrapping old plants and erecting new ones on a regional basis. Nucor's major facilities are in South Carolina, Nebraska, Texas, and Utah, areas hardly known in the past for steelmaking, but which are close to scrap sources and markets.

By 1983, the corporation had a capacity of more than 1.1 million tons per year, and its revenues came to $540 million. Nucor is highly efficient and consistently profitable. The company averages 700-800 tons of steel per employee per year, which is twice that of the older, integrated companies. Labor costs at Nucor come to $48 a ton; those at the majors are approximately $185. For these reasons, the mini-mills have not only taken market share from the larger companies, but have also managed to turn back the foreigners as well.[15]

On the whole, these companies are leaner and more progressive than the integrated firms. Their long-term debt services are far less onerous than those of the majors. The debt as a percentage of equity for the new firms is usually under 40

14. Darwin Brown, "Mini and Medium Steel Plants of North America," *Iron and Steel Engineer*, November 1975, pp. 1-29.
15. Leslie Wayne, "The Going Gets Tough at the Nucor Minimill," *New York Times*, August 7, 1983.

percent, as compared with better than 80 percent for the increasingly impoverished old-line operations. This pattern is likely to continue, since the plants for the mini-mills are so new: the average age of Nucor facilities is three years, and Florida Steel's operations are five years old; in contrast, the Inland plants average 5 years, and Republic's are 17 years old.

The future for steel, then, rests on the abandonment of old facilities and the erection of new ones, the acceptance and employment of new technologies, and an acceptance of the fact that in the future domestic steel production will be less than it has been in the past and the plants more widespread.

Steel, then, is in the process of drastic reshaping, while the automobile industry is in the process of reviving. In both, the American companies have been challenged successfully by foreigners. In contrast, information processing in its modern shape is a relatively new industry, in which the American companies have had signal successes. More so than in almost any other industry—and certainly more so than in autos and steel—it is in the midst of constant and rapid evolution, with some industry experts expecting that, prior to the end of the 1980s, it will be the largest single manufacturing and service industry in the world.

As has been seen, International Business Machines dominated the industry in the mid-1960s, followed by a handful of seven medium-sized firms with varying reputations. Industry observers tagged the group "Snow White and the Seven Dwarfs." All but one of the smaller firms had ambitions to challenge the leader across the line.

In 1965, IBM led the pack, accounting for two-thirds of the market. It was followed by Sperry Rand, whose Univac Division had 12.1 percent of sales, and then in order by Control Data (5.4), Honeywell (3.8), Burroughs (3.5), General Electric (3.4), Radio Corporation of America (2.9), and National Cash Register (2.9), with the rest being taken by peripheral companies such as Philco, Hewlett-Packard, Varian Associates, Scientific Data, and Digital Equipment.[16]

In the late 1960s, the major companies concentrated upon large and medium-sized machines (or mainframes, as they were called), tape drives, which store the data, and printers, which spew out information. This equipment was known as hardware, distinguished from software, or the programs through which the data was processed. Hardware was deemed paramount in this period, while software was usually created for each customer's use by the vendor. That was one of the major reasons for IBM's great success. No company in the industry was better at hand-holding than IBM. In those early days of data processing, when the concept still was esoteric, romantic, and not a little mysterious, the presence of those three letters on a giant computer and the knowledge that help was literally minutes away inspired the kind of confidence no other company could match.

Data processing was still a relatively small industry during this period; in 1965, IBM had gross revenues of $2.5 billion, with most of this accounted for by such non-computer items as the ubiquitous IBM cards, sorters, punches, and calculators. Control Data, the only one of the seven dwarfs totally committed to computers, had revenues of $160 million that year and working capital of less than $100 million.

Such was the situation at a time when the industry was about to undergo a severe shakeout. As indicated, General Electric abandoned the field in 1970, selling its computer business to Honeywell, and the following year, RCA disposed of its operations, selling to Sperry Rand. Burroughs and NCR went into decline, unable to assay the switch from electromechanical to electronic equipment with ease. Control Data concentrated upon the very large machines that IBM ignored and, as a result, was able to carve out a niche for itself, which eluded the others. In the process, the seven dwarfs were transformed into "the

16. Unless otherwise indicated, the material in this section has been drawn from Robert Sobel, *IBM: Colossus in Transition* (New York, 1981) and Katharine Davis Fishman, *The Computer Establishment* (New York, 1981).

BUNCH'' (an acronym for Burroughs, Univac, NCR, Control Data, and Honeywell.)

IBM's tremendous power, the failure of six of the original seven dwarfs to achieve any real measure of success, and the gains made by the seventh—Control Data—provided others with two valuable lessons. No company could afford to mount such a direct across-the-board confrontation against IBM. Moreover, success might be achieved by attacking IBM at its flanks, namely those areas which, for one reason or another, it chose to ignore or where it had little representation. Control Data had achieved a dominant position in very large marchines; other companies might do as well in similar peripheral markets.

Then, too, would-be entrepreneurs in information processing recognized that this was an exploding industry, with new ideas and products arriving annually and sometimes even more rapidly. No single company—not even IBM—had the resources to achieve domination up and down the line. During the 1970s, some of these individuals were able to create major enterprises simply by accepting this situation and creating products and services that fit the pattern.

For example, Digital Equipment Corp., which began as a parts supplier, created the PDP-1 computer in 1960, which sold for $120,000 at a time when this was deemed an extremely low price. Five years later, DEC presented the PDP-8, offered at $18,000, and this small computer swept the field. It was a fast and inexpensive machine, but more to the point, IBM had nothing like it to offer its customers, since the company didn't believe there was much of a market for such hardware. DEC became known as "the IBM of minicomputers," and by the time the industry leader entered the field, the market was so well entrenched it couldn't be crushed. By 1980, DEC could boast that it was the second largest computer manufacturer in the world (behind IBM, of course), and in fact it was turning out more machines than anyone else. Later on, Cray would achieve domination in huge "super-computers," and a host of firms did well in sub-minis, or "micros," due to the failure of Control Data and DEC—and IBM—to exploit these fields.

For a while, Scientific Data Systems dominated a segment of the market for specialized scientific computers. Led by Max Palevsky, it reported revenues of over $100 million by 1968 and turned back several challenges from IBM. However, Palevsky sold his company to Xerox and went on to other things. Xerox started to transform its newly renamed Xerox Data Systems into a full-line operation, where it met with little success. In time, XDS was dismantled, the parent writing it off as a loss, and the industry learned once again the difficulties of attempting to win market share from IBM and recognized the need to uncover and then exploit weaknesses in that giant firm's facade.

The wisdom of mounting indirect challenges was best illustrated by the experiences of a group of firms which in the 1960s and afterwards recognized a flaw in IBM's price structure. Under terms of a 1956 consent decree, IBM was obliged to sell as well as lease its machines, the latter practice being the norm until then. While large numbers were purchased thereafter, most continued to be leased on terms that brought substantial cash flow to the parent. Several firms were organized with the intention of purchasing computers from IBM and then offering them to customers at more advantageous rates. It started with Management Assistance Inc., which entered the computer-leasing business in 1961. Others followed—Booth, Itel, Randolph, Data Processing Financial & General, and Levin-Townsend being among the largest and most successful—while IBM considered countermeasures. In the end, most went out of business due to the rapid development of the industry. When IBM introduced a new line of computers, making its old machines either overpriced or obsolete, leasees broke their agreements with the leasing companies, obliging them to repossess the machines at a time when their values and marketability were sharply reduced. Leasing continued in the 1980s, but on a much more cautious basis.

Similar experiences were had by those companies that concentrated on manufacturing and/or marketing peripheral equipment that was priced competitively with IBM hardware and could be used with its mainframes. In the early 1960s, Mohawk Data Sciences, Telex, and Memorex advertised that their peripheral devices not only were superior in performance to IBM counterparts but offered savings of from 20 to 60 percent. Several of the manufacturers of peripheral equipment enjoyed short-term successes, but only one—Storage Technology, a manufacturer of tape drives and related memory systems—prospered for more than a short period.

Most were brought down by the combination of two factors. First, they lacked the necessary financial strength to maintain themselves in the face of rapid technological change. They drained resources to develop and manufacture equipment that often became obsolete in a matter of months and thus failed to make a return on investment sufficient to fund ongoing projects and new research. Second, IBM retaliated by slashing prices and offering attractive leasing arrangements to customers so as to woo them from the competition.

More lasting success was enjoyed by manufacturers of plug-compatible mainframes. IBM software could be used with these machines, which usually were both faster and less expensive than the models they emulated. The key figure here was Gene Amdahl, who as an IBM engineer had helped develop several of the firm's most important large computer systems. He left IBM in 1970 to form Amdahl Corp., whose first PCM was shipped five years later. Within a year, Amdahl had won several key placements from old IBM customers—American Telephone & Telegraph, NASA, and other government agencies—and had shipped seventeen machines. At the end of the decade, Amdahl Corp., was doing $300 million a year in business, and Amdahl together with other PCM manufacturers accounted for revenues of close to a billion dollars. By then, however, IBM was able to strike back by releasing new machines and reducing prices.

Amdahl and the others responded by offering their own versions of the next generation and matching IBM's price cuts, but it seemed quite evident that the PCM business was quite risky. After failing to bring about mergers that would have strengthened his company, Amdahl left it to organize yet another computer firm. This firm, called Trilogy, would concentrate on developing new technologies in addition to exploiting the plug-compatible market.

The most important new development of the 1970s was the appearance of the microcomputer, a device that literally brought information processing within the reach not only of small offices, but also of novices, as well as experts, who wanted to use computers at home. Here too new, small companies were able to establish beachheads while IBM was engaged in other activities. Several of them had become quite large and well established by the time IBM entered the field in the early 1980s.

Microcomputers had their origins in microelectronics, the creation of electronic games, and most important, the development of the hand-held calculator, all of which took place in the late 1960s and early 1970s. In 1974, a New Mexico-based electronic firm, Micro-Instrumentation Telemetry, turned out the Altair 8800 micro, designed to sell for $400. It met with a good reception, encouraging Radio Shack, then the largest American retailer of electronic products to the general public, to enter the field. Its micro was introduced in 1977 and accounted for half the approximately 200,000 small computers sold that year. Dozens of firms had sprung up before the end of the decade. Led by Radio Shack, Commodore, and Apple, the micro market was growing at a rate of better than 50 percent per annum. By then, too, IBM and most of the other old-line companies had their own micro programs underway.

IBM introduced its Personal Computer in August 1981, at that time opening company stores and announcing that the machines would be sold through Sears Roebuck, and later on selling them elsewhere as well. IBM soon became the dominant company in this subindustry, but it was growing so rapidly that not only were the others able to survive and grow, but newcomers entered the field. By 1984, there were some 200 manufacturers of micros, and the more successful of them were offering machines that were able to use IBM software—in effect, a marriage of the micro with the PCM. By then, too, the Japanese companies were coming to the United States with their micros.

Fujitsu, a major Japanese electronics firm, was one of Amdahl's early backers, and some Fujitsu hardware was used in the Amdahl PCMs. While technology sharing took place, Amdahl denied having a hand in helping the Japanese catch up with the Americans in information processing. Nonetheless, by the early 1970s, it had become evident that Japan meant to mount as serious a challenge in this new field as it had in the older ones of automobiles and steel.

IBM World Trade dominated foreign markets just as the domestic firm dominated the market in the United States. In 1961, IBM World Trade was the largest factor in all countries in which it operated, including Japan and Germany. In that year, the six major Japanese computer companies—Nippon Electric, Hitachi, Fujitsu, Toshiba, Oki Denki, and Mitsubishi—came together to organize the Japan Electronic Computer Company. That company had three basic tasks: to purchase machines from the member companies for placement at end users, to harmonize research and development efforts, and to study the possibilities for overseas sales, all of which was aimed at IBM, both in Japan and elsewhere.

Initially at least, the American information-processing firms had little difficulty keeping the Japanese at bay, not only in micros (an area where the Japanese had been expected to carve out an important market share) but in all other fields. In fact, outside of office copiers and later on small printers and electronic typewriters, the Japanese had little impact on the American market. In the early 1980s, most of their successes were in the area of components (such as microchips) and not end-use products. But the Japanese persisted, and at the same time entered into additional agreements with the Americans to share technology, and even products, in a manner similar to but much more limited than that in the automobile industry. Moreover, so rapidly was the industry developing and expanding that even IBM couldn't go it alone, either overseas or domestically. In 1982, IBM agreed to market a copier manufactured by Minolta, a transaction not dissimilar to one entered into earlier with Matsushita.

This partnership—and indeed the entire relationship between the information-processing industries of both countries—soon became clouded by scandal. In late June 1982, the news broke that with IBM's assistance, the Federal Bureau of Investigation had uncovered of a plot by Hitachi and Mitsubishi Electric to purchase stolen IBM secrets. Hitachi later pleaded guilty and paid a fine. While some claimed the Japanese had been entrapped, what was more significant to others was the fact that they had been obliged to enter into such shady operations, and that this demonstrated that IBM was still the leading corporation in high technology. It even became a badge of honor in Armonk. "They had to steal from us," bragged one IBMer. "They didn't go to DEC, Control Data, or any of the others." 'More important, however, was the fact that at a time when Detroit was slavishly copying Toyota, Honda, and Nissan models and production techniques, the Japanese were still looking to the American companies for ideas in high technology.

Yet IBM continued to seek partners. In 1982, the company announced it would purchase certain software from independent vendors rather than rely completely upon in-house developments, and it soon became known that many of the parts in the Personal Computer had also been purchased from suppliers. Later that year, IBM purchased a quarter interest in Intel, a pioneer in microprocessor technology and a major supplier for several key IBM products. In 1983, IBM took an important position in Rolm Corp., a fast-growing factor in telecommunications, this a signal that it meant to expand rapidly in that field.

These two purchases wouldn't have been possible in the 1970s, for at that time IBM was engaged in defending itself against a government antitrust action. In early January 1982, the Justice Department dropped its prosecution. Now IBM was relatively free to compete aggressively in a rapidly expanding information- and data-processing and distribution industry.

A settlement was reached in the AT&T case that same year, under the terms of which that huge enterprise was to be broken into its component parts, leaving a newly born enterprise freed from constraints to compete in many areas where IBM was dominant. But the information-processing and distribution industry was so huge and rapidly growing that there appeared to be room for both. Nonetheless, IBM now became more aggressive than ever, slashing prices, introducing new models (among them additional versions of the personal computer), and entering into new joint ventures, such as one with Sears Roebuck and CBS in the area of videotext.

That the Justice Department had no response to developments in the industry was yet another indication that the American information-processing companies would be freer to combine to compete internationally than had been enterprises in other fields. More important, however, it was taken as a sign that the Americans were being tacitly encouraged by Washington to unite against the Japanese invasion in high technology. This isn't to suggest that an "America Inc." was being created in this industry to match "Japan Inc." Rather, the implication was that the Japanese wouldn't easily make beachheads into IBM's turf as they did a generation ago into those of such giants as General Motors, General Electric, and RCA. Nonetheless, they would try, for not to do so would be to abandon the world's most dynamic industry. Most forecasters believe that, by the end of the decade, information processing will be a trillion-dollar industry, the cutting edge of business developments for the foreseeable future.

Coda, Summary, and Conclusion

The industrial evolutions described in this book are consistent with a five-phase process through which almost all industries seem to pass.

The first of these might be called "inception," when the new concepts appear only to be rejected by leaders of the old Establishment, partly because of lack of imagination but also because they have the most to lose if the new products and services are accepted, since they would then be forced out of business.[17] Young people, often technicians, amateurs, and dilettantes, rather than businessmen lead the way.

In the second stage, they organize companies and start turning out the product or providing the service, which meets with slow and then rapid acceptance. Others perceive the appeal of the innovation and enter the field. Soon it is crowded with scores, even hundreds, of small entities. Technological progress is rapid, almost always outpacing those products available in the marketplace. Price cuts resulting from technological advances and the struggle for market share become epidemic. (Generally speaking, declining unit prices are a hallmark of young industries, increasing ones of the mature industry). All of this leads to declining profit margins, which are often masked by rising net returns resulting from higher volume.

In time, the products reach the third stage, one marked by chronic glut. Large numbers of firms disappear due to faulty leadership, capital shortages, and inability to stand the pace of technological progress, the departure of key personnel, the

---

17. Of the buggy manufacturers, only Studebaker embraced the automobile, and IBM, then the largest manufacturer of calculators, produced computers only after Thomas Watson Jr.'s long campaign to sway his father, who opposed the changeover.

pressures of temporary twists in the business cycle. There are literally dozens of factors that can cause the demise of a new venture in a young and exciting industry.

This leads to the fourth stage, one of consolidation, which in the nineteenth century was often accomplished by banks stepping in to refinance and amalgamate several failed enterprises upon which they had foreclosed. Takeovers, either friendly or contested, are more often the case today. Some firms become parts of larger enterprises seeking entry into the new field; more unite with similar concerns seeking strength through size. In some cases, a viable enterprise might pick up the pieces and add them to its own divisions. The ending is invariably the same: the emergence of several giant corporations, functioning almost as an oligopoly and certainly behaving as one. These are lead by managers who are usually capable but bland and conservative, with a stake in evolutionary rather than bold and sudden growth. The bureaucracy takes over; corporate leaders now prize the M.B.A. from an Ivy League university more than the brilliant insights of eccentrics with a technological bent, amateurs with a feel for the marketplace, and oddballs who simply find corporate life stifling and yearn for greater freedom.

Finally, we have the fifth stage. Now that industry which once was yeasty, overcrowded, and marked by rapid change is complaisant and settled, with leaders who perceive that their interests rest with preventing their main products from becoming obsolete. In the fifth stage, corporate leaders become defensive, a sure sign of stagnation. And it's then that those aforementioned eccentrics, oddballs, and amateurs start organizing to displace them, staring the cycle once again.

An awareness of this process may assist a corporation and even an industry to avoid such a fate. What is required is a serious effort to understand problems and, more important, a willingness to scrap old ways, slash bureaucracies, and seek fresh approaches to new problems and possibilities. One group of scholars has called this approach "reindustrialization."[18]

The history of the steel industry in the nineteenth and twentieth centuries well illustrates this cycle, and a still better example would be what transpired in automobiles. Around the turn of the century, there were many small companies with cars on the roads, most of which turned out fewer than a score of them a year. In 1903, Oldsmobile, which was one of the largest in the field, manufactured 3,922 sedans and sold them within a six-state area. The auto industry might have emerged out of buggies or railroading, but the tycoons of those industries ignored the new technology. Instead, leadership came from tinkerers and opportunists. Henry Ford was one of the former, while William Durant, the genius who put together General Motors, fell into the latter category. The founders of almost all the auto companies of this period were one or the other, and only later on did they give way to the managers. In the case of GM, Durant was elbowed aside by the DuPont interests represented by Alfred Sloan.

Many firms failed in this period, while others entered into consolidations. But even then it appeared mergers would result in the formation of several giants, each offering a wide variety of models to appeal to the entire market. For example, Durant united such firms as Buick, Cadillac, Oakland, and later on Chevrolet, Pontiac and Oldsmobile as well. Not all of these amalgamations were successful; United States Motors, comprised of eight companies including Columbia, Stoddard-Dayton and Brush Runabout collapsed, only to be incorporated into Chrysler later on, and Chrylser then purchased Dodge Brothers. After World War II came the union of Studebaker and Packard to form Studebaker-Packard, while Nash and Hudson came together to create American Motors. At one time, there

18. William Abernathy, Kim Clark, and Alan Kantrow, *Industrial Renaissance: Producing a Competitive Future for America* (New York, 1983).

were some 300 companies in the field; today America has only four.

Of course, the auto giants are still with us, but in the 1950s, the Japanese literally reinvented the automobile, doing so while scorned, ignored, and ridiculed by Detroit. Had this continued for just a few more years, Japan might now be the center of a reborn auto industry. As it is, the American auto makers will survive by becoming more entrepreneurial and less managerial than they were in the 1960s and early 1970s. In short, they are in the process of reindustrialization. A similar development is taking place in steel, which is rapidly evolving into a quite different industry from what it was in the old fifth stage.

The process may also be studied in several aspects of the information-processing and transmission industry. For example, microcomputers as a subindustry really began in the mid-1970s, when several of those eccentrics and technology whizzes experimented with chips and calculators, coming up with very small and inexpensive minis. As has been noted, the advent of Micro-Instrumentation Telemetry Systems' Altair 8800 may be said to have marked the subindustry's beginning. Other firms followed suit, with most of these small operations centered in the Far West, headed by technicians rather than managers. This, of course, was the first stage.

The second may be said to have begun in 1974, when Radio Shack entered the field and then started to expand rapidly. Others followed, with Apple and Commodore the best known and most successful of the lot.

We are in the third phase right now, with glut, price-cutting, rapid technological development—all the classic symptoms. Amalgamations may soon be expected, along with the appearance of professional managers to replace the entrepreneurs. A sign of this can be seen at Apple, which took on an outsider, a management-marketing expert, to replace the founder-president, whose background is in technology.

The American experience with information processing and

distribution is one of the more encouraging aspects of the business scene in the mid-1980s, but there are signs of industrial reawakening elsewhere as well. After one of the most jarring decades in American business history, the nation's major industries appear to be better equipped to handle both domestic and international challenges, more of which may be expected in the near future. In the future old industries will either reindustrialize or fade away, while more new ones will appear than at any time since the late nineteenth century. If the outlook at the beginning of the 1970s was grim and forbidding, that of the present is exciting and encouraging.

Selected Bibliography

This book is a study of microeconomic history and so concentrates on specific businessmen and corporations within industries and selected periods in their development. This presented both problems and opportunities regarding sources. The conventional works in economic history have been explored, and several have been quoted in the text or referred to elsewhere. But most economic historians focus their attention upon issues broader than microeconomics, and so I have had to delve more deeply into monographic and periodical literature than I thought necessary when I began my research. The books most useful to this work, some of which are in the field of microeconomic and business history, may be found following this brief essay. More important, however, have been journal articles. I have made extensive use of the *Journal of Economic and Business History, Explorations in Economic History,* and *Business History. The Business History Review* and its predecessor, *Bulletin of the Business History Society,* have been invaluable. Rather than list the articles used in the preparation of this work, I will say that almost every issue of the *Review* contains material of this nature, but I especially recommend Ralph Hidy's article, "Business History: Present Status and Future Needs," *Business History Review,* 44 (Winter 1970), 483-497. It is an excellent survey of recent work in the field, a landmark in the subject. A copy should be in the hands of every student of microeconomic history.

I have gone through every issue of *Fortune* and *Business Week* since their foundings, and have mined these magazines generously. *Forbes* and *Barron's* have been most useful for the post–World War II period. Finally, I have drawn upon the materials and experience of several investment consultants, who have been most helpful with both their time and materials.

Abernathy, William. *The Productivity Dilemma: Roadblock to Innovation.* Baltimore, 1978.

Adelman, Morris. *A & P: A study in Price-Cost Behavior and Public Policy.* Cambridge, 1959.

American Tobacco Company. *"Sold American!": The First Fifty Years.* New York, 1954.

Arnold, Thurman. *Folklore of Capitalism.* New Haven, 1937.

Barnes, Julius. *The Genius of American Business.* New York, 1924.

Barnouw, Erik. *A Tower in Babel: A History of Broadcasting in the United States.* New York, 1966.

———. *The Golden Web: A History of Broadcasting in the United States, 1933 to 1953.* New York, 1968.

Barton, Bruce. *The Man Nobody Knows.* New York, 1924.

Baruch, Bernard. *American Industry in the War.* New York, 1941.

———. *Baruch: The Public Years.* New York, 1960.

Beaton, Kendall. *Enterprise in Oil: A History of Shell in the United States.* New York, 1957.

Berle, Adolf, Jr., and Means, Gardiner. *The Modern Corporation and Private Property.* New York, 1932.

Bernstein, Jeremy. *The Analytical Engine: Computers—Past, Present, and Future.* New York, 1966.

Bogan, Edwin A. *Handbook of War Products.* New York, 1942.

Brock, Gerald. *The U.S. Computer Industry: A Study of Market Power.* New York, 1975.

Carr, Charles. *Alcoa: An American Enterprise.* New York, 1952.

Carr, William. *The Du Ponts of Delaware.* New York, 1964.

Chandler, Alfred D., Jr. *Strategy and Structure: Chapters in the History of the Industrial Enterprise.* Cambridge, 1962.

Chandler, Lester. *Benjamin Strong: Central Banker.* Washington, 1958.

————, ed. *Giant Enterprise: Ford, General Motors, and the Automobile Industry.* New York, 1964.

————. *The Visible Hand: The Managerial Revolution in American Business.* Cambridge, 1977.

Clark, Grosvener. *Industrial America in the World War.* New York, 1923.

Cleland, Robert, and Putnam, Frank. *Isias W. Hellman and the Farmers and Merchants Bank.* San Marino, 1965.

Cole, Arthur H. *Business Enterprise in its Social Setting.* Cambridge, 1959.

Crandall, Robert. *The U.S. Steel Industry in Recurrent Crisis.* Washington, 1981.

Crowell, Benedict, and Wilson, Robert. *How America Went to War: The Great Hand.* New Haven, 1921.

Crowther, Samuel, ed. *A Basis for Stability.* Boston, 1932.

Dana, Julian. *A. P. Giannini: Giant in the West.* New York, 1947.

De Seversky, Alexander. *Victory Through Air Power.* New York, 1942.

Douglas, Paul. *Controlling Depressions.* New York, 1935.

Drucker, Peter. *The New Society: The Anatomy of Industrial Order.* New York, 1962.

Durand, Edward. *American Industry and Commerce.* New York, 1930.

Edwards, Charles. *Dynamics of the United States Automobile.* Columbia, S. C., 1965.

Ezekiel, Mordecai. *Jobs for All Through Industrial Expansion.* New York, 1939.

Fainsod, Merle; Gordon, Lincoln; and Palamountain, Joseph, Jr. *Government and the American Economy.* New York, 1959.

Feigenbaum, Edward, and McCorduck, Pamela. *The Fifth Generation: Artificial Intelligence and Japan's Computer Challenge to the World.* New York, 1983.

Finn, David. *The Corporate Oligarch.* New York, 1969.

Fishman, Katharine Davis. *The Computer Establishment.* New York, 1981.

Ford, Henry. *My Life and Work.* New York, 1923.

Gibb, George S., and Knowlton, Evelyn N. *History of Standard Oil Company (New Jersey): The Resurgent Years, 1911–1927.* New York, 1956.

Gibney, Frank. *Miracle by Design: The Real Reasons Behind Japan's Economic Success.* New York, 1982

Girdler, Tom. *Boot Straps.* New York, 1943.

Goldberg, Alfred, ed. *A History of the United States Air Force.* New York, 1957.

Goldstine, Herman. *The Computer from Pascal to von Neumann.* Princeton, 1972.

Gras, N.S.B., and Larson, Henrietta. *Casebook in American Business History.* New York, 1939.

Hall, Courtney. *History of American Industrial Science.* New York, 1954.

Hall, Max, ed. *Made in New York: Case Studies in Metropolitan Manufacturing.* Cambridge, 1959.

Harris, Seymour. *Economics of the Kennedy Years and a Look Ahead.* New York, 1964.

Harvard University. Graduate School of Business Administration. George F. Baker Foundation. *The Radio Industry: The Story of its Development.* New York, 1928.

Hawley, E. W. *The New Deal and the Problem of Monopoly.* New York, 1966.

Hogan, William. *The 1970s: Critical Years for Steel.* Lexington, 1972.

———. *Economic History of the Iron and Steel Industry in the United States.* 5 vols. Lexington, 1971.

Holley, Irving Jr. *United States Army in World War II, Special Studies, Buying Aircraft: Material Procurement for the Army Air Forces.* Washington, 1964.

Hoover, Calvin. *The Economy, Liberty, and the State.* New York, 1959.

Hoover, Herbert. *An American Epic.* 2 vols. Chicago, 1960.

Ickes, Harold. *Secret Diary of Harold Ickes: The First Thousand Days, 1933–1936.* New York, 1953.

Ingham, John. *The Iron Barons: A Social Analysis of an American Urban Elite.* Westport, 1978.

Janeway, Eliot. *The Struggle for Survival.* New Haven, 1951.

Kelly, Charles, Jr. *The Sky's the Limit: A History of the Airlines.* New York, 1963.

Laidler, Harry. *Concentration of Control in American Industry.* New York, 1931.

Larson, Henrietta, and Porter, Kenneth. *History of Humble Oil and Refining Company.* New York, 1959.

Lawrence, David. *Beyond the New Deal.* New York, 1934.

Lawrence, Joseph. *Wall Street and Washington.* Princeton, 1929.

Lawrence, Paul, and Dyer, Davis. *Renewing American Industry.* New York, 1983.

Lay, Bernie, Jr. *Someone Has to Make it Happen: The Inside Story of Tex Thornton, the Man Who Built Litton Industries.* New York, 1969.

Lebhar, Godfrey M. *Chain Stores in America: 1859–1959.* New York, 1959.

Livesay, Harold. *Andrew Carnegie and the Rise of Big Business.* Boston, 1975.

Lund, Robert; Coffin, Howard; and Burkett, Charles. *Truth about the New Deal.* New York, 1936.

Lutz, Freidrich. *Corporate Cash Balances: 1914–1943.* New York, 1945.

Lynd, Robert S, and Lynd, Helen M. *Middletown: A Study in Modern American Culture.* New York, 1956.

McLaughlin, Glenn. *Growth of American Manufacturing Areas.* Pittsburgh, 1938.

McNair, M. P. *Expansion and Profits in the Chain Store Business.* Harvard, 1929.

Mansfield, Harold. *Vision: A Saga of the Sky.* New York, 1956.

———. *Vision: The Story of Boeing.* New York, 1966.

Marsburg, Theodore. *Small Business in Brass Fabricating: The Smith & Griggs Manufacturing Co. of Waterbury.* New York, 1956.

Marcosson, Isaac. *Anaconda.* New York, 1957.

Miller, John. *Men and Volts at War.* New York, 1947.

Mitchell, Sidney. *S. Z. Mitchell and the Electrical Industry.* New York, 1960.

Mitchell, Wesley. *Business Cycles: The Problem and its Setting.* New York, 1927.

Moritz, Michael, and Seamon, Barry. *Going for Broke: The Chrysler Story.* New York, 1981.

Morris, Lloyd, and Smith, Kendall. *Ceiling Unlimited.* New York, 1953.

Myers, William, and Newton, Walter. *The Hoover Administration:*

A Documented Narrative. New York, 1936.

Nelson, Donald. *Arsenal of Democracy: The Story of American War Production.* New York, 1946.

Nevins, Allan, and Hill, Frank. *Ford: Expansion and Challenge, 1915–1933.* New York, 1957.

Niemeyer, Glenn. *The Automotive Career of Ranson E. Olds.* East Lansing, 1963.

Peck, Merton, and Scherer, Frederic. *The Weapons Acquisition Process: An Economic Analysis.* Boston, 1962.

Peek, George, and Crowther, Samuel. *Why Quit Our Own?* New York, 1936.

Perlo, Victor. *Militarism and Industry: Arms Profiteering in the Missile Age.* New York, 1963.

Pfeiffer, John. *The Thinking Machine.* New York, 1962.

Pound, Arthur. *Industrial America: Its Way of Work and Thought.* Boston, 1936.

Prothro, James. *The Dollar Decade: Business Ideas in the 1920s.* Baton Rouge, 1954.

Rae, John B. *The American Automobile.* Chicago, 1956.

————.*American Automobile Manufacturers: The First Forty Years.* New York, 1959.

————. *Climb to Greatness: The American Aircraft Industry, 1920–1960.* Cambridge, 1968.

Rosenman, Samuel, ed. *The Public Papers and Addresses of Franklin D. Roosevelt.* New York, 1938.

Silk, Leonard. *The Research Revolution.* New York, 1960.

Simmons, John, and Mares, William. *Working Together.* New York, 1983.

Simonson, G. R. *The History of the American Aircraft Industry.* Cambridge, 1968.

Sloan, Alfred, Jr. *My Years With General Motors.* New York, 1964.

Sobel, Robert. *IBM: Colossus in Transition.* New York, 1981.

Sorenson, Charles E. *My Forty Years With Ford.* New York, 1956.

Steckler, Herman. *The Structure and Performances of the Aerospace Industry.* Berkeley, 1965.

Stettinius, Edward, Jr. *Lend Lease: Weapon for Victory.* New York, 1944.

Sutton, Francis; Harris, Seymour; Kaysen, Carl; and Tobin, James. *The American Business Creed.* Cambridge, 1956.

Temin, Peter. *Iron and Steel in Nineteenth Century America: An Economic Inquiry.* Cambridge, 1964.

———, Federal Trade Commission, *The United States Steel Industry and Its International Rivals: Trends and Factors Determing International Competitiveness.* Washington, 1978.

Thompson, John, and Beasley, Norman. *For the Years to Come: A Story of International Nickel of Canada.* New York, 1960.

U.S. Department of Commerce. *U.S. Industrial Outlook: 1969.* Washington, 1968.

———. Report of the Committee on Recent Economic Changes of the President's Conference on Unemployment. *Recent Economic Changes in the United States.* New York, 1929.

———. Temporary National Economic Committee. *Investigation of Concentration of Economic Power.* Washington, 1941.

Urofsky, Melvin. *Big Steel and the Wilson Administration.* Columbus, Ohio, 1969.

Vatter, Harold. *The U.S. Economy in the 1950s.* New York, 1963.

Wagoner, Harless D. *The U.S. Machine Tool Industry from 1900 to 1950.* Cambridge, 1966.

Wall, Joseph. *Andrew Carnegie.* New York, 1970.

Walton, Francis. *Miracle of World War II.* New York, 1956.

White, Lawrence. *The Automobile Industry Since 1945.* Cambridge, 1970.

Whitney, Simon. *Antitrust Policies: American Experience in Twenty Industries.* 2 vols. New York, 1958.

Williamson, Harold; Andreano, Ralph; Daum, Arnold, and Klose, Gilbert. *The American Petroleum Industry: The Age of Energy, 1899–1959.* Evanston Ill., 1953.

Wiltz, John. *In Search of Peace: The Senate Munitions Inquiry, 1934–1936.* Baton Rouge, 1963.

Woodbury, David. *Battlefronts of Industry.* New York, 1949.

Woytinsky, Emma S. *Profile of the U.S. Economy.* New York, 1967.

Index

About the Author

ROBERT SOBEL is a Professor of History at New College, Hofstra University. His most recent books include *IBM: Colussus in Transition*, *Inside Wall Street: Continuity and Change in the Financial District*, and *ITT: The Management of Opportunity*.